给孩子最美的教育
——麦加菲美德读本

[美] 威廉 · H. 麦加菲　编著　　依妮 苍松　译

新世界出版社
NEW WORLD PRESS

献给所有喜爱孩子的中国父母

我有一个梦想

“给孩子最好的教育”或许是每一个中国父母最大的愿望。可是，什么样的教育是最好的呢？卢梭说：“教育就是成长。”那么，最好的教育就应该帮助孩子最好的成长。于是，我又产生一个疑问：什么样的成长对于孩子来说是最好的呢？尤其是不久前我光荣的成为一名父亲之后，寻找这个问题的答案就成了我最迫切的目标。

起初，我觉得为小生命设计一条成长之路并不是一件困难的事情。我还记得初次抱起她时那种柔软的感觉，仿佛一不小心就会融化在我的掌心里，也还记得她第一次握住我的大拇指时的那份依恋……但很快，我就发现，小生命并不是像我想的那么简单柔弱。尤其是在一个晴朗的夏日里，当我们四个大人威逼利诱、软硬兼施，花了快一个小时的时间，都没能让小家伙穿上我们选定的那双缀满漂亮装饰的小凉鞋——一岁多的她坚定地选择了一双花色暗淡的红色小雨靴。看着她穿着雨靴快乐地跑来跑去的身影，我不禁问自己：我们的选择真的是孩子自己的需要吗？

好吧，我承认，我有可能并不真正了解我的孩子。我所能做的，或许只能如埃默森所说：“保存儿童的天性，并且正是按照它所指出的方向，用知识把儿童天性武装起来。”但我总得做点什么，因为我还记得培根的一句话：“毫无疑问，从幼年开始的好习惯是最完美

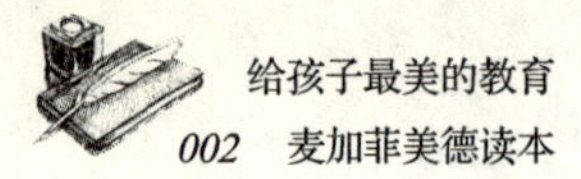

的，我们把这叫做‘教育’，因为教育其实就是一种早年开始的习惯。所以我们看到与以后的时期相比，幼年时代学语言，舌头学习表达方式和发音时更柔顺，学各种技巧动作时，关节更灵活。”用邓爷爷的话来说，就是“教育要从娃娃抓起”。

我有点明白了，如果我不能明白孩子真正想要什么，那我至少应该让她自己能够明白自己想要什么；如果我不能给孩子“最好的教育”，那我至少应该给孩子“最美的教育”。让她的世界充满美善而不是丑恶，让好的习惯占据她人生的高地。就如我们的老祖宗所做的那样：让孩子的人生从《弟子规》、《三字经》开始。

于是，我开始行动起来。不过，请先原谅做父母的一点点小小的私心。虽然我已经放弃了让孩子复制我的人生或者弥补我生命中某种缺憾的想法，但我还是对她存在着一点点小小的期望：期望她能够健康成长，开心快乐，长大后能够成为地球村里一位合格的村民，在村里自由地转来转去。

怀着这一点点国际化的期望，我将目光投向了国外。功夫不负有心人，我找到了一本书，看起来十分符合我的要求：美德、美语、美式教育。

威廉·霍尔姆斯·麦加菲（William Holmes McGuffey），美国著名教育家，他曾经用了二十多年的时间为美国的学生们编写了一套“语文”教材——《麦加菲美德读本》。这套教材为当时美国的大多数学校所采用，并持续销售了一百多年，到1960年累计销量就高达1.22亿册，直至今日，仍被许多学校选为最佳课外读物。美国媒体称：“它至少影响了美国五代人，如果你能找到一个五世同堂的大家庭，你会惊奇地发现，从高祖到重孙，他们能异口同声地背诵《麦加菲美德读本》中的优秀篇章。”《出版商周刊》将其评为“人类出版史上第三大畅销书”，认为它对美国青年的心灵塑造与道德培养产生了史无前例的影响。

但令我心折的并不是因为它是美国小学生的“国语”课本，或是它骄人的销量，而是它贴近人性的编选。与中国当前的教材不同，《麦加菲美德读本》中并没有选录很多的寓言或者童话，在这里，人是绝对的主角，生活是当然的舞台，生活中的许多场景都被收录到了课文之中。有写不出老师布置的作文，最后却发现窗外的风景就是最好的作文的苏茜，有因为贫穷而被同学嘲笑的戴维，有为了证明自己“勇敢”，而在大孩子的教唆下朝教室门口扔雪球的乔治……当然，为了让那些高年级的同学欣赏文学的优美，其中也有不少狄更斯、华盛顿·欧文等著名作家的名篇节选。而且，除了真、善、美，麦加菲先生也没有回避生活中的艰难与困苦，但是更突出了困境之下的个人的坚守与成长。这样的文章，更容易引起心灵的共鸣，于无声处滋养心灵的成长。

“从生活中来，到生活中去”，这正是我所期盼的教育。我将把这本书当做礼物送给我亲爱的女儿，作为陪伴她成长的礼物。不过，为了不让她被这厚厚的六卷本所吓倒，我倒是可以发挥一下我的作用——从中精选出一些最为优秀的文章作为她最早的启蒙。

依照《麦加菲美德读本》的编选思路，我将这本书分成了“温暖的家庭”、“美丽的世界”、“可爱的大自然”、“幸福的童年”、“美好的品德”、“五味的人生”和“培养良好的习惯”七个章节。每个章节都按照由浅入深的程度精选了多个小故事。在翻译的过程中，为了更好地让孩子们理解英文，首先追求“信”，基本采取直译的方式，只是每个章节的后几篇才部分采取意译的方式，以追求“雅”的境界。为了保留原书中英文的原汁原味，书中一些早期现代英语的用法也给予了保留。在这里，我必须要感谢我的朋友依妮，正是她帮助翻译完成了书中最难的部分，并让它变得更“美”。

什么是最好的教育？每个人的答案可能都不相同。我只想让我的孩子接受最美的教育，让她自己去判别什么是好，什么是坏。我相信，这本书可以帮助我做到这一点。

我希望，我的孩子能够喜欢我为她准备的礼物，并且永远记住人生最初的这点美丽。在漫长的人生旅途中，无论经历欢笑或是挫折，高潮或是低谷，都能够微笑着去面对。我并不期望她能够做到最好，但至少，她的心中，要葆有一份美丽——这就是我的梦想。

同时，也将这本书送给中国所有的父母，希望孩子们都能拥有一个美丽的童年。

> 教育是人们灵魂的教育，而非理智知识和认识的堆积。教育的本质意味着：一棵树摇动另一棵树，一朵云摇动另一朵云，一个灵魂唤醒另一个灵魂。
>
> ——［德］雅斯贝尔斯

苍松

2011年10月

Contents

目录

CHAPTER 1
温暖的家庭

Contents

目录

CHAPTER 2
美丽的世界

CHAPTER 3
可爱的大自然

CHAPTER 4
幸福的童年

CHAPTER 5
美好的品德

CHAPTER 6
五味的人生

CHAPTER 7
培养良好的习惯

CHAPTER 1

温暖的家庭

对于孩子来说，家庭应是歇憩的场所，培养丰富的人性的土壤以及明亮无比的孩子之梦的温床。

——[日]池田大作

小鸟的晨曲

你是否也曾在母亲温情的呼唤中赖在床上不肯起来，享受着亲情的纵容？任何时候，家庭总会给我们最温暖的怀抱。儿时的歌谣很久不曾响起，但母亲的爱却永留心间。昔日的小鸟渐渐羽翼丰满，什么时候让我们也为母亲唱一首歌，只愿，她能忘却一天的劳累，在歌声中安心入眠。

醒一醒，小宝贝，小鸟们都出来了，
而你还在巢里安睡！
连最懒惰的小鸟都在四处蹦蹦跳跳，
你该起来和它们一块儿玩耍。
醒一醒，小宝贝，快醒醒！

哦，看看在你贪睡时所错过的，
闪亮的露珠，美丽的天空！
你错过的东西，我在歌中连一半也唱不完。
你却连“哼”都不“哼”一声，
醒一醒，小宝贝，快醒醒！

妈妈已经唤了你很久，
我再也没有耐心为你歌唱，
小鸟们已经做完它们要做的事，
或许，它们就要来啄醒你！
醒一醒，小宝贝，快醒醒！

Birdie's Morning Song

Wake up, little darling, the birdies are out,
And here you are still in your nest!
The laziest birdie is hopping about;
You ought to be up with the rest.
Wake up, little darling, wake up!

Oh, see what you miss when you slumber so long,
The dewdrops, the beautiful sky!
I can not sing half what you lose in my song;
And yet, not a word in reply.
Wake up, little darling, wake up!

I've sung myself quite out of patience with you,
While mother bends o'er your dear head;
Now birdie has done all that birdie can do:
Her kisses will wake you instead!
Wake up, little darling, wake up!

George Cooper

围炉夜话

单纯的玩耍会让你收获快乐，而更多时候，在学习和工作的过程中，你能获取到更大的快乐。这快乐不仅包括达成目的后的成功喜悦，也包括在过程中汲取的点滴感受与能力的培养，更重要的是，它让你认识到了自身的价值。

当你解开一道难题，当你学会一件乐器，你都为自己的人生宝藏中放入了一样珍宝。你的人生将会有多么绚丽？这取决于你今天放进去多少珍宝。

这是冬天的一个晚上，在劳德夫人温馨的家中，她和两个小女儿坐在明亮的炉火旁。两个女孩在做针线活，劳德夫人则忙着织毛衣。

卡蒂做完了自己手头的活。她抬起头来说：“妈妈，我觉得今天的炉火比平时的要明亮些。听，木柴发出的‘噼啪’声多么好听。”

“是啊，这正是我想说的，”玛丽也叫起来，“今晚的灯光要比昨晚的亮许多。”

“亲爱的孩子们，”劳德夫人笑着说，“你们今天晚上一定感觉比平时快乐。所以你们才会认为火比平时更大，灯比往日更亮！”

“但是妈妈，”玛丽说，“我不明白，为什么今天我们会觉得比从前更快乐。昨晚还有简表姐在这里，我们一起玩‘捉迷藏’和‘摸瞎子’，一直到我们都累了才结束呢。”

“我知道，我知道为什么！”卡蒂说，“这是因为今天晚上我们在干一些有意义的事情。我们之所以感到幸福，是因为我们一直在忙碌着。”

“说得对，亲爱的！”劳德夫人说，“我真高兴你们两个都能认识到，做些有意义的事情要比单纯的玩耍更令人愉快，受益更多。”

人生格言

在一切道德品质之中，善良的本性在世界上是最重要的。

——[英]罗素

家是世界上唯一隐藏人类缺点与失败的地方，它同时也蕴藏着甜蜜的爱。

——[英]萧伯纳

习惯真是一种顽强而巨大的力量，它可以主宰人生。因此，人自幼就应该通过完美的教育，去建立一种好的习惯。

——[英]培根

合理生活的目的就在于：懂得什么是正义的东西，感受什么是奇妙的东西，渴求什么是美好的东西。

——[德]普拉顿

与人共事，要学吃亏。俗云：终身让畔，不失一段。

——[清]左宗棠

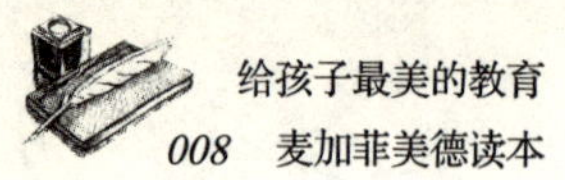

The Fireside

One winter night, Mrs. Lord and her two little girls sat by a bright fire in their pleasant home. The girls were sewing, and their mother was busy at her knitting.

At last, Katie finished her work, and, looking up, said, "Mother, I think the fire is brighter than usual. How I love to hear it crackle!"

"And I was about to say," cried Mary, "that this is a better light than we had last night."

"My dears," said their mother, "it must be that you feel happier than usual to-night. Perhaps that is the reason why you think the fire better, and the light brighter."

"But, mother," said Mary, "I do not see why we are happier now than we were then; for last night cousin Jane was here, and we played 'Puss in the corner' and 'Blind man' until we all were tired."

"I know! I know why!" said Katie.

"It is because we have all been doing something useful to-night. We feel happy because we have been busy."

"You are right, my dear," said their mother. "I am glad you have both learned that there may be something more pleasant than play, and, at the same time, more instructive."

晚安

有多少人会在睡觉前跟大家道声“晚安”？也许你会觉得这是一件讨厌的任务，或者难为情地不好意思说出口。其实，这只是一句简单的祝福。如果你希望你的父母、好朋友们还有这个世界晚上做个好梦，那么就请在临睡前轻轻地说一声“晚安”。

太阳躲出了我们的视线，
鸟儿也都停止了歌唱，
是跟大家道晚安的时候了，
请给每一个人一个甜蜜的吻。

晚安，我亲爱的爸爸、妈妈！
请来吻一下你们的小儿子。
晚安，我的朋友们，无论你们远在天边还是近在眼前！
晚安的祝福送给每一个人。

欢快的鸟儿，晚安。
祝你一觉睡到天明！

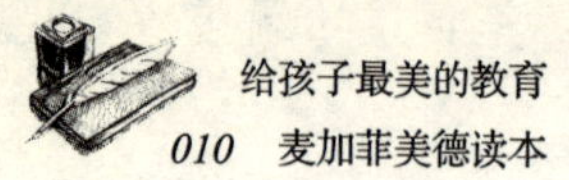

或许，如果你也能用人的语言歌唱，
你也会说声“晚安”。

晚安，我美丽的花儿们！
我入睡时你们在悄然绽放；
星星们闪着明亮的光，
他们整夜醒着与你们同在。

月亮照亮整个天空，
星星在天空闪烁，
是闭上疲劳双眼的时候了，
同时说出我们今夜的祝福。

Good Night

The sun is hidden from our sight,
The birds are sleeping sound;
'T is time to say to all, "Good night!"
And give a kiss all round.

Good night, my father, mother, dear!
Now kiss your little son;
Good night, my friends, both far and near!
Good night to every one.

Good night, ye merry, merry birds!
Sleep well till morning light;
Perhaps, if you could sing in words,
You would have said, "Good night!"

To all my pretty flowers, good night!
You blossom while I sleep;

And all the stars, that shine so bright,
With you their watches keep.

The moon is lighting up the skies,
The stars are sparkling there;
'T is time to shut our weary eyes,
And say our evening prayer.

Mrs. Follen

下面的这些单词你认识吗?

thou=you （你，主格） thee=you（你，宾格）
thy=your（你，属格） ye=you（你们，主格）
you=you（你们，宾格） your=your（你们的，属格）
o'er=over ne'er=never 'T =it

它们都是早期现代英语中的单词。如果你喜欢看英文的诗歌，你会经常在其中发现它们的身影。

谁最爱妈妈

行动往往比言语更有力量。母亲或许不会每天告诉你她有多爱你，但她会永远无微不至的来照顾你。每当你遇到困难的时候，为你遮风挡雨的总是你的家庭。

爱不仅需要表达，更需要行动。做一些力所能及的小事情，也是我们表达爱意的最好的体现。

“我爱你，妈妈，”小约翰说。可是他却忘记了干活，帽子还扔在那里，自己却晃悠悠地去花园里玩耍，留下妈妈一个人在那里搬木柴。

“我爱你，妈妈，”漂亮的内尔说，“我无法用语言表达出我对你的爱意。”她噘着小嘴讨了妈妈半天欢心，终于让妈妈高兴后，自己出去玩了。

“我爱你，妈妈，”小范妮说，“真高兴今天不用上学，我可以在家帮你干活了。”她摇着小宝宝一直到他入睡。

接着，她轻轻地走进房间，拿起一把扫帚，把地扫了一遍，又把整个房间清扫了一下。一整天她都快乐地在给妈妈帮忙。

“我爱你，妈妈。”睡觉前，三个孩子又都对妈妈说。

你觉得他们当中谁最爱妈妈呢?

Which Loved Best?

"I love you, mother," said little John;
Then, forgetting work, his cap went on,
And he was off to the garden swing,
Leaving his mother the wood to bring.

"I love you, mother," said rosy Nell;
"I love you better than tongue can tell;"
Then she teased and pouted full half the day,
Till her mother rejoiced when she went to play.

"I love you, mother," said little Fannie;
"To–day I'll help you all I can;
How glad I am that school doesn't keep!"
So she rocked the baby till it fell asleep.

Then, stepping softly, she took the broom,
And swept the floor, and dusted the room;

Busy and happy all day was she,
Helpful and cheerful as child could be.

"I love you, mother," again they said—
Three little children going to bed;
How do you think that mother guessed
Which of them really loved her best?

Joy Allison

三字经（节选）

为人子，方少时，亲师友，习礼仪。
香九龄，能温席。孝于亲，所当执。
融四岁，能让梨。弟于长，宜先知。
首孝悌，次见闻，知某数，识某文。

——《三字经》

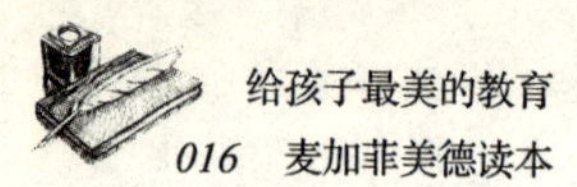

好哥俩

如果你是哥哥，你会把篮子往哪边移多一些呢？一段小小的距离，就体现出了兄弟之间的深厚情谊。哥哥的行为，很好地诠释了什么是兄长的担当和责任。

为所爱的人多付出一些，并不会会让我们失去什么，相反，我们会收获更多的幸福。

一次，一个男孩要给他的奶奶送一篮子东西。篮子装得很满，所以非常重。他的弟弟决定和他一起去，帮他提篮子。他们用一根木棍从篮子提手下面穿过，然后每人抬着棍子的一端，这样，他们就能很轻松地抬起篮子了。

在路上，哥哥心里想，我弟弟汤姆可能并不知道这根棍子是起什么作用的。

“如果我把篮子向他那边移近一点，他那边就会变重一些，而我这边就会轻一些。如果篮子处于棍子中间，我这边就会和他那边一样重。”

“如果我把篮子往他那边移的话，他肯定不知道。但是我不能那样做，因为这样是不对的，我不能做明知是错误的事情。”

于是，他偷偷地把篮子往自己这边移了许多，现在他承担的分量比弟弟的要重很多。尽管如此，他仍然很高兴，因为他觉得自己的行为是正确的。假如他欺骗了自己的弟弟，他根本无法觉得高兴。

英文中的分号

与中文一样，分号用于分隔地位平等的独立子句。在某些情况下，使用分号比使用句号更能显出子句之间的紧密联系，另外分号也经常与连接副词 thus, however, therefore 一起使用(放在这些词语之前)。如：I realize I need exercise; however, I'll lie down first to think about it.

在句子中如果已经使用过逗号，为了避免歧义的产生，就用分号来分隔相似的内容。如 The employees were Tom Hanks, the manager; Jim White, the engineer; and Dr. Jack Lee.

需要注意的是：一个完整的句子以大写字母开始，以句号结束。写英文时用逗点代替句号、分号、冒号或破折号叫“逗号错”，这正是我们所要避免的。请比较下列例句：

误：It was raining hard, they could not work in the fields.

正：It was raining hard; they could not work in the fields.

或 It was raining hard. They could not work in the fields.

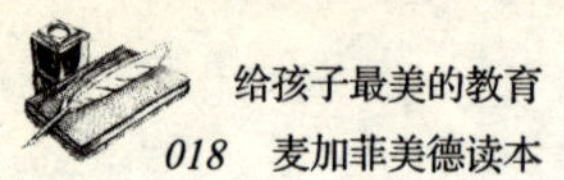

A Kind Brother

A boy was once sent from home to take a basket of things to his grandmother.

The basket was so full that it was very heavy. So his little brother went with him, to help carry the load.

They put a pole under the handle of the basket, and each then took hold of an end of the pole. In this way they could carry the basket very nicely.

Now the older boy thought, "My brother Tom does not know about this pole.

"If I slip the basket near him, his side will be heavy, and mine light; but if the basket is in the middle of the pole, it will be as heavy for me as it is for him.

"Tom does not know this as I do. But I will not do it. It would be wrong, and I will not do what is wrong."

Then he slipped the basket quite near his own end of the pole. His load was now heavier than that of his little brother.

Yet he was happy; for he felt that he had done right. Had he deceived his brother, he would not have felt at all happy.

乔治的盛宴

你并不能决定你出生在什么样的家庭，但是你可以决定你心中有多少爱，又把多少爱留给你的家人。

幸福并不取决于你拥有的财富，而取决于你爱着多少人，又正被多少人爱着。

乔治的家里非常穷。冬天里，他们无法生起明亮而温暖的炉火。因为他们买不起木柴，只能烧一些乔治从树下或路边捡来的干枝。

七月晴朗的一天，妈妈让乔治到两英里外的树林去。乔治要在那里待上一整天，尽可能地捡更多的柴。

天气真好，乔治拾柴也很卖力。太阳越升越高，乔治也觉得越来越热。他需要一个凉爽的地方休息一下，顺便吃他的午餐。于是他来到小溪边，却意外地在苔藓中间发现了许多熟得通红的野草莓。

“它们配上我的面包和黄油一起吃，那味道一定好极了！”乔治想着。于是他在帽子里垫了一层树叶，把他所能找到的草莓都装在了里面，最后乔治坐在了小溪边。

那是一个很美的地方，乔治感到非常愉悦和舒畅。他想，如果妈妈不是在林子里又黑又小的房子里，而是也在这里，那该有多好啊！

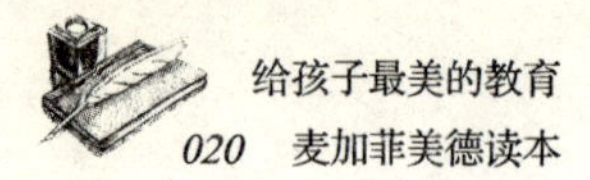

乔治这样想着，一边把第一颗草莓往嘴里送。突然，他停住了，并把草莓放回到帽子里。乔治自言自语地说："妈妈会多喜欢这些草莓啊！"

"我还是把它们留给妈妈吧！"他边说边想着妈妈开心的样子，同时又用渴望的眼神看着那些草莓。

犹豫了半天，乔治终于决定。"我可以吃一半，把另一半留给妈妈。"于是他把草莓分成两堆。但是，每一堆看起来都那么小，于是他又将它们拢到了一起。

"那我只尝一个好了。"他这样想。但是，就在他拿起一颗草莓准备送进嘴里时，发现那是最好的一颗，于是他又把草莓放了回去。"算了，我还是把它们全都留给妈妈吧。"说着他精心地将它们包好，一颗也没有吃。

太阳要落山了，乔治准备回家。他显得多么快活啊！他把所有的草莓都留给了他生病的母亲，离家越近，他就越不想去吃草莓。

乔治刚刚把柴火放下，就听见屋里传来妈妈微弱的声音。"是你吗，乔治？我真高兴你回来，我渴了，很想喝茶。"

乔治跑进屋去，高兴地把野草莓递到妈妈面前。"这都是你留给妈妈的吗？"妈妈问。她眼里含着泪水，用手疼爱地抚摸着乔治的头。"上帝会为你的行为而祈福的，我的孩子。"

想想吧，如果乔治吃了这些草莓，他还能感受到哪怕一半此刻的幸福吗？

George's Feast

George's mother was very poor. Instead of having bright, blazing fires in winter, she had nothing to burn but dry sticks, which George picked up from under the trees and hedges.

One fine day in July, she sent George to the woods, which were about two miles from the village in which she lived. He was to stay there all day, to get as much wood as he could collect.

It was a bright, sunny day, and George worked very hard; so that by the time the sun was high, he was hot, and wished for a cool place where he might rest and eat his dinner.

While he hunted about the bank he saw among the moss some fine, wild strawberries, which were a bright scarlet with ripeness.

"How good these will be with my bread and butter!" thought George; and lining his little cap with leaves, he set to work eagerly to gather all he could find, and then seated himself by the brook.

It was a pleasant place, and George felt happy and contented. He thought how much his mother would like to see him there, and to be there herself, instead of in her dark, close room in the village.

George thought of all this, and just as he was lifting the first strawberry to his mouth, he said to himself, "How much mother would like these;" and he stopped, and put the strawberry back again.

"Shall I save them for her?" said he, thinking how much they would refresh her, yet still looking at them with a longing eye.

"I will eat half, and take the other half to her," said he at last; and he divided them into two heaps. But each heap looked so small, that he put them together again.

"I will only taste one," thought he; but, as he again lifted it to his mouth, he saw that he had taken the finest, and he put it back. "I will keep them all for her," said he, and he covered them up nicely, till he should go home.

When the sun was beginning to sink, George set out for home. How happy he felt, then, that he had all his strawberries for his sick mother. The nearer he came to his home, the less he wished to taste them.

Just as he had thrown down his wood, he heard his mother's faint voice calling him from the next room. "Is that you, George? I am glad you have come, for I am thirsty, and am longing for some tea."

George ran in to her, and joyfully offered his wild strawberries. "And you saved them for your sick mother, did you?" said she, laying her hand fondly on his head, while the tears stood in her eyes. "God will bless you for all this, my child."

Could the eating of the strawberries have given George half the happiness he felt at this moment?

妈妈的礼物

上天赐给父母最好的礼物，就是他们的小宝宝了。杰西给了妈妈一个很棒的惊喜，他无疑就是妈妈最好的圣诞礼物。

“千里送鹅毛，礼轻情意重”。只要礼物里包含着你深深的情意，即使它并不贵重，你也可以大大方方的拿出手。因为，别人希望收到的是你的心意，而不是金钱。

杰西和妈妈开了一个很棒的玩笑，让我来讲述给你听。

圣诞节就要到了，杰西、杰米和乔一起到树林里去采集装饰房间用的绿色松枝。

杰西戴着她的小帽子，身穿白色的皮衣和红色的套裤。她是一个快乐的小姑娘，但是那天早晨她却不是很开心，因为她听到妈妈说：“所有的孩子都会得到圣诞礼物，除了我这个妈妈，我们今年的日子实在不好过。”

杰西把妈妈的话告诉了她的兄弟们，他们立刻热烈地谈论开了。“妈妈这么好，这么慈爱，竟然没有圣诞礼物，这简直太糟糕了！”

小杰西含着眼泪说。“我不喜欢这样。”

“噢！她还有你呀！”乔说。

“但我并不是新的呀！”杰西说。

“嗯，等你再回到家的时候，你就会是新的了。”乔说，“因为她已经有一个小时没有看到你了。”

杰西笑着跳起来，“那就把我放进篮子里带给妈妈吧，对她说‘我是她的圣诞礼物’。”

于是杰米和乔把杰西放进篮子里，在她的周围放满绿色的松枝，高兴地抬着杰西往回家走。这真是一段愉快的行程。到家了，他们把篮子放在门口的台阶上，冲进门对妈妈说：“妈妈，外面有一份给您的圣诞礼物。”

妈妈跑出去一看，在一篮翠绿的松枝中间，她可爱的小女儿正坐着冲她笑呢！

“宝贝，你是我最想要的礼物。”妈妈惊喜地说。

“亲爱的妈妈，”杰西从树枝丛中跳出来说，“我觉得，对妈妈们来说，每天都应该是圣诞节，因为她们每天都可以看到自己的女儿！”

Mamma's Present

Jessie played a good joke on her mamma. This is the way she did it.

Jessie had gone to the woods with Jamie and Joe to get green branches to trim up the house for Christmas. She wore her little cap, her white furs, and her red leggings.

She was a merry little girl, indeed; but she felt sad this morning because her mother had said, "The children will all have Christmas presents, but I don't expect any for myself. We are too poor this year."

When Jessie told her brothers this, they all talked about it a great deal. "Such a good, kind mamma, and no Christmas present! It's too bad."

"I don't like it," said little Jessie, with a tear in her eye.

"Oh, she has you," said Joe.

"But I am not something new," said Jessie.

"Well, you will be new, Jessie," said Joe, "when you get back. She has not seen you for an hour."

Jessie jumped and laughed. "Then put me in the basket, and carry me to mamma, and say, 'I am her Christmas present.' "

So they set her in the basket, and put green branches all around

her. It was a jolly ride. They set her down on the doorstep, and went in and said, "There's a Christmas present out there for you, mamma."

Mamma went and looked, and there, in a basket of green branches, sat her own little laughing girl.

"Just the very thing I wanted most," said mamma.

"Then, dear mamma," said Jessie, bounding out of her leafy nest, "I should think it would be Christmas for mammas all the time, for they see their little girls every day."

二十四孝

“孝”是中国古代重要的伦理思想之一，元代郭居敬辑录历代二十四个孝子从不同角度、不同环境、不同遭遇行孝的故事，编成《二十四孝》，序而诗之，用训童蒙，成为宣传孝道的通俗读物。由于后来的印本大都配以图画，故又称《二十四孝图》。

孝感动天	戏彩娱亲	鹿乳奉亲	百里负米
啮指痛心	芦衣顺母	亲尝汤药	拾葚异器
埋儿奉母	卖身葬父	刻木事亲	涌泉跃鲤
怀橘遗亲	扇枕温衾	行佣供母	闻雷泣墓
哭竹生笋	卧冰求鲤	扼虎救父	恣蚊饱血
尝粪忧心	乳姑不怠	涤亲溺器	弃官寻母

苏茜的作文

苏茜写出了一篇很好的作文，但实际上，她只是写出了她眼中看到的景色。没错，写作文并不是让我们去编故事，文字的作用就是帮我们记录下身边或者世界上发生的事情，还有自己内心的感受。

当你把写作文当做任务时，它会是只难以逾越的拦路虎；而当你以平常心去看待它，你会发现它不过是只纸老虎。在人生的路上，你还会遇到很多类似的事情，比如考试，它将是拦路虎还是纸老虎，一切都取决于你。

一天，苏茜·史密斯放学回家，一进门就哭了起来。妈妈一边把女儿搂到身边，一边笑着问道：“怎么了，我的宝贝？”

“噢，妈妈，麻烦大了。”苏茜啜泣着，“所有同学明天早上都要交作文，我从来就写不出来。我们至少要写十二行，可我憋了快一个下午才写了几个字。看看我才写了点什么啊！”

史密斯太太拿起苏茜手里皱巴巴、浸着泪渍的纸，看看上面都写了什么。苏茜慎重地写下了三个主题：时间、自制和勤奋。

“时间是短暂的，我们都应该充分利用时间。”“自制是非常有

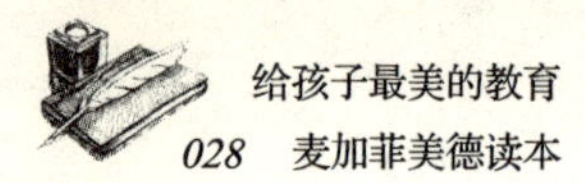

用的。”“在这个世界上我们想做任何事情都要很勤奋。”这就是她写下的所有的句子。

苏茜说，“对这些主题我再也想不出一个词了，我知道，明天上学一定交不出写好的作文，我可不想从书上抄一篇或是求爸爸或你帮我写。”

“这就对了，亲爱的，”妈妈说，“自己写的作文再糟糕，也比请别人代写的漂亮文章让你感觉更好。不过，开心起来吧。你没有开好头，你是在尝试着写自己根本不了解的题目。去花园里玩吧，半小时后我会叫你的。”

“可是我的作文……”妈妈打断苏茜的话，说：“玩的时候别想作文的事，只管开心地去玩。”

好像只不过玩了几分钟，苏茜就听到妈妈喊她。她立刻跑回屋里，手里捧着花，小脸红扑扑的。

“现在，苏茜，我要你坐在窗前，取一张空白的纸和一支铅笔，写下你看到的东西。”妈妈吩咐说。

“可是我的作文呢，妈妈，我什么时候开始写我的作文啊？”苏茜问道。妈妈说：“别想你的作文了，亲爱的，先做我告诉你的，我们之后再谈作文的事。”

苏茜虽然觉得妈妈的要求有点奇怪，但是她知道妈妈不论做什么事情总是有她的道理的。所以她拿起纸笔，坐到窗前。

“不要和我讲话，往窗外看，写下对你所看到的东西的感受。”

苏茜禁不住笑起来，这真是一件好玩的事情。她向外望去，首先看到的是西边的天空和绚烂的晚霞。“哦，妈妈，多壮观的落日啊！”苏茜忍不住惊叹道。

“不要说，而是写下来。”妈妈回答。

“那我就写落日好了。”铅笔开始在纸上飞快地划过。几分钟后她说：“妈妈，我念给你听我写的东西好吗？”

“不，现在不行。我要去餐厅了，你坐下来继续写，等我回来。”妈妈嘱咐说。

苏茜继续写下去。她开始对自己做的事情感兴趣了。有那么一会儿，她完全忘了可怕的作文。她描写了晚霞，那远处的山丘、树木、河流，写下了开满鲜艳花朵的花园和飞过窗口的小鸟。

就在她都快写满一张纸的时候，妈妈进来了，笑着问：“苏茜，你的作文怎样了？”苏茜惊道：“作文？你可是告诉我别去理会作文的啊，我还没有想呢。我刚才只是非常开心地写下了我从窗户里看到的一切。”

史密斯太太拿过苏茜的稿纸，大声朗读起苏茜写的文字：“我坐在窗前的一张小矮凳上，窗户半开着，从这里可以闻到花园里飘来的缕缕花香。天空被落日染得绚烂极了，呈现出紫色、粉色和金色的颜色。我相信没有谁的颜料盒里会有这么漂亮的颜色。”

“我看到一朵云彩，高高在上，像一艘大轮船航行在蔚蓝的海面上。若是它不会让我眩晕的话，我真想坐在云彩上。现在，就在我写下这些的时候，云彩正变幻着不同的颜色和形状，每次都非常漂亮。”

“绿色山丘的山尖上镶着金边，看上去像披着金色的外衣。我可以看到远处的河流，远远看去非常宁静，尽管我知道它正飞快地奔向大海。”

“鸟儿飞过窗口，急着赶回家照顾小宝宝。我真高兴小鸟一点都不害怕住在我家花园里，它还在我家的树上筑巢呢。”

“我们的花园里种满了各种花：石竹、百合和玫瑰。我的生日再有一周就到了。到那时我们就可以用我们想要的花来编花环装饰野餐会了。”

史密斯太太说：“苏茜，你看，这其实是一篇很好的作文。”

“一篇作文！”苏茜激动地喊道：“可以称得上作文吗？”

“是的，亲爱的，还是一篇好作文呢。”妈妈回答说。“就是还差一个题目。”

“我们来给它安一个题目吧。我确信你的老师会和我一样非常喜欢这篇作文的。你看，亲爱的，”妈妈接着说：“如果你描写自己感兴趣的事物，写作文其实是件很容易的事情。”

第二天早晨，苏茜整整齐齐誊抄了作文，高高兴兴地准备去上学了。当她和妈妈吻别的时候，苏茜说：“亲爱的妈妈，想想多有意思啊，我写了那么长的一篇作文，自己竟然都没有意识到。”

英语的起源

英语的语源其实是德语。公元410年，罗马人结束了对英国的占领。随后，来自德国北部平原的三个日耳曼部落：盎格鲁人、撒克逊人和朱尔特人开始到不列颠定居。英语就是盎格鲁-撒克逊人的语言。但是后来这个民族曾经被很多个民族征服过，所以它包含了很多外来词汇，很多又难又拗口的词多数来自拉丁语和法语。

语言学家们一般把英语的历史分为三个时期：古英语，中古英语，现代英语。古英语时期（又称盎格鲁-撒克逊时期 the Anglo-Saxon Period）：公元450年至1150年；中古英语时期：公元1150年至1500年；现代英语时期：公元1500年至今。

现代英语时期又细分为：早期现代英语时期——1500年至1700年；后期现代英语时期——1700年至今。

Susie's Composition

Susie Smith came home from school one day, and had no sooner entered the sitting room than she burst into tears. "What is the matter, my dear child?" said her mother, drawing her daughter to her side and smiling.

"O mother, matter enough," sobbed Susie. "All our class must bring in compositions to-morrow morning, and I never, never can write one. We must write twelve lines at least, and I have written only a few words after trying nearly all the afternoon. See what work I have made of it!"

Mrs. Smith took the rumpled, tear-stained paper which Susie held in her hand, and glanced at what she had written. In a careful hand she had tried to write upon three themes: "Time," "Temperance," and "Industry."

"Time is short. We should all improve our time." "Temperance is a very useful thing." "We should all be industrious if we wish to do anything in the world." These sentences were all she had written.

"Now," said Susie, "I can't think of another word to say upon any of these subjects, and I know I shall have to go to school without a composition, for I won't be so mean as to copy one from a book, or to ask you or papa to write one for me."

"That is right, my dear," said her mother. "You will be far happier with a poor composition, if it is all your own, than with a fine one written by somebody else. But cheer up. You have not begun right—you have been trying to write upon subjects that you know nothing about. Run into the garden and play. I will call you in half an hour."

"But my composition," began Susie. "Don't think about your composition while you are gone," said Mrs. Smith, "but have as pleasant a time as you can."

It seemed but a few minutes to Susie before she heard her mother's voice calling her. She went into the house at once—her hands full of sweet flowers, and her cheeks rosy with exercise.

"Now, Susie," said her mother, "I want you to sit by the window with this nice sheet of paper and a pencil, and write something about what you can see." "But my composition, mother," said Susie; "when shall I begin that?" "Never mind your composition, my dear; do this to please me, and we will talk about that by and by."

Susie thought her mother's request was a strange one; but she knew that she always had a good reason for everything she did: so she took the paper and pencil, and sat by the window.

"Do not talk to me at all," said her mother. "Look out of the window, and then write down your thoughts about everything you see."

Susie could not help laughing, it seemed such a funny thing to be doing. As she looked out, she first saw the western sky and some bright, sunset clouds. "O mother!" she exclaimed, "what a splendid sunset!" "Don't talk," said her mother, "but write."

"I'll write about the sunset, then," said she, and the pencil began to move rapidly across the paper. In a few moments she said, "Mother, shall I read you what I have written?" "No, not now," answered her mother; "I am going into the dining room. You may sit and write until I return."

As Susie went on writing, she became very much interested in her occupation, and for a time forgot all about the dreaded composition. She wrote about the sunset clouds, the appearance of the distant hills, the trees, the river, the garden with its gay flowers, and the birds flying past the window.

Just as she had reached the bottom of the page, her mother came in. "Well, Susie," said she, with a smile, "how does that composition come on?" "Composition!" exclaimed Susie; "you told me not to think about my composition, and I have not thought of it once; I have had such a nice time writing about what I could see from the window."

Mrs. Smith took the paper and read aloud what Susie had written: "I am sitting on a low seat at the bay window, one half of which is open, so that I can smell the sweet flowers in the garden. The sky is all bright with sunset; I can see purple, and pink, and golden. I do not believe that anyone on earth has a paint box with such lovely colors in it."

"I can see one cloud, far above the rest, that looks like a ship sailing in the blue sea. I should like to sail on a cloud, if it would not make me dizzy. Now, while I have been writing, the clouds have changed in color and form, but they are just as beautiful as they were before."

"The green hills are tipped with light, and look as if they were wearing golden crowns. I can see a river a great way off, and it looks quite still, although I know it is running as fast as it can to get to the ocean."

"The birds are flying past the window to go home and take care of their little ones. I am glad the birds are not afraid to live in our garden, and to build nests in our trees."

"Our garden is full of flowers—pinks, lilies, and roses. Mother calls this the month of roses. My birthday will come in a week, and we can have all the flowers we wish for wreaths and bouquets."

"There, Susie," said Mrs. Smith, "that is a very nice composition, indeed." "A composition!" exclaimed Susie, "is that a composition?" "Yes, my dear, and a very good one, too," replied her mother. "When it hasn't even a subject?"

"We can find one for it, and I do not doubt it will please your teacher, as it does me. You see, my dear," continued her mother, "that it is easy enough to write if you have anything interesting to write about."

The next morning Susie copied her composition very neatly, and started to school with a happy heart, saying, as she gave her mother a kiss, "Just think how funny it is, dear mother, that I should have written so long a composition without knowing it."

CHAPTER 2

美丽的世界

人是世界的主人，年轻、美丽，征服了世界，改造了大地，会使草木生长，能和树木、野兽、天神谈心。

——[法]罗曼·罗兰

春日

你可曾仔细看过外面的世界？飞鸟划过天空，小草悄悄地钻出地面，水面一圈圈的涟漪，荡漾在心头。啊，生活平实而美好！

大自然是美好的，但这美好的一切都需要我们去悉心爱护。因为我们，还有我们的子孙后代，都将生活在这个地球上。而环境一旦被破坏，将留下难以平复的创伤。

河边的赤杨轻轻舒展着，
仿佛笼着一层淡淡的粉，
柳芽探出头，给柳树镶上一道漂亮的银边，
孩子们在快乐的玩耍。

小鸟飞过天空，
听，它们唱的多么动听！
像是要告诉孩子们，
春天，又回来了。

绿茸茸的小草悄悄探出地面，
脚下的泥土多么柔软，
青蛙跃出水面，
唱起响亮而甜蜜的歌曲。

瞧那些可爱的毛茛，
还有那鲜红的猫爪花，
阳光铺洒在草地上，
蒲公英熠熠的闪着光。

那些可爱的白色、黄色的小花，
是雏菊在遍地绽放，
孩子们用那柔软的小手，
快乐的采个不停。

三叶草也乐的弯下了腰，
红色的海洋中不小心闪出紫罗兰的身影，
哦，快乐的孩子们，
这一切都是造物主的奇迹。

Spring

The alder by the river
Shakes out her powdery curls;
The willow buds in silver
For little boys and girls.

The little birds fly over,
And oh, how sweet they sing!
To tell the happy children
That once again 't is Spring.

The gay green grass comes creeping
So soft beneath their feet;
The frogs begin to ripple
A music clear and sweet.

And buttercups are coming,
And scarlet columbine,

And in the sunny meadows
The dandelions shine.

And just as many daisies
As their soft hands can hold,
The little ones may gather,
All fair in white and gold.

Here blows the warm red clover,
There peeps the violet blue;
Oh, happy little children!
God made them all for you.

Celia Thaxter

让雨下吧

雨点会打湿我们的头发，溅起的污泥会弄脏我们漂亮的衣服，雨天里我们不能到外边自由玩耍。但同时，雨水能够浇灌树木，清洗城市，帮助万物成长。

任何事情都有它有利的一面，也有它不利的一面，并且是可以相互转换的。别让那些消极的因素影响自己的心情，正确评估每一件事情，并努力促使事情向好的方向发展，这样，你的道路将越走越宽。

“哦，怎么开始下雨了！爸爸，爸爸，快看，天多暗啊！我只能整天待在家里了吗？”露丝向爸爸抱怨道。

“露丝，你会抱怨今天早餐的面包和乳酪吗？”

“看您说的，爸爸，多奇怪的一个问题！我怎么会抱怨呢？其实，如果我吃不到它们，我才会抱怨呢。”

“那么，我的女儿，当你看到花园里树木和花朵在生长的时候，你会抱怨吗？”

“抱怨？不，当然不。实际上，刚才我还很想到外边去仔细地欣赏它们呢，它们看起来好可爱啊！”

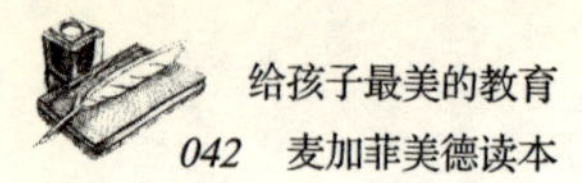

“好。那你看到马儿和牛羊在小溪边开怀畅饮的时候，你会感到遗憾吗？”

“噢，爸爸，你一定以为我是一个残忍的小姑娘，会希望那些辛勤劳作的马儿，给我们送来可口的牛奶的漂亮的小牛，还有那些可爱的小羊羔一直受到口渴的煎熬。”

“如果没有水喝，它们会死掉吗？”爸爸严肃地问。

“当然，我确信它们会渴死的。光是想想这个事情就让我感到难过。”

“我看小露丝对下雨感到十分的遗憾。可是你觉得，如果没有水，树木和花朵能够生长吗？”

“不，爸爸，它们会在阳光下枯萎的。那样，我们就看不到可爱的花了，我也没有办法给妈妈编漂亮的花圈了。”露丝难过地说。

“还有，我们的面包是用什么做成的呢？”

“我知道，是用面粉做成的。面粉是小麦在磨坊里磨出来的。”

爸爸摸摸露丝的头，赞许地说：“你说的没错，露丝。雨水帮助小麦生长，是水推动水磨将小麦磨成面粉。你还对下雨感到遗憾吗？”

“爸爸，我从来没想过这些事情，现在，我才知道下雨是多么快乐的事情。”

Let It Rain

Rose: See how it rains! Oh dear, dear, dear! how dull it is! Must I stay in doors all day?

Father: Why, Rose, are you sorry that you had any bread and butter for breakfast, this morning?

Rose: Why, father, what a question! I should be sorry, indeed, if I could not get any.

Father: Are you sorry, my daughter, when you see the flowers and the trees growing in the garden?

Rose: Sorry? No, indeed. Just now, I wished very much to go out and see them,—they look so pretty.

Father: Well, are you sorry when you see the horses, cows, or sheep drinking at the brook to quench their thirst?

Rose: Why, father, you must think I am a cruel girl, to wish that the poor horses that work so hard, the beautiful cows that give so much nice milk, and the pretty lambs should always be thirsty.

Father: Do you not think they would die, if they had no water to drink?

Rose: Yes, sir, I am sure they would. How shocking to think of such a thing!

Father: I thought little Rose was sorry it rained. Do you think the trees and flowers would grow, if they never had any water on them?

Rose: No, indeed, father, they would be dried up by the sun. Then we should not have any pretty flowers to look at, and to make wreaths of for mother.

Father: I thought you were sorry it rained. Rose, what is our bread made of?

Rose: It is made of flour, and the flour is made from wheat, which is ground in the mill.

Father: Yes, Rose, and it was rain that helped to make the wheat grow, and it was water that turned the mill to grind the wheat. I thought little Rose was sorry it rained.

Rose: I did not think of all these things, father. I am truly very glad to see the rain falling.

与水有关的诗句

落霞与孤鹜齐飞，秋水共长天一色。（王勃《秋日登洪府滕王阁饯别序》）

君不见黄河之水天上来，奔流到海不复回。（李白《将进酒》）

江作青罗带，山如碧玉簪。（韩愈《送桂州严大夫同用南字》）

日出江花红胜火，春来江水绿如蓝。（白居易《忆江南》）

水光潋滟晴方好，山色空蒙雨亦奇。（苏轼《饮湖上初晴后雨》）

山重水复疑无路，柳暗花明又一村。（陆游《游山西村》）

泉眼无声惜细流，树阴照水爱晴柔。（杨万里《小池》）

树叶的私语

自然规律是奇妙的，它维持着这个星球微妙的平衡。树叶飘落就如人生总会走到尽头一样，并不值得过早地去担忧。我们应享受人生每个阶段的精彩，坦然地面对成功与失败，快乐地度过每一天。

保尔·柯察金说："人最宝贵的是生命，生命每个人只有一次。人的一生应当这样度过，当你回首往事的时候，不会因为虚度年华而悔恨，也不会因为卑鄙庸俗而羞愧……"

当轻风吹过树林，隐隐约约地，仿佛听到小叶子哭泣和叹息的声音。

细枝关心地问："小叶子，你怎么了？"

"都是风，"小叶子回答："它刚才对我说，有—天它会把我拽下来，扔到地上，让我等死。"

细枝把这些话儿告诉了树杈，树杈又将它们转告给了大树。大树听到这些话，微微一笑，发出沙沙的响声，又把话儿传给了正在害怕地发抖的小叶子。

"不要害怕。"大树说，"紧紧地抓牢我，你准备好了，我才会让你离开呢。”

于是，小叶子停止了叹息，又继续开心地唱起歌来。整个夏天它都在快乐地成长，不知不觉就到十月。秋高气爽的日子里，小叶子看到周围所有的树叶都变得非常漂亮，一些是金黄色的，一些是褐色的，还有许多树叶上有五颜六色的条纹。于是，小叶子好奇地问大树这究竟是怎么回事儿。

大树回答说：“所有这些树叶都已做好了要飞的准备。它们都欣喜地穿上了自己最喜欢的颜色的衣服。”

听了大树的话，小叶子也想要飞走了。当它这样想时，它发现自己也开始变得漂亮起来。但当它为自己穿上彩衣而高兴时，却发现树杈并没有穿上鲜艳的衣服。于是小叶子问：“咦，树杈，为什么我们都是漂亮的金黄色，而你还是铅色的呢？”

“我们的工作还没有做完”大树替树杈回答说，“所以，我们必须继续穿着自己的工作服。而你们之所以穿上了节日礼服，是因为你们的任务已经完成了。”

就在这时，一阵微风吹来，还没等叶子回过味来，它发现自己就飘了起来。风儿托着小叶子在空中飞舞起来。

后来，叶子轻轻回旋着飘落下来，落在篱笆边的草地上，落在成百上千片的叶子当中。它再也没有醒过来，告诉我们它梦到了什么。

What the Leaf Said?

Once or twice a little leaf was heard to cry and sigh, as leaves often do, when a gentle wind is blowing. And the twig said, "What is the matter, little leaf?"

"The wind," said the leaf, "just told me that one day it would pull me off, and throw me on the ground to die."

The twig told it to the branch, and the branch told it to the tree. When the tree heard it, it rustled all over, and sent word back to the trembling leaf.

"Do not be afraid," it said; "hold on tight, and you shall not go off till you are ready."

So the leaf stopped sighing, and went on singing and rustling. It grew all the summer long till October. And when the bright days of autumn came, the leaf saw all the leaves around growing very beautiful.

Some were yellow, some were brown, and many were striped with different colors. Then the leaf asked the tree what this meant.

The tree said, "All these leaves are getting ready to fly away, and they have put on these colors because of their joy."

Then the little leaf began to want to go, and grew very beautiful in thinking of it. When it was gay in colors, it saw that the branches of the tree had no bright colors on them.

So the leaf said, "O branch! why are you lead-colored while we are all beautiful and golden?"

"We must keep on our working clothes," said the tree, "for our work is not yet done; but your clothes are for holidays, because your task is now over."

Just then a little puff of wind came, and the leaf let go without thinking, and the wind took it up and turned it over and over.

Then it fell gently down under the edge of the fence, among hundreds of leaves, and has never waked to tell us what it dreamed about.

浪花

小浪花完成了自己的工作，并在工作中获得了很多乐趣。工作意味着责任和付出，每个人来到世界上，都要承担一定的责任，接受着他人的付出，也要为这个世界付出自己的一份努力。

很多时候，你面对困难选择逃避，不是因为它无法战胜，而是害怕付出。

“我们要去哪里呀？”浪花问深沉的大海妈妈。

“亲爱的孩子，我们要去金黄的沙滩，你要去那里做你的事儿。”

“可我想去玩。”一个小浪花说，“我想去比赛，看我们谁能跳得最高。”

“不行，走吧，快走，我们得出发了。”另一个比较热心的浪花说，“妈妈说得一定没错，我们要去工作。”

“哦，我可不敢去。”还有一个浪花说，“看看沙滩边那些巨大的黑色岩石吧，它一定会把我撕成碎片的，我可不去那儿。”

“拉紧我的手，妹妹。”那个比较热心的浪花说，“让我们一起出发吧，你要知道做这类工作有多么的光荣。”

“我们还能回到妈妈身边吗？”

“当然了，我们一把工作完成就回来。”

于是大家急匆匆地出发了。即使那个最想玩的小浪花也觉得他们的工作才是最有趣的。那个胆子比较小的浪花也不甘落后，奋勇地奔向沙滩。

的确，这太有趣了！他们一个紧挨着一个，跳着，笑着，涌向岸边，冲上那闪闪发光的沙滩。

首先，他们涌入一幢美丽的沙滩城堡。扑通！扑通！他们冲进去又退出来。“噢，太有趣了。”他们叫道。

“妈妈让我带了一些海藻来，我要给它们找一个好地方。”一个浪花在岸边跑了好远，把海藻留在了鹅卵石上。鹅卵石嚷道：“欢迎你们的到来，我正想洗澡呢。”

“妈妈让我带来一些海贝，我不知道该放在哪里？”一个小浪花烦恼地说。“把它们一个挨一个放到沙滩上吧，小心不要弄破了。”一个年纪最大的浪花说。

小浪花做着自己的工作，把海贝轻轻地放到地上，小心极了，生怕摔坏一个。

“我做些什么呢？”一个身材高大的浪花说，“这和玩差不多嘛，小个子都能轻松地做完这些。妈妈还说这是我的工作呢！”说着，它冲上了岸边那巨大的岩石。

穿过岩石，它来到一个小池子里，听到鱼儿说：“海水来了。真的，太感激你了，亲爱的大海，你总是在暴风雨来临之前让大浪来给我们送信。也感谢你，亲爱的浪花，我们在这里已经准备好了。”

之后，浪花们全都从湿漉漉的沙滩上退了回来，看得出它们累了，动作缓慢而小心。

“我的贝壳全都完好无损。”一个说。

“我的海藻也留到了上面。”另一个说。

“我给所有的鹅卵石都洗了澡。”第三个抢着说。

“我——冲过了岸边的岩石，到了一个小水池里。”那个曾经想去做点大事的浪花说，“我没有做好，妈妈，那里没有什么事情可做。”

“嘘，安静一下，孩子们。”大海说话了。这时，他们听到一个在岸边散步的小男孩说：“妈妈，海水都已经漫过来了！看，沙滩又干净又漂亮，连那个小水池里的水也清澈无比。”

接着大海说：“听！”远远的，他们听见了风呼啸的声音，暴风雨要来了。

“走吧，我亲爱的孩子们。”大海妈妈说，“你们已经完成了你们的任务。现在让暴风雨去做他该做的事吧。”

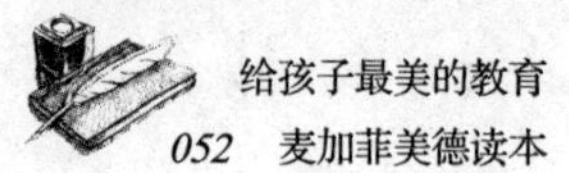

The Waves

"Where are we to go?" said the little waves to the great, deep sea.

"Go, my darlings, to the yellow sands: you will find work to do there."

"I want to play," said one little wave; "I want to see who can jump the highest."

"No; come on, come on," said an earnest wave; "mother must be right. I want to work."

"Oh, I dare not go," said another; "look at those great, black rocks close to the sands; I dare not go there, for they will tear me to pieces."

"Take my hand, sister," said the earnest wave; "let us go on together. How glorious it is to do some work."

"Shall we ever go back to mother?" "Yes, when our work is done."

So one and all hurried on. Even the little wave that wanted to play, pressed on, and thought that work might be fun after all. The timid ones did not like to be left behind, and they became earnest as they got nearer the sands.

After all, it was fun, pressing on one after another—jumping, laughing, running on to the broad, shining sands.

First, they came in their course to a great sand castle. Splash, splash! they all went over it, and down it came. "Oh, what fun!" they cried.

"Mother told me to bring these seaweeds; I will find a pretty place for them," said one—and she ran a long way over the sands, and left them among the pebbles. The pebbles cried, "We are glad you are come. We wanted washing."

"Mother sent these shells; I don't know where to put them," said a little fretful wave. "Lay them one by one on the sand, and do not break them," said the eldest wave.

And the little one went about its work, and learned to be quiet and gentle, for fear of breaking the shells.

"Where is my work?" said a great, full-grown wave. "this is mere play. The little ones can do this and laugh over it. Mother said there was work for me." And he came down upon some large rocks.

Over the rocks and into a pool he went, and he heard the fishes say, "The sea is coming. Thank you, great sea; you always send a big wave when a storm is nigh. Thank you, kind wave; we are all ready for you now."

Then the waves all went back over the wet sands, slowly and carelessly, for they were tired.

"All my shells are safe," said one.

And, "My seaweeds are left behind," said another.

"I washed all of the pebbles," said a third.

"And I—I only broke on a rock, and splashed into a pool," said the one that was so eager to work. "I have done no good, mother—no work at all"

"Hush!" said the sea. And they heard a child that was walking on the shore, say, "O mother, the sea has been here! Look, how nice and clean the sand is, and how clear the water is in that pool."

Then the sea, said, "Hark!" and far away they heard the deep moaning of the coming storm.

"Come, my darlings," said she; "you have done your work, now let the storm do its work."

面朝大海，春暖花开

从明天起，做一个幸福的人
喂马、劈柴，周游世界
从明天起，关心粮食和蔬菜
我有一所房子，面朝大海，春暖花开

从明天起，和每一个亲人通信
告诉他们我的幸福
那幸福的闪电告诉我的
我将告诉每一个人

给每一条河每一座山取一个温暖的名字
陌生人，我也为你祝福
愿你有一个灿烂的前程
愿你有情人终成眷属
愿你在尘世获得幸福
我只愿面朝大海，春暖花开

——海子

荨麻的故事

大自然里有无尽的宝库，土地、矿产、牛羊，还有和我们关系最为密切的植物。你了解那些千奇百怪的植物吗？你知道那些身边的小草叫什么名字吗？我们一起来看看父亲教了安娜哪些植物学的知识吧。

安娜：噢，爸爸！那棵荨麻扎了我的手。

父亲：亲爱的，这可不是个好消息。不过，把荨麻边上那片大草叶子揪起来，挤出叶子里面的汁擦在扎伤的地方，是不是感觉没那么疼了？

安娜：确实好多了，几乎都不疼了。但是我希望世界上没有荨麻就好了。我不知道它们能有什么用。

父亲：安娜，你要是知道一点植物学就不会这么说了。

安娜：爸爸，植物学是什么？

父亲：亲爱的，植物学是关于植物的知识。

安娜：有一些植物长得非常漂亮。要是百合长在我们的花园里，我才不会抱怨呢。可是这种荨麻多丑呀！我真不知道荨麻有什么好看的，它又能有什么用。

父亲：可是，宝贝，荨麻远比百合美丽、有用，我们能从它身上学到很多东西。

安娜：哦？爸爸，你为什么这么说呢？

父亲：戴上手套，拔起那棵荨麻，我们来仔细观察一下。先看看它的花。

安娜：爸爸，花在哪儿？我可看不到什么花，除非这些小小的疙疙瘩瘩的小团可以称为花。它们既没有颜色又没有香味，比别针头大不了多少。

父亲：给，再用放大镜看看。

安娜：噢，我现在看到了，每个小团都包在叶子里面，像玫瑰花骨朵一样。也许里面包着花儿呢。

父亲：试试用别针触这个小团，你看到了什么？

安娜：多奇妙啊！

父亲：什么很奇妙？

安娜：我一碰它，它就张开了。好像变魔术一样，腾起一朵小小的云雾，四片美丽的小小的花瓣伸展开来，如同是有生命的一般。现在通过镜片再仔细看，我看到一朵雅致的小花，和百合一样漂亮完美。

父亲：好的，现在来看看叶子。

安娜：我看到叶子上布满了刺。用放大镜观察每根刺的底部，它都有一个小小的盛满水一样液体的小包囊。哈！这就是刚才扎了我的东西。

父亲：现在用针尖去碰一下这个小包。

安娜：我挤压底部小包的时候，液体从刺顶端的小口渗了出来，所以我想这些小刺是中空的，可是它们比我的缝衣针的尖要硬多了。

父亲：所有的叶子都有刺吗？

安娜：不是的，爸爸，一些嫩叶是绿绿的，软软的，像天鹅绒一样，我即使握着它们也不会受到伤害。

父亲：现在来看茎，折断它。

安娜：很容易就折断了，可是却很难把它们分离开，因为外面的皮很坚韧地把它们连在了一起。

父亲：嗯，你看，荨麻身上有远超出你想像的有趣的东西。

安娜：真是这样的。但是你经常告诉我每一种东西都有它的用处，可是这些我都看不出来有什么用？

父亲：那我们现在来想一想。你刚才看到一朵小花绽开，有一团雾升了起来，你说就像变魔术一样。所有这些对植物来说都是必需的。世界上有成千上万种植物，上帝用他的智慧，让它们有自己的特色而与其他的种类相区分。现在看看长在路对面的荨麻吧，你发现它们和你刚才研究过的那种并不完全一样了吧。

安娜：是的，爸爸，不一样。这颗有小小的扁扁的籽，而不是花朵。

父亲：非常正确，亲爱的。现在，为了使这些种子能够生长，需要让这株荨麻的花和那株荨麻的种子结合在一起，如同其他大多数植物一样。由于植物不能像动物一样走路，上帝用他的智慧对此进行了补救。当这朵小花绽开的时候，它会抛出一种细细的粉，就是你看到的雾一样的东西。花粉由空气带到其他植株上，落在种子上，给它力量生长，使它成为一颗真正的种子。而当种子落在土里时，就会长出一棵新的植物来。要是没有这种花粉，种子永远也无法真正成熟。

安娜：太奇妙了。我知道那团小雾和花的作用了，可是刺伤我的叶子，会有什么用呢？爸爸，让你回答这个问题，会不会太为难你了？

父亲：就是这些刺对人们才有用呢。一些国家的穷人在生病的时候就用它们来治病。有些人用那些没有刺的叶子当食物。荨麻茎可以制造一种纤维，它和亚麻的用途一样。所以，你所看到的看似不起眼的荨麻也不是毫无用途的。

The Nettle

Anna: O papa! I have stung my hand with that nettle.

Father: Well, my dear, I am sorry for it; but pull up that large dock leaf you see near it; now bruise the juice out of it on the part which is stung. Well, is the pain lessened?

A: Oh, very much indeed, I hardly feel it now. But I wish there was not a nettle in the world. I am sure I do not know what use there can be in them.

F: If you knew anything of botany, Nanny, you would not say so.

A: What is botany, papa?

F: Botany, my dear, is the knowledge of plants.

A: Some plants are very beautiful. If the lily were growing in our fields, I should not complain. But this ugly nettle! I do not know what beauty or use there can be in that.

F: And yet, Nanny, there is more beauty, use, and instruction in a nettle, than even in a lily.

A: O papa, how can you make that out?

F: Put on your gloves, pluck up that nettle, and let us examine it. First, look at the flower.

A: The flower, papa? I see no flower, unless those little ragged knobs are flowers, which have neither color nor smell, and are not much larger than the heads of pins.

F: Here, take this magnifying glass and examine them.

A: Oh, I see now; every little knob is folded up in leaves, like a rosebud. Perhaps there is a flower inside.

F: Try; take this pin and touch the knob. Well, what do you see?

A: Oh, how curious!

F: What is curious?

A: The moment I touched it, it flew open. A little cloud rose out like enchantment, and four beautiful little stems sprung up as if they were alive; and, now that I look again with the glass, I see an elegant little flower as nice and perfect as a lily itself.

F: Well, now examine the leaves.

A: Oh, I see they are all covered over with little bristles; and when I examine them with the glass, I see a little bag, filled with a juice like water, at the bottom of each. Ha! these are the things which stung me.

F: Now touch the little bag with the point of the pin.

A: When I press the bag, the juice runs up and comes out at the small point at the top; so I suppose the little thorn must be hollow inside, though it is finer than the point of my cambric needle.

F: Have all the leaves those stings?

A: No, papa; some of the young ones are quite green and soft, like velvet, and I may handle them without any danger.

F: Now look at the stem, and break it.

A: I can easily crack it, but I can not break it asunder, for the bark is so strong that it holds it together.

F: Well, now you see there are more curious things in the nettle than you expected.

A: Yes, indeed, I see that. But you have often told me that God makes nothing without its use; and I am sure I can not see any use in all these things.

F: That we will now consider. You saw the little flower burst open, and a cloud rose, you say, like enchantment. Now all this is necessary for the nature of the plant. There are many thousand plants in the world, and it has pleased God, in his wisdom, to make them all different. Now look at this other nettle, which grew on the opposite side of the road; you see that it is not exactly like the one you have just examined.

A: No, papa; this has little flat seeds instead of flowers.

F: Very right, my dear. Now, in order to make those seeds grow, it is necessary that the little flower of this plant and the seed of that should be together, as they are in most others. But plants can not walk, like animals. The wisdom of God, therefore, has provided a remedy for this. When the little flower bursts open it throws out a fine powder, which you saw rise like a cloud; this is conveyed by the air to the other plant, and when it falls upon the seed of that plant it gives it power to grow, and makes it a perfect seed, which, in its turn, when it falls to the ground, will produce a new plant. Were it not for this fine powder, that seed would never be perfect or complete.

A: That is very curious, indeed; and I see the use of the little cloud and the flower; but the leaf that stung me, of what use can that be? There, dear papa, I am afraid I puzzle you to tell me that.

P: Even these stings are made useful to man. The poor people in some countries use them instead of blisters, when they are sick. Those leaves which do not sting are used by some for food, and from the stalk others get a stringy bark, which answers the purpose of flax. Thus you see that even the despised nettle is not made in vain.

荨 麻

中文学名:	荨麻	门:	被子门
拉丁学名:	Nettle	科:	荨麻科
别称:	蜇人草、咬人草、蝎子草	属:	荨麻属
界:	植物界	分布区域:	广泛分布于亚欧大陆

杂交荨麻是多年生草本植物，主要以地上嫩茎嫩叶供食用，其营养丰富，独具特色，素炒作汤、凉拌作馅均可，还可速冻或脱水长期贮藏。杂交荨麻因其丰富的营养价值而流行欧美。每100克嫩茎叶中含水分77.88克、粗蛋白4.66克、脂肪0.62克、粗纤维4.34克、碳水化合物9.64克。还含有较高的铁、钙等无机盐及丰富的胡萝卜素和维生素C，它含有的叶绿素也高于其他任何蔬菜。

杂交荨麻的根的醇提取物在欧洲特别是法国一直用于治疗前列腺肥大，其水溶性部位主要含有多糖类成分，能调解T淋巴细胞免疫功能，阻止上皮组织癌细胞的分化与扩散。

暴风雨

华盛顿·欧文（1783～1859），美国著名作家，生于纽约，他的著作滋养了美国文学。他受过常规教育，19岁时开始他的文学生涯，为他的哥哥创办的一份刊物写稿。1807年，他出版了第一本书《杂烩》。两年后，他出版了《纽约见闻录》。1815年，他旅居欧洲，并在那待了17年之久，在此期间，他完成了几部著作。1842～1846年间，他出任美国驻西班牙大使。他生命的最后时光是在纽约达里镇附近的森尼赛德度过的。他一生未婚。他的最后一部著作《华盛顿传》完成于他生命的最后一年。欧文的写作风格幽默、情感淳朴、追求文雅正确的表述。下面的文字节选于《布雷斯布里奇庄园》中的“道尔夫”。

旅程的第二天，他们来到海兰德。这是一个寂静、闷热的下午，他们随着海浪的起伏，在峻峭的群山间漂浮。在夏日的炙烤下，万物沉寂无声。木板的颤动声，或是船桨偶尔碰在船板上的声音，都在群山间引起回荡，回声沿着海岸一遍遍激荡着。每次船长喊出一道命令之后，好像无数无形的舌头就会从每处悬崖中伸出来，重复着他刚才的话。

道尔夫瞪大眼睛四处张望，静静地欣赏着这大自然的奇观，品味其中的愉悦和奇妙。在他的左侧，顿德斯堡耸立在树木繁茂的峭壁上，岩壁一层高过一层，树木层层叠叠，直抵高远的夏日天际。右侧，险峻的安东尼岬远远的矗立着，一只孤独的雄鹰正展翅飞过。再远一些，只见群山叠嶂，绵延起伏。

这时，道尔夫注意到有一团明亮、雪白的云朵，隐现于西方的山顶之上。云朵层层堆积，每一层都好像在将前面的一层用力往前推着，它们散发着炫目的光亮一直垒进到茫茫的蓝天里，隐约可以听到群山后面雷声滚滚。水面刚才还像镜子一样平静光滑，倒映着蓝天和高山，这时也被一阵风吹起暗色的波浪。鱼鹰盘旋鸣叫着，飞上干燥的树顶栖息。乌鸦乱作一团，飞向岩石的缝隙。自然界的万物都意识到，一场暴风雨就要来临了。

山顶的云朵这时聚做一团，虽然云尖还是明亮雪白的，但其余的地方已如泼墨般乌黑。大颗雨点没头没脑地砸下来，风儿清新，卷起层层浪花。不久，厚厚的云朵好像被尖耸的山峰刺穿了一样，大雨倾盆而下。闪电在云层之间穿越，岩石都跟着颤抖起来，树木仿佛要被撕裂一般。雷声接踵而至，在群山间回响着。它们先冲上了顿德斯堡，又沿着山间隘路上了海兰德，沿途在每个山头都留下新的回声。老布尔山也向暴风雨怒吼着。

有一段时间，疾风、迷雾和倾盆大雨遮蔽了眼前的一切。四周是一片让人恐惧的昏暗，大雨中不时闪耀的闪电更让人心惊。道尔夫还从未见识过如此狂暴的自然界，就好像暴雨在山崖中生生撕开一道裂缝，用天堂中所有的武器开始作战。

The Thunderstorm

Washington Irving (b. 1783, d. 1859). This distinguished author, whose works have enriched American literature, was born in the city of New York. He had an ordinary school education, and began his literary career at the age of nineteen, by writing for a paper published by his brother. His first book, "Salmagundi," was published in 1807. Two years later he published "Knickerbocker's History of New York." In 1815 he sailed for Europe, and remained abroad seventeen years, during which time he wrote several of his works. From 1842 to 1846 he was minister to Spain. The last years of his life were passed at "Sunnyside," near Tarrytown, N.Y. He was never married. "The Life of Washington," his last work, was completed in the same year in which he died. Mr. Irving's works are characterized by humor, chaste sentiment, and elegance and correctness of expression. The following selection is from "Dolph" in "Bracehridge Hall."

In the second day of the voyage, they came to the Highlands. It was the latter part of a calm, sultry day, that they floated gently with the tide between these stern mountains. There was that perfect quiet which prevails over nature in the languor of summer heat. The turning of a plank, or the accidental falling of an oar, on deck, was echoed from the mountain side and reverberated along the shores; and, if by chance the captain gave a shout of command, there were airy tongues that mocked it from every cliff.

Dolph gazed about him, in mute delight and wonder, at these scenes of nature's magnificence. To the left, the Dunderberg reared its woody precipices, height over height, forest over forest, away into the deep summer sky. To the right, strutted forth the bold promontory of Antony's Nose, with a solitary eagle wheeling about it; while beyond, mountain succeeded to mountain, until they seemed to lock their arms together and confine this mighty rive in their embraces.

In the midst of this admiration, Dolph remarked a pile of bright, snowy clouds peering above the western heights. It was succeeded by another, and another, each seemingly pushing onward its predecessor, and towering, with dazzling brilliancy, in the deep blue atmosphere; and now muttering peals of thunder were faintly heard rolling behind the mountains. The river, hitherto still and glassy, reflecting pictures of the sky and land, now showed a dark ripple at a distance, as the wind came creeping up it. The fishhawks wheeled and screamed, and sought their nests on the high, dry trees; the crows flew clamorously to the crevices of the rocks; and all nature seemed conscious of the approaching thunder gust.

The clouds now rolled in volumes over the mountain tops; their summits still bright and snowy, but the lower parts of an inky blackness. The rain began to patter down in broad and scattered drops; the wind freshened, and curled up the waves; at length, it seemed as if the bellying clouds were torn open by the mountain tops, and complete torrents of rain came rattling down. The lightning leaped from cloud to cloud, and streamed quivering against the rocks, splitting and rending the stoutest forest trees. The thunder burst in tremendous explosions; the peals were echoed from mountain to mountain; they crashed upon Dunderberg, and then rolled up the long defile of the Highlands, each headland making a new echo, until old Bull Hill seemed to bellow back the storm.

For a time the scudding rack and mist and the sheeted rain almost hid the landscape from the sight. There was a fearful gloom, illumined still more fearfully by the streams of lightning which glittered among the raindrops. Never had Dolph beheld such an absolute warring of the elements; it seemed as if the storm was tearing and rending its way through the mountain defile, and had brought all the artillery of heaven into action.

太阳的影响

约翰·廷德尔（1820～1893年），爱尔兰裔英国物理学家，现代最著名的科学家之一，法拉第的优秀学生。1853年，他接受英国皇家研究所的聘请，担任自然哲学教授。廷德尔因其关于气体的透明度和大气吸收辐射热量的著作而著名，他还著有一两本有关阿尔卑斯山脉及其冰川的趣味读物。他曾到美国访问，在此期间做了几场科学方面的报告，并演示了几次出色的物理实验，博得了美国科学界人士的喝彩。廷德尔一生为人类的科学事业做出了众多重要的发现。

就像转动钟表指针的力量确信无疑地来自于发条一样，地球上的所有力量都来自于太阳。不考虑火山爆发以及潮汐的涨落和流动等，地球表面所有的机械作用，所有力量的展示，无论是有机物的还是无机物的，无论是生物的还是物质的，都是由太阳产生的。它的高温使海水保持液体状态，大气层保持气体状态，所有风暴的形成都来自于太阳的作用。它将河水和冰川运动到高山上，瀑布和雪崩的巨大能量也都直接来自于太阳。

雷电也来自它的力量。每一场燃起的大火和每一束发光的火炬都

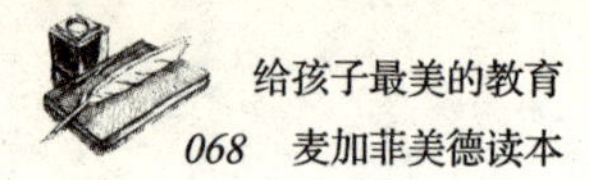

会发出光和热，而这些光和热最初都来自太阳。如今这个时代，我们不幸地经常听说战争的消息，但每次射击和装弹都是对太阳的机械能的利用或误用。它吹响了号角，它发射出子弹，它引爆了炸弹。别忘了，这不是诗歌，而是太阳机械能铁的事实。

就如我所说的，太阳滋养了所有的植物，并通过它们养活了所有的动物。田野里的百合花、青翠的牧场、山坡上成千上万的牛群等，都是太阳杰出的工艺品。太阳铸就了动物的肌肉，它推动血液进行循环，它促进了动物的智力发育。太阳的迅猛体现在狮子的腿上，它让豹子在林间跳跃、苍鹰在空中翱翔、蛇在草丛间滑行。它抚育了森林并把它砍倒，栽种树木和挥动斧头的力量实际上都是同一种能量。苜蓿发芽并且开花，割草人挥动镰刀等，使用的其实也是同一种能量。

太阳从我们的矿井中挖出了矿石，它使铁器变形，使水沸腾，它驱动了火车，不但种植了棉花还纺出了线并织成了网。高举的锤子、转动的车轮或抛出的梭子等，无一不是太阳举起、转动或抛出的。

太阳的能量在太空中自由释放，但是我们这个世界的点面上，能量被以各种形式利用了。仿若普罗特斯（希腊神话传说中的海神，他最大的特点就是能够任意改变自己的外形）施展着他的魔力。本质上完全相同的东西竟然能够演变出上百万种形状和颜色，并最终回归到它最初的、不易察觉的状态。太阳以热的形式来到我们身边，又以热的形式离我们而去，就在这一来一去之间，地球上产生了多种形式的能量。它们都是特殊形式的太阳能，这些模式的优势在于其能量来源是无穷无尽的。

The Influences of the Sun

John Tyndall, 1820–1893, one of the most celebrated modern scientists, was an Irishman by birth. He was a pupil of the distinguished Faraday. In 1853 he was appointed Professor of Natural Philosophy in the Royal Institution of London. He is known chiefly for his brilliant experiments and clear writing respecting heat, light, and sound. He also wrote one or two interesting books concerning the Alps and their glaciers. He visited America, and delighted the most intelligent audiences by his scientific lectures and his brilliant experiments. The scientific world is indebted to him for several remarkable discoveries.

As surely as the force which moves a clock's hands is derived from the arm which winds up the clock, so surely is all terrestrial power drawn from the sun. Leaving out of account the eruptions of volcanoes, and the ebb and flow of the tides, every mechanical action on the earth's surface, every manifestation of power, organic and inorganic, vital and physical, is produced by the sun. His warmth keeps the sea liquid, and the atmosphere a gas, and all the storms which agitate both are blown by

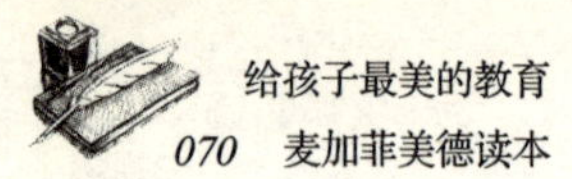

the mechanical force of the sun. He lifts the rivers and the glaciers up to the mountains; and thus the cataract and the avalanche shoot with an energy derived immediately from him.

Thunder and lightning are also his transmitted strength. Every fire that burns and every flame that glows, dispenses light and heat which originally belonged to the sun. In these days, unhappily, the news of battle is familiar to us, but every shock and every charge is an application or misapplication of the mechanical force of the sun. He blows the trumpet, he urges the projectile, he bursts the bomb. And, remember, this is not poetry, but rigid mechanical truth.

He rears, as I have said, the whole vegetable world, and through it the animal; the lilies of the field are his workmanship, the verdure of the meadows, and the cattle upon a thousand hills. He forms the muscles, he urges the blood, he builds the brain. His fleetness is in the lion's foot; he springs in the panther, he soars in the eagle, he slides in the snake. He builds the forest and hews it down, the power which raised the tree, and which wields the ax, being one and the same. The clover sprouts and blossoms, and the scythe of the mower swings, by the operation of the same force.

The sun digs the ore from our mines, he rolls the iron; he rivets the plates, he boils the water; he draws the train. He not only grows the cotton, but he spins the fiber and weaves the web. There is not a hammer raised, a wheel turned, or a shuttle thrown, that is not raised, and turned, and thrown by the sun.

His energy is poured freely into space, but our world is a halting place where this energy is conditioned. Here the Proteus works his spells; the selfsame essence takes a million shapes and hues, and finally dissolves into its primitive and almost formless form. The sun comes to us as heat; he quits us as heat; and between his entrance and departure the multiform powers of our globe appear. They are all special forms of solar power—the molds into which his strength is temporarily poured in passing from its source through infinitude.

太 阳

太阳是距离地球最近的恒星，是太阳系的中心天体。太阳系质量的99.87%都集中在太阳。太阳系中的八大行星、小行星、流星、彗星、外海王星天体以及星际尘埃等，都围绕着太阳进行公转。

但在茫茫宇宙中，太阳只是一颗非常普通的恒星，在广袤浩瀚的繁星世界里，太阳的亮度、大小和物质密度都处于中等水平。只是因为它离地球较近，所以看上去是天空中最大最亮的天体。其他恒星离我们都非常遥远，即使是最近的恒星，也比太阳远27万倍，看上去只是一个闪烁的光点。

太阳每时每刻都在向地球传送着光和热，有了太阳光，地球上的植物才能进行光合作用。据计算，整个世界的绿色植物每天可以产生约4亿吨的蛋白质、碳水化合物和脂肪，与此同时，还能向空气中释放出近5亿吨的氧，为人和动物提供了充足的食物和氧气。

考试

丹尼尔·皮尔斯·汤普森（1793～1868），生于马萨诸塞州的查尔斯镇，后随父搬到佛蒙特，二十岁之前一直生活在那里的一个农场里。他并没有什么机会接受教育，但汤普森志向远大，并善于把握每个机会。通过自身努力，他挣到了足够的钱支持自己进入米德伯瑞学院学习，并于1820年从那里毕业。随后，他作为私人教师去了弗吉尼亚，并在那里开始从事律师业。不久以后汤普森回到了佛蒙特，在蒙皮利开了一家律师事务所。随后被选举为法官，后来成为美国国务卿。从大学开始，汤普森就开始为多家杂志写稿，其小说代表作有《洛克·阿姆斯顿校长》、《掘金者梅·马丁》、《绿山男孩》和《女子军或托利的女儿》。

“您还有别的什么要问我的吗？先生？”洛克问道。

“没什么啦。”邦克·阿姆斯顿回答，“我可不懂那些阅读、写作、语法什么的，那些方面我就当你不错好了，当然，如果我发现你在别的方面都思维敏锐，这猜测很大程度上也就有根据了。你懂哲学吗？”

“先生，你是指哪方面的哲学？”

“就是那唯一的一方面啊。”

“但是你知道哲学可以分为很多种，比如说自然方面、道德方面或智力方面。”

“胡说！哲学就是哲学，就是研究我们所看见事物的前因后果，无论是应用于一个疯狂的梦境或是土豆的腐烂过程。你对此有了解吗？”

“是的，先生，相当程度上。”

“那么如果你愿意，我会提一两个问题。有一种现象，如果人同时向两把刀上吹气，锻造得好的那把刀上的湿气消散的比较快，这是什么原因呢？”

“大概是由于两把刀打磨程度的不同吧。”洛克这样回答。

“啊哈！这是个仅仅停留在表面的回答。”邦克幽默地反驳道。“你显然是个不错的思考者，但我想你一定没有思考这个问题。我总共花了一个星期努力思考这个问题，并在铁匠铺里做实验以找到它的原因，这与打磨的程度无关。就算拿两片打磨程度相同的刀，湿气一样会较快的从那把较好的刀上消散，这是因为两片刀在材质上有紧密和疏松的差别。”

“首先，我查明通过锤打和锻造可以使钢变得致密，而且锤打得越多，钢就变得越致密。当然，刀上的孔隙也会同比例减小。想到这里我立即就知道这就是我想找的答案。因为我们知道一块湿海绵的干燥时间比一块刚砍下来的湿木头的干燥时间要久得多，因为前者的孔隙更大。一块风干的木头或陈木比带着绿叶的木头容易干燥，道理也是一样的。”

“或者你可以在一块木头上用手钻钻出大孔，而另一块钻出小孔，在孔中注满水，把它们搁在那儿直至水分全部蒸发，它们所需时间的不同会更明显的证明这一点。所以就刀而言，水汽会在那片锻造得更为粗糙的刀上停留更久，因为它的空隙较大，吸收了更多的水汽微粒，所以需要更长的时间来变干。”

“这起码是个有独创性的理论，”洛克评论道，“这让我想起了另一个自然现象，对此我还没有找出让自己满意的解释。是这样的：为什么被踩过的土壤会比旁边没有被踩过的土壤冻得更硬更深呢？我询问过许多人，他们都说是因为被踩过的土壤更为致密，您觉得这是个充分的理由吗？”

“不是，”邦克说，“但我会告诉你是怎么回事，因为很久之前我就想出这个问题的答案了。你知道在寒冷的季节里，我们所获得的温暖多数是由地面散发出来的。就算不是一直如此，但至少在一定程度上，温暖的水汽会从地面土壤里散发出来与空气混合，从而缓解地面上的寒冷空气。”

“现在，这些上升的温暖气流基本会被踩实的致密土壤所阻隔，那自然，气流会在地面下分道从两旁较为疏松的土壤里散发出来。这样，被踩实的道路下面相当深的地方就是一片冰冷和死寂，这就为霜冻的侵袭和蔓延提供了条件，地表下的暖空气对此也不会有任何影响。暖空气会不受阻碍地从两边升上来，从而阻碍它们所作用的那块区域形成冰冻。”

“这就是这个现象的合理解释了，先生，你应该相信它。但我们将不再讨论这些问题了，因为我已完全相信你不仅有丰富的知识，更懂得如何自己思考问题。现在，我想进一步了解的是，你是否能够教导别人去思考，这是当好一个老师的关键。但由于我在注意观察其他方面的时候已经留意到了这一点，也许我要求你做的只是在这里的一个孩子身上做个小小的实验就可以了。”

“请便，先生。”洛克说道。

“好的。”邦克转过身面对壁炉，木材燃烧产生的烟雾形成了一个烟柱往上升去，邦克继续说，“你看见那儿烟雾在上升吧？你我都明白为何烟雾会向上扩散，但我这里最小的孩子还不懂得这个道理。

现在去吧，看看你能不能让他明白。”

洛克沉思了一会儿，环顾了一下屋子四周，看看有什么东西可以作为有用的教具。他在架子上意外发现了一些可用的东西，这套铸铁是最小的一套，就是人们常说的空心圆管，马车的轮轴可以在里面转动。然后他选了一个刚好能容纳那铁管的锡杯，将杯子里注上适量的水，他预计把铁管放进去后杯里的水刚好满溢。洛克把这些分别拿给那个孩子看，并问道：

“你瞧，小家伙，告诉我这两件东西哪个更重些？”

“嗯，一定是这个圆管了。”孩子一手拿着半满的杯子，一手拿着空心铁管回答道。

“那么你觉得这铁管比等体积的水要重，是吗？”洛克继续问。

“嗯，是的，还是要重的，我知道这一点。”孩子立刻就给出了回答。

“那现在看清楚我做了什么！”洛克接着把铁管放入了杯子中，水立即上涨到了杯子的边缘。

“看到了吗？水上升到杯子的顶部了！”

“是的，我看到了。”

“很好，这是什么引起的呢？”

“嗯，这么简单，我再清楚不过啦！因为铁管更重一些，而且它的四周都是水，水不能向别处流散，就只能上升了。”

“十分正确！那现在能不能告诉我是什么引起了烟雾沿着烟囱向上升呢？”

“嗯，我想，”孩子迟疑着。回答说，“我想——我想我不知道。”

“那么你以前有没有在冬天为了看清高架子上有什么东西而踩上椅子，结果头快要接近暖和的屋子的顶部的事呢？你注意到屋子上方的空气和下方的空气有什么不同吗？”

“有啊，我记得有过。我发现上方的空气十分温暖，而我下来以后低头捡东西的时候，我觉得那里的空气寒冷极了。”

“事实就是这样的。但我希望你能告诉我为什么冷空气总是在停留在屋子下方，而同时暖空气却在上方呢？”

“因为，因为，重的东西会下沉，嗯，冷空气——有了！我有答案了！我肯定——冷空气比较重，所以下沉，暖空气就上升了！”

“很好。你已经明白冷空气比热空气重的道理了，就像铁要比水重一样。现在让我们回头看看这个问题——什么导致了烟雾上升呢？”

“噢！我现在十分清楚了！冷空气沉在四周，就像那个铁管，推动被火加热的空气上升，就像杯中的水。烟雾被热空气带了上去，就像旋风中的羽毛和物品。哎呀！我已找出了烟雾上升的原因了，真是太奇妙了！”

“干得真像个哲学家！”邦克叫道，“问题都解决了！我相信你会是千里挑一的好老师！你不仅能够自己思考，还可以启发别人思考，所以你可以尽早来上任了。”

美国中小学学制

“六-三-三制”是美国当前最重要的学制，在美国占主导地位，城市和经济较发达的农村地区以及规模较大的学区普遍实行这种学制；19世纪60年代以后在“六-三-三制”基础上出现的“四-四-四制”或“五-三-四制”，由于更加符合学生身心发展的特点，所以备受人们的青睐，许多州纷纷创办。与中国不同的是，在美国，一律是几年级学生，从1至12级学生。

The Examination

Daniel Pierce Thompson (b. 1795, d. 1868) was born at Charlestown, Mass., but soon removed with his father to Vermont, where he lived until twenty years of age, on a farm. His means of schooling were most limited, but he was very ambitious and seized every opportunity. By his own efforts he earned enough money to carry him through Middlebury College, where he graduated in 1820. He then went to Virginia as private tutor, and while there was entered at the bar. He shortly returned to Vermont, and opened a law office in Montpelier. In time he was elected a judge, and later secretary of state. From his college days Mr. Thompson was a writer for the various magazines. Among his novels may be mentioned "Locke Amsden, the Schoolmaster," "May Martin, or the Money Diggers," "The Green Mountain Boys," and "The Rangers, or the Tory's Daughter."

"Have you any questions to ask me in the other branches, sir?" asked Locke.

"Not many," replied Bunker. "There is reading, writing, grammar, etc., which I know nothing about; and as to them, I must, of course, take you by guess, which will not be much of a guess, after all, if I find you have thought well on all other matters. Do you understand philosophy?"

"To what branch of philosophy do you allude, sir?"

"To the only branch there is."

"But you are aware that philosophy is divided into different kinds; as, natural, moral, and intellectual."

"Nonsense! philosophy is philosophy, and means the study of the reasons and causes of the things which we see, whether it be applied to a crazy man's dreams, or the roasting of potatoes. Have you attended to it?"

"Yes, to a considerable extent, sir."

"I will put a question or two, then, if you please. What is the reason of the fact, for it is a fact, that the damp breath of a person blown on a good knife and on a bad one, will soonest disappear from the well-tempered blade?"

"It may be owing to the difference in the polish of the two blades, perhaps." replied Locke.

"Ah! that is an answer that don't go deeper than the surface," rejoined Bunker, humorously. "As good a thinker as you evidently are, you have not thought on this subject, I suspect. It took me a week, in all, I presume, of hard thinking, and making experiments at a blacksmith's shop, to discover the reason of this. It is not the polish; for take two blades of equal polish, and the breath will disappear from one as much quicker than it does from the other, as the blade is better. It is because the material of the blade is more compact or less porous in one case than in the other.

"In the first place, I ascertained that the steel was, made more compact by being hammered and tempered, and that the better it was tempered the more compact it would become; the size of the pores being made, of course, less in the same proportion. Well, then, I saw the reason I was in search of, at once. For we know a wet sponge is longer in drying than a wet piece of green wood, because the pores of the first are bigger. A seasoned or shrunk piece of wood dries quicker than a green one, for the same reason.

"Or you might bore a piece of wood with large gimlet holes, and another with small ones, fill them both with water, and let them stand till the water evaporated, and the difference of time it would take to do this would make the case still more plain. So with the blades: the vapor lingers longest on the worst wrought and tempered one, because the pores, being larger, take in more of the wet particles, and require more time in drying."

"Your theory is at least a very ingenious one," observed Locke, "and I am reminded by it of another of the natural phenomena, of the true explanation of which I have not been able to satisfy myself. It is this: what makes the earth freeze harder and deeper under a trodden path than the untrodden earth around it? All that I have asked, say it is because the trodden earth is more compact. But is that reason a sufficient one?"

"No," said Bunker, "but I will tell you what the reason is, for I thought that out long ago. You know that, in the freezing months, much of the warmth we get is given out by the earth, from which, at intervals, if not constantly, to some extent, ascend the warm vapors to mingle with and moderate the cold atmosphere above.

"Now these ascending streams of warm air would be almost wholly obstructed by the compactness of a trodden path, and they would naturally divide at some distance below it, and pass up through the loose earth on each side, leaving the ground along the line of the path, to a great depth beneath it, a cold, dead mass, through which the frost would continue to penetrate, unchecked by the internal heat, which, in its unobstructed ascent on each side, would be continually checking or overcoming the frost in its action on the earth around.

"That, sir, is the true philosophy of the case, you may depend upon it. But we will now drop the discussion of these matters; for I am abundantly satisfied that you have not only knowledge enough, but that you can think for yourself. And now, sir, all I wish to know further about you is, whether you can teach others to think, which is half the battle with a teacher. But as I have had an eye on this point, while attending to the others, probably one experiment, which I will ask you to make on one of the boys here, will be all I shall want."

"Proceed, sir," said the other.

"Ay, sir," rejoined Bunker, turning to the open fireplace, in which the burning wood was sending up a column of smoke, "there, you see that smoke rising, don't you? Well, you and I know the reason why smoke goes upward, but my youngest boy does not, I think. Now take your own way, and see if you can make him understand it."

Locke, after a moment's reflection, and a glance round the room for something to serve for apparatus, took from a shelf, where he had espied a number of articles, the smallest of a set of cast–iron cart boxes, as are usually termed the round hollow tubes in which the axletree of a carriage turns. Then selecting a tin cup that would just take in the box, and turning into the cup as much water as he judged, with the box, would fill it, he presented them separately to the boy, and said,

"There, my lad, tell me which of these is the heavier."

"Why, the cart box, to be sure," replied the boy, taking the cup, half-filled with water, in one hand, and the hollow iron in the other.

"Then you think this iron is heavier than as much water as would fill the place of it, do you?" resumed Locke.

"Why, yes, as heavy again, and more too—I know it is," promptly said the boy.

"Well, sir, now mark what I do," proceeded the former, dropping into the cup the iron box, through the hollow of which the water instantly rose to the brim of the vessel.

"There, you saw that water rise to the top of the cup, did you?"

"Yes, I did."

"Very well, what caused it to do so?"

"Why, I know well enough, if I could only think: why, it is because the iron is the heavier, and as it comes all around the water so it can't get away sideways, it is forced up."

"That is right; and now I want you to tell what makes that smoke rise up the chimney."

"Why,— I guess," replied the boy, hesitating, "I guess,—I guess I don't know."

"Did you ever get up in a chair to look on some high shelf, so that your head was brought near the ceiling of a heated room, in winter? and did you notice any difference between the air up there and the air near the floor?"

"Yes, I remember I have, and found the air up there as warm as mustard; and when I got down, and bent my head near the floor to pick

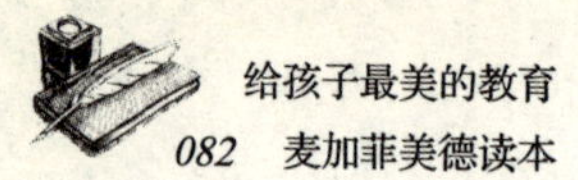

up something, I found it as cold as could be."

"That is ever the case; but I wish you to tell me how the cold air always happens to settle down to the lower part of the room, while the warm air, somehow, at the same time, gets above."

"Why, why, heavy things settle down, and the cold air—yes, yes, that's it, I am sure—the cold air is heavier, and so settles down, and crowds up the warm air."

"Very good. You then understand that cold air is heavier than the heated air, as that iron is heavier than the water; so now we will go back to the main question—what makes the smoke go upwards?"

"Oh! I see now as plain as day; the cold air settles down all round, like the iron box, and drives up the hot air as fast as the fire heats it, in the middle, like the water; and so the hot air carries the smoke along up with it, just as feathers and things in a whirlwind. Well! I have found out what makes smoke go up—isn't it curious?"

"Done like a philosopher!" cried Bunker. "The thing is settled. I will grant that you are a teacher among a thousand. You can not only think yourself, but can teach others to think; so you may call the position yours as quick as you please."

CHAPTER 3

可爱的大自然

我不是不爱人类，而是更爱大自然。

——[英]拜伦

麻雀先生

一个孩子在向麻雀表达他的善意。孩子们对一切都充满着好奇，在他们的眼睛里，没有等级，没有贵贱，他们只看到生命，而生命是平等的。

很高兴见到你，麻雀先生！
我听到你叽叽喳喳的叫声，
你想要说什么？
天寒地冻你需要些食物？

我早都为你准备好了，
看这，多么丰盛的宴席，
请不要害怕，这都是为了款待你，
我会等在这里，看着你吃掉它们。

我听到一些关于你的可怕传闻，
那些都是真的吗？

他们说你是夏日里的大盗，
你一定觉得那很荒谬吧？

托马斯说你偷走了他的小麦，
约翰叔叔抱怨你啄食了他的李子，
你只选那些最好的下嘴，
全不顾它们的主人是谁。

但是我现在并不在意，
你以前都做过什么，
这是你的早餐，请吃光它们，
欢迎你来看我，请每天都来。

The Sparrow

Glad to see you, little bird;
Twas your little chirp I heard:
What did you intend to say?
"Give me something this cold day"?

That I will, and plenty, too;
All the crumbs I saved for you.
Don't be frightened—here's a treat:
I will wait and see you eat.

Shocking tales I hear of you;
Chirp, and tell me, are they true?
Robbing all the summer long;
Don't you think it very wrong?

Thomas says you steal his wheat;
John complains, his plums you eat—

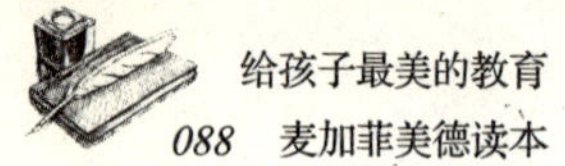

Choose the ripest for your share,
Never asking whose they are.

But I will not try to know
What you did so long ago:
There's your breakfast, eat away;
Come to see me every day.

与麻雀有关的歇后语

麻雀嫁女——细吹细打

麻雀饮河水——干不了

麻雀搬家——唧唧喳喳

麻雀飞进照相馆——见面容易说话难

麻雀飞到旗杆上——鸟不大，架子倒不小

麻雀飞到糖堆上——空欢喜

麻雀掉在面缸里——糊嘴

麻雀开会——细商量

麻雀飞大海——没着落

麻雀鼓肚子——好大的气

讲故事的人

品达叔叔要讲的故事里的地方叫做北极，是地球的最北端。北极生活着爱斯基摩人和他们的阿拉斯加雪橇犬。在那里，狗在人们生活中扮演着重要的角色。格陵兰岛的歌中有这样的歌词："没有狗的猎人只能算是半个猎人。"它们不仅帮着人们打猎、拉雪橇，也是搜救的好帮手。

彼得·品达可是个讲故事的高手，孩子们都喜欢围着他转。这不，当他路过学校时，孩子们又围住了他。"请给我们讲一个没有听过的故事吧。"孩子们七嘴八舌地要求。内德大声喊："最好是关于男孩和小狗的故事。"

"好，好"彼得说，"你们都是好孩子，而且非常的有礼貌，我就给你们讲一个新故事。讲些什么呢？满足内德的愿望，就讲一个男孩和一只狗的故事吧。"

"不过，在我们开始之前，我们能不能找一个比较阴凉的地方。约翰，一会你要像小老鼠一样的安静噢。还有你，玛丽。你得管好你那只大狗，别让它叫个不停。"

彼得带着孩子们来到一棵大树下，这正是个讲故事的好地方。

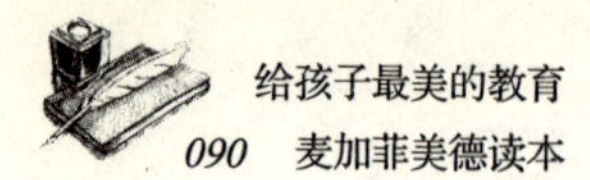

“在一个很远很远的地方，有一处非常寒冷的陆地，那里经常下雪。那儿的山好高，去那旅行的人时常会迷失在山里面。当地人养了许多个头很大的狗，他们还教会了这些狗去搜救在雪中迷路的人们。你们知道，狗的嗅觉是非常灵敏的，它们仅靠气味就能够找到迷路的人们。”

“有时天真是漆黑一片，伸手不见五指。经常会有人迷了路，走得精疲力竭，被埋在雪堆下面。”

“也是在这样一个寒冷的夜晚，大雪急急地下着，狂风呼呼地吹着。外边一片漆黑，天空中看不到一颗星星。当地的好心人把家里的狗放了出去，看看有没有需要帮助的人。一、两个小时后，人们就听到狗跑回来了。

“他们向屋外一看，发现狗驮着一个男孩。这个可怜的孩子已经冻僵了，好在他仍能勉强坚持着趴在狗的背上。”

“一看就知道，他已在雪地里躺了很长时间，虚弱得连走路的力气都没有了。恍恍惚惚间，他感到有东西在拖他的外套，听到狗的吠声，他挣扎地伸出了手，碰到了狗的身体，这只狗又用力拖了拖他。

“狗给了男孩一线希望。求生的本能让他紧紧地抓住狗，一点一点的，狗把男孩拖出了雪堆，但他太虚弱了，站都站不起来，更别说走动了。”

“他勉强爬上狗背，用手臂环着狗的脖子，紧紧搂住它，他知道狗丝毫没有伤害他的意思。于是男孩骑着这只狗，一直坚持到了这个好心人的家。

“这家好心人悉心地照顾着他，直到雪停了，才把他送回他自己的家。”

The Story–Teller

Peter Pindar was a great storyteller. One day, as he was going by the school, the children gathered around him.

They said, "Please tell us a story we have never heard." Ned said, "'Tell us something about boys and dogs."

"Well," said Peter, "I love to please good children, and, as you all appear civil, I will tell you a new story; and it shall be about a boy and some dogs, as Ned asks.

"But before we begin, let us sit down in a cool, shady place. And now, John, you must be as still as a little mouse. Mary, you must not let Towser bark or make a noise.

"A long way from this place, there is a land where it is very cold, and much snow falls.

"The hills are very high there, and traveler's are often lost among them. There are men there who keep large dogs. These are taught to hunt for people lost in the snow.

"The dogs have so fine a scent, that they can find persons by that alone.

"Sometimes it is so dark, that they can not see anything. Those who are lost often lie hid in the snowdrifts. "

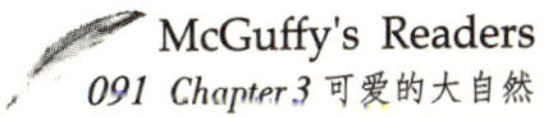

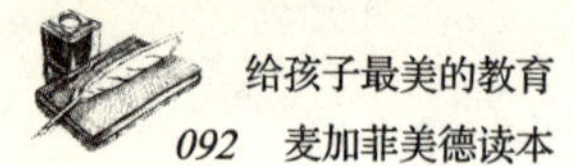

"One cold, bleak night, the snow fell fast, and the wind blew loud and shrill. It was quite dark. Not a star was to be seen in the sky.

"These good men sent out a dog, to hunt for those who might want help.In an hour or two, the dog was heard coming back.

"On looking out, they saw him with a boy on his back. The poor child was stiff with cold. He could but just hold on to the dog's back.

"He had lain for a long time in the snow, and was too weak to walk.

"He felt something pull him by the coat, and heard the bark of a dog. He put out his hand, and felt the dog. The dog gave him another pull.

"This gave the poor boy some hope, and he took hold of the dog. He drew himself out of the snow, but ho could not stand or walk.

"He got on the dog's back, and put his arms round the dog's neck, and held on. He felt sure that the dog did not mean to do him any harm.

"Thus he rode all the way to the good men's house.

"They took care of him, till the snow was gone. Then they sent him to his home."

詹妮的呼唤

万物皆有灵性。你以什么样的态度对待对方，对方就会以什么样的态度对待你。不要以为人比动物更聪明，就可以无情地驾驭驱使它们。我们也是动物界中的一员，只不过在进化的道路上多走了几步。何况，人类的一些行为，要比动物更凶残和愚昧。

“没用的，泰姆波拉夫人。我们花了将近一个小时去抓那匹撒野的马，但它是不可能被逮住的。”

五月的一个令人愉快的早晨，当泰姆波拉夫人计划骑马出行的时候，佣人告诉她这样一个的消息。

“我知道它难以驯服，但我就是想骑它。”她转身说道。

“你想要什么，妈妈？”詹妮问。詹妮是一个活泼可爱、长着褐色头发、有双褐色眼睛的十二岁女孩。此时，她正好走到屋子里。

“我需要芳妮，”妈妈说，“多么好的一个早晨。我想骑着它到镇上去，去杂货店买一些东西，顺便拜访你的姑妈安，和她一起去河边骑会儿马，之后邀请她到家里一块吃晚饭。但是，你父亲整天都在外面，佣人们用了将近一个小时，连马毛都没有给我带回来一根，他们中甚至有人声称那匹马根本就无法被抓住。”

“可能它是不会让他们抓住它的，”詹妮说，露出一个轻快的微笑，“不过，妈妈，你尽管做出行前的准备吧。假如你真想骑它，我会为它套上马具的。”

“什么！我的孩子，他们说它总是轻松地跃过壕沟，就像一匹野马。如果你花时间去抓它的话，可能一无所获，而且还会让自己筋疲力尽，耽误去学校上课。”

“这不会花费我多长时间的，妈妈，芳妮会自动跑到我身边来。”詹妮一边快乐地说着，一边戴上她的大草帽，立即动身到山下的牧场去了。

马儿一听到詹妮衣裙的沙沙声，便竖起耳朵，打了个响鼻，警惕地抬起头，像是随时准备要逃开似的。

“芳妮！噢，芳妮！”詹妮大声呼叫着马儿的名字，这匹漂亮的马把头转了过来。这温柔的呼唤是马儿熟悉的，看到它的朋友更让马儿高兴。芳妮立刻跑到栅栏边，用它的头亲热地蹭着小女孩的肩。栅栏门被打开了，马儿随着詹妮到了马棚。

佣人们总是很粗暴地对待它，它记着呢！但它也记着詹妮总是很温柔的声音，和她轻轻爱抚它的双手。它用爱回报詹妮的爱，而且也乐意为朋友服务。

Jenny's Call

"It's of no use, Mrs. Templar; I have been trying the greater part of an hour to catch that rogue of a horse. She won't be caught."

Such was the report the hired man brought in to Mrs. Templar one pleasant May morning, when she had been planning a ride.

"I suppose it can not be helped, but I wanted her very much," she said, as she turned away.

"What was it you wanted, mother?" asked Jenny Templar, a bright, brown-haired, brown-eyed girl of twelve, who had just come into the room.

"Fanny," said the mother. "It is such a beautiful morning, I meant to drive down to the village, get some groceries, then call for your Aunt Ann, have a nice ride up the river road, and bring her home to dinner.

"But father is away for all day, and the men have been trying nearly an hour to catch Fanny; one of the men says she can't be caught."

"Maybe she can't by him," said Jenny, with a merry laugh. "But, get ready, mother; you shall go if you like. I'll catch Fanny, and harness her, too."

"Why, my child, they say she jumped the ditch three or four times, and acted like a wild creature. You'll only be late at school, and tire yourself for nothing."

"It won't take me long, mother. Fanny will come to me," said Jenny, cheerily. She put on her wide straw hat, and was off in a moment, down the hill, to the field where the horse was grazing.

The moment Fanny heard the rustle of Jenny's dress, she pricked up her ears, snorted, and, with head erect, seemed ready to bound away again.

"Fanny! O Fanny!" called Jenny, and the beautiful creature turned her head. That gentle tone she well knew, and, glad to see her friend, she carne directly to the fence, and rubbed her head on the girl's shoulder. As soon as the gate was opened, she followed Jenny to the barn.

The men had treated her roughly, and she remembered it. But she knew and loved the voice that was always kind, and the hand that often fed and caressed her. She gave love for love, and willing service for kindness.

猫头鹰

如果你看过《哈利·波特》，你一定记得哈利的那只宠物——白猫头鹰，它是魔法世界里最高贵的宠物。智慧女神雅典娜的爱鸟也是一只小鸮（猫头鹰的一种），象征着智慧。在日本，猫头鹰被称为福鸟。但在中国，猫头鹰通常被看做是“不详之鸟”，被叫做逐魂鸟、报丧鸟。

猫头鹰大多数是夜行动物，在夜晚，它的能见度比人高出一百倍。再加上它羽毛柔软，飞行无声，能够悄悄地接近猎物，进行闪击，一般落入它眼中的猎物很少能够逃脱。猫头鹰是捕鼠能手，一年能吃掉一千多只老鼠，帮人们节约了不少的粮食。

“你从哪儿抓到那只猫头鹰的，哈瑞？”一个小伙伴羡慕地问。

“我和弗瑞德在一棵空心的老橡树里发现它的。”哈瑞得意地说。

“可是，你怎么发现它在那儿的呢？”

“我来告诉你吧。有天黄昏，我和弗瑞德围着一个旧的谷仓在玩捉迷藏。当我正要爬进一个角落时，听到一声尖叫，一只大鸟飞过我的头顶，爪子上还抓着一个什么东西。我也顾不得玩游戏了，马上叫来弗瑞德，我们看到它飞到了这棵树周围。弗瑞德认为，这只鸟是一

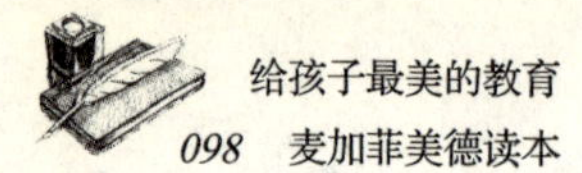

只猫头鹰，它的窝就安在那棵老橡树上。第二天，我们就去橡树那找它，果然，它就在那儿。”

“但是你们是如何逮住它的？它有那样锋利的喙，真要啄起人来一定很厉害。”

“它醒着的时候当然很厉害，可是，它在白天却看不清东西，而且还会时不时地打盹。我们在橡树洞里看到它的时候，它睁着一双大眼，羽毛支楞着，不时‘咕咕’地叫。可弗瑞德说：‘不要怕它。’毫不犹豫地把它塞进了袋子里。”

“弗瑞德可真胆大。哈瑞，你现在想把它怎么办？”小伙伴问。

“我想放飞它。它在老橡树里呆惯了，不会喜欢这个笼子的。如果是一只小猫头鹰的话，驯养起来还比较容易，但这只太老了。”

“但是它不会抓你的小鸭子和小鸡吗？”

“不会的，这周围有好多老鼠。我爸说猫头鹰是捕鼠能手，一只猫头鹰的捕鼠能力，要顶得上五六只猫呢。”

“真不错，在你放飞它之前我还能看到它，瞧，它的毛是多么柔软！”

“是的，当它在飞的时候，你几乎发现不了它的动静。正是由于这一点，它才能非常容易地捕获到猎物。”

“但它看起来很滑稽，大眼睛眨啊眨的，头总是晃来晃去的。”

“呵呵，那是它在观察你的狗呢，喂，安静一点，小狗。你知道吗？我们发现它吃起东西来可非常有趣。它先把老鼠的骨头咬碎，然后整个吞下去。过一两个小时，它才把团成一团的骨头和毛皮吐出来。”

“谢谢你告诉我这么多，哈瑞。原来猫头鹰是这样的，真有趣。”

The Owl

"Where did you get that owl, Harry?"

"Fred and I found him in the old, hollow oak."

"How did you know he was there?"

"I'll tell you. Fred and I were playing 'hide and seek' round the old barn, one night just at dusk.

"I was just creeping round the corner, when I heard a loud squeak, and a big bird flew up with something in his claws.

"I called Fred, and we watched him as he flew to the woods. Fred thought the bird was an owl, and that he had a nest in the old oak.

"The next day we went to look for him, and, sure enough, he was there."

"But how did you catch him? I should think he could fight like a good fellow with that sharp bill."

"He can when he is wide awake; but owls can't see very well in the daytime, and he was taking a nap.

"He opened his great eyes, and ruffled up his feathers, and said, "Whoo! Whoo!' 'Never mind who,' Fred said, and slipped him into a bag."

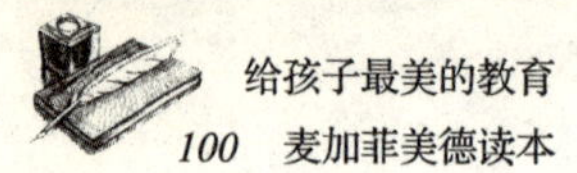

"What are you going to do with him, Harry?"

"Let him go. He doesn't like this cage half so well as his old oak tree. A young owl can be tamed easily, but this one is too old to tame."

"But won't he catch all your ducklings and little chickens?"

"No, not while there are any rats or mice around. Father says an owl is a good mouser, and can catch more mice than half a dozen cats."

"I'm glad I had a look at him before you let him go. What soft feathers he has!"

"Yes, he can fly so softly that you can scarcely hear him, and for this reason he can easily surprise and capture his prey."

"How comical he looks, winking his big eyes slowly, and turning his head from side to side!"

"Yes; he is watching your dog. Be still. Bounce!

"We have just found out a funny thing about his way of eating. He breaks the bones of a mouse, and then swallows it whole. After an hour or two, he throws up the bones and fur rolled up in a little ball."

蜜蜂之歌

蜜蜂是一种群居性昆虫，过着母系氏族生活。一个蜂巢由1～2只蜂王、近千只雄蜂和2～5万只工蜂组成。你所看到的勤劳的小蜜蜂都是工蜂，筑巢、采蜜、育儿、守卫等工作都是由工蜂来完成的。

8字舞是蜜蜂们传递蜜源信息的特殊方式，采蜜可是项辛苦活，一只蜜蜂要采一千多朵花才能获得一蜜囊蜂蜜，一生只能采获0.6克蜂蜜。但蜜蜂对人类最大的贡献，是它在采蜜的同时，完成了植物相互间的授粉工作，世界上76%的粮食作物和84%的植物依靠它们传授花粉。

蜜蜂管自己住的地方叫做蜂房。

根据工作的不同，它们可以分为三种：工蜂、雄蜂和蜂王。蜂王在每个蜂房里只能有一只，它是这里真正的王。如果蜂王失踪或死掉了，其他蜜蜂就不知道该干什么好了。

它们是一群非常聪明而又勤劳的小生灵。它们齐心协力为蜂宝宝们建造蜂巢。每只蜜蜂都能找到自己的位置，做自己分内的工作。一些忙着出外采花蜜，一些则待在家中在蜂巢里辛勤地工作。

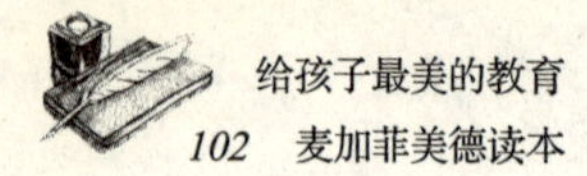

蜜蜂们为自己建造的房间可以称为一件伟大的艺术品。每一个小巢室的形状和尺寸都一模一样，巢室并不是圆的，它是一个正六边形，巢室与巢室之间连一丝空隙都没有。

如果蜂房是透明的，你就可以看到蜜蜂工作时的情景。一大群小家伙总是忙忙碌碌地在蜂房里爬进爬出，真是有趣。

不过，所有的雄蜂都会在冬天来临之前被赶出蜂房或者被杀死，因为它们并不采蜜。冬天万物凋零，蜜蜂们没有食物来源，只能靠积蓄的花蜜度过漫长的冬季。

可是，孩子们，千万不要因为蜜蜂很可爱，就冒冒失失地用手去抓它们。蜜蜂有令人生畏的螫，它们很清楚应如何在防御中使用它。

让我们一起来唱这首蜜蜂之歌吧。

嗡嗡嗡，那是蜜蜂在欢唱，
多么快乐的小家伙，
它有金黄色的小腿，
它还是一个伟大的工程师。

阳光明媚，它出门采蜜，
天气阴沉，它就在家酿蜜，
一会落在洁白的百合上，一会停在粉红色的喇叭花上，
百花盛开的季节，正是采蜜的好时光。

嗡嗡嗡，这里有三叶草的清香，
蜜蜂边唱边工作，翅膀上还带着玫瑰的香气，
从不偷懒的小家伙，整日从早忙到晚，
无论荆条还是雏菊，都是它无尽的宝藏。

嗡嗡嗡，那是蜜蜂在欢唱，
太阳刚探头，它歌儿唱得欢，
黑夜将到来，它依然在歌唱，
边唱边采蜜，夏天就这样快乐地过。
哦！我们会疲倦，感觉工作好沉闷，
但辛勤工作远比无所事事要好得多。

英语的标点符号（一）

英语的标点符号与汉语的标点符号在形式上与使用上大同小异。容易疏忽的地方，大致有以下几处：

1．英语句号是实心点，而不是小圆圈，如果英语的句号也和汉语一样，则容易和字母“o”相混淆。

2．英语的省略号一般使用“…”是3点，不是像汉语那样用6点“……”

3．当句子最后一个单词后有表示缩写的点“.”或者句末是省略号时，一般不再加句号。如：The class meeting will begin at 3 p.m.

She is a teacher, beautiful and…

4．包含直接引语的句子，说话人和表示“说”的动词可放在句首、句中和句末。一定要注意标点符号的不同。如：She said, “All of us are very interested in going abroad.”

“All of us are very interested in going abroad,” She said.

“All of us,” she said, “are very interested in going abroad.”

5．作“也”的too，多位于句末，一般前边要加逗号，位于句中时，前后均须加逗号；作“请”讲的please位于句末时，其前要加逗号；however等副词无论在句首、句中还是句末都要用逗号把它与句子的其他部分分开。如：

I’ ll work hard, too.

You, too, should be quiet in class.

Sit down, please.

Later, however, he decided to go.

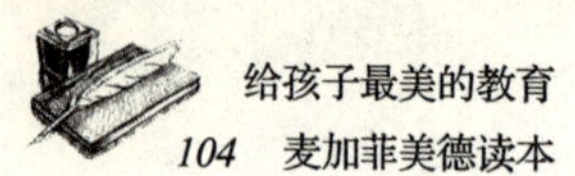

The Bee

Bees live in a house that is called a hive. They are of three kinds,—workers, drones, and queens.

Only one queen can live in each hive. If she is lost or dead, the other bees will stop their work.

They are very wise and busy little creatures. They all join together to build cells of wax for their honey.

Each bee takes its proper place, and does its own work. Some go out and gather honey from the flowers; others stay at home and work inside the hive.

The cells which they build, are all of one shape and size, and no room is left between them.

The cells are not round, but have six sides.

Did you ever look into a glass hive to see the bees while at work? It is pleasant to see how busy they always are.

But the drones do not work. Before winter comes, all the drones are driven from the hive or killed, that they may not eat the honey which they did not gather.

It is not quite safe for children to handle bees. They have sharp stings that they know well how to use in their defense.

The song of the bee

Buzz! buzz! buzz!
This is the song of the bee.
His legs are of yellow;
A jolly, good fellow,
And yet a great worker is he.

In days that are sunny
He's getting his honey;
In days that are cloudy
He's making his wax:
On pinks and on lilies,
And gay daffodillies,
And columbine blossoms,
He levies a tax!

Buzz! buzz! buzz!
The sweet–smelling clover,
He, humming, hangs over;
The scent of the roses
Makes fragrant his wings:
He never gets lazy;
From thistle and daisy,

And weeds of the meadow,
Some treasure he brings.

Buzz! buzz! buzz!
From morning´s first light
Till the coming of night,
He´s singing and toiling
The summer day through.
Oh! we may get weary,
And think work is dreary;
´Tis harder by far
To have nothing to do.

英语的标点符号（二）

6. 美国英语中，在书信称呼后可用冒号亦可用逗号，而在英国英语里一般用逗号。如：

Dear Mr. Smith: /Dear Mr. Smith,（美国英语）

Dear friends,（英国英语）

7. 字符号不要写得太长，写长了容易跟破折号混淆。其长度应该与一个字母的宽度相当。破折号的长度约占两个字母的位置。书写破折号时，与前后的单词应有一定的距离。

8. 英语中没有顿号“、”。要表示句中较短的并列词语之间的停顿，汉语习惯用顿号，而英语只能用逗号,汉语中连词“和”、“及”等之前不可用顿号，而英语中连接一系列并列项目的“and”或“or”之前往往可以用逗号。

9. 英语中没有书名号《》，书名一般用引号。如：Yesterday she saw an English film “Gone with the Wind”. 或书名大写Have you read Red Star Over China? 或用斜体Have you read Red Star Over China?

狮子

即便是世界上最强大的猛兽，也可以成为人类的朋友，只要你对它付出足够的耐心和善意。时间和精力，这是每个人都拥有的两样法宝，只要你能够很好的运用它，世界上就没有什么不可能完成的任务。只要努力，一切皆有可能。

狮子常被称为“百兽之王”。它通常有3～4英尺高，6～9九英尺长。它的毛皮有浅黄的、棕色的，还有黄褐色的。脖子周围有一大片粗而密的鬃毛，这使它更具威严。

狮子拥有巨大的力量，它的巨爪可以很轻易地撕碎牛或马的头颅。没看过从一只成年狮子嘴里取出的牙齿的人很难想像它到底有多大。一颗牙齿就需用一只手来握，你很可能误认为它是一只小像的牙齿。

狮子的故乡在亚洲和非洲的丛林里，它对于人还是动物来说都是一种威胁。白天它通常不出去活动，当黑暗降临的时候，它会潜伏在其他动物捕食饮水的地方，在最不经意的时候突然跳出来，伴随着如雷鸣般的吼声。

有些狮子能活很久。一只叫庞培的狮子1760年在伦敦去世，死时已经七十岁了。如果在很小的时候就开始加以训练，狮子是可以驯化

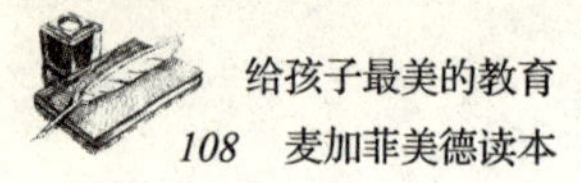

的，而且它还会和主人十分亲近。

在布鲁塞尔的一个动物园里，曾经养过一只叫做唐科的狮子。狮舍恰巧需要修补，于是那个叫威廉的驯狮人请了一个木匠来修补。木匠来了，但是他太害怕狮子了，坚持不肯独自一人靠近那个小屋。

于是威廉进了屋子，把狮子带到上面一层，以便让木匠对底层进行修补。威廉与狮子玩了一会儿，直到他和狮子都累了，不知不觉地睡着了。木匠还在不停地工作，当他终于完成的时候，便大声叫威廉来看一看。

他喊了一遍又一遍，就是不见威廉答应。这个可怜的木匠开始感到害怕了，他担心狮子已把驯狮人当成了晚餐，或是已把他撕成了碎片。他悄悄地爬到上面一层，透过栏杆，他看见狮子和威廉正肩并肩地睡在一起，惬意得就像是一对兄弟。

他太惊奇了，禁不住大声叫了出来。狮子被他的叫声惊醒了，愤怒地盯着木匠，把爪子放在驯兽人的胸上，样子似乎是说："看你敢碰一碰他！"之后这头威武的雄狮倒下继续睡了。木匠被吓坏了，他不知道怎样才能叫醒威廉，最后只好跑出了那间小屋，把他所看到的一切告诉给了其他人。

一些人闻讯来到小屋。他们打开门，想办法唤醒了威廉。他揉了揉眼睛，看了看四周，对这些人说他美美地睡了一觉。他抓住狮子的爪子，轻轻地晃了晃，然后安然无恙地从小屋中走了出来。

The Lion

The lion is often called the "king of beasts," His height varies from three to four feet, and he is from six to nine feet long. His coat is of it yellowish brown or tawny color, and about his neck is a great shaggy mane which gives his head a majestic appearance.

The strength of the lion is so great that he can easily crush the skulls of such animals as the horse or ox with one blow of his paw. No one who has not seen the teeth of a full grown lion taken out of their sockets can have any idea of their real size; one of them forms a good handful, and might easily be mistaken for a small elephant's tooth.

The home of the lion is in the forests of Asia and Africa, where he is a terror to man and beast. He generally lies concealed during the day, but as darkness comes on he prowls about where other animals are accustomed to go for food or drink, and springs upon them unawares, with a roar that sounds like the rumble of thunder.

The lion sometimes lives to a great age. One by the name of Pompey died at London, in the year 1760, at the age of seventy years. If taken when young the lion can be tamed, and will even show marks of kindness to his keeper.

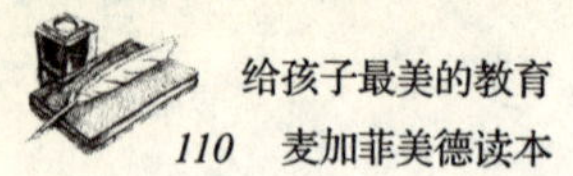

In a menagerie at Brussels, there was a cell where a large lion, called Danco, used to be kept. The cell happened to be in need of repair, and the keeper, whose name was William, desired a carpenter to come and mend it. The carpenter came, but was so afraid of the lion, that he would not go near the cell alone.

So William entered the cell, and led the lion to the upper part of it, while the other part was refitting. He played with the lion for some time; but, at last, being wearied, both he and the lion fell asleep. The carpenter went on with his work, and when he had finished he called out for William to come and see it.

He called again and again, but no William answered. The poor carpenter began to be frightened, lest the lion had made his dinner of the keeper, or else crushed him with his great paws. He crept round to the upper part of the cell, and there, looking through the railing, he saw the lion and William sleeping side by side as contentedly as two little brothers.

He was so astonished that he uttered a loud cry. The lion, awakened by the noise, stared at the carpenter with an eye of fury, and then placing his paw on the breast of his keeper, as if to say, "Touch him if you dare," the heroic beast lay down to sleep again. The carpenter was dreadfully alarmed, and, not knowing how he could rouse William, he ran out and related what he had seen.

Some people came, and, opening the door of the cell, Contrived to awaken the keeper, who, rubbing his eyes, quietly looked around him, and expressed himself very well satisfied with his nap. He took the lion's paw, shook it kindly, and then retired uninjured from the cell.

大象

动物们也是有智慧的，而且情感在它们的世界中占有重要的地位。它们并不会倚强凌弱，也不会因为自己更聪明就将自己置于更高的地位。人类或许会认为它们的顺从是因为软弱或者愚笨，但对动物们来说，它们更认可友谊这个说法。

大象是陆地上最大的四足动物，高8～14英尺，长10～15英尺。它身形像大型机车，眼睛小小的却很灵活，垂着两个蒲扇般的大耳朵，长有两颗长长的牙齿，象牙也成为一种贸易品。它还有一个长长的鼻子，可以用来取食物，还可以用来进攻或防卫。大象的皮肤呈深灰褐色。

大象喜欢成群活动，当他们出去觅食时，脚下的大地好像都颤动起来。它们吃树叶、青草，也吃植物的根茎和谷物、水果，但它们却不吃鱼，也不吃肉。它们天性安静、温和，却也不乏勇敢。只有它们在自卫或保护同类时，才会展现它们的威力。

亚洲和非洲都有大象，但它们属于不同种群。亚洲象有五个脚趾，而非洲象却只有三个。大象一旦被捉住并受到驯化，它们将会是四足动物中最温驯、最顺从、最有耐性、最聪明和最容易教化的。它们既可用来负重，也可用来旅行。它们非常依恋主人，好像生来就是服务并听从于主人似的。它们总是跪下来让人坐上去或者把货物放在它们的背上。

有关大象性格的轶事真是举不胜举。比如，在伦敦参加展览会的大象，如往常的博览会一样，人们要求用它长长的鼻子将扔在地上的钱捡起来。一个人丢过去了个六便士，但硬币却滚到了离墙不远的地方，这样，它就有点够不着了。为了捡起硬币，它不得不几次伸长鼻子，结果都没有够到，它就站在那里几秒钟一动不动，显然在那里思考怎样才能捡起来。

接下来，它将鼻子笔直地伸展开，尽可能地伸长，直到硬币上面稍稍远一点的地方，然后用力地对着墙吹气。结果，正如它所希望的，气流遇到墙的阻碍，反作用于硬币，于是人们惊奇地看着硬币朝它滚过去，被它捡了起来。

还有一个印度士兵，经常给一头大象喝亚力酒。有一天，士兵喝醉了，突然发现卫兵在追着他打算将他关进监狱，于是士兵躲在大象身旁寻求保护。卫兵很快发现了他的踪迹，但发现要将士兵从大象身边带走是不可能的，因为大象奋力地用鼻子护卫着他，只好放弃了。

当士兵从醉酒中醒过来，突然发现自己处于这样一个庞然大物的身下，不禁吓得手脚一动都不敢动。而大象很快就消除了他的恐惧，它用鼻子轻轻地拍着他，好像在说，“不要怕，走吧。”

还有一则令人称道的故事，与勒克瑙地方长官的大象有关。一次，勒克瑙城发生了一场骚乱，城中遭受了可怕的浩劫。通往宫殿门口的路上躺满了病倒和垂死的人，这时，地方长官正好从此地经过。

地方长官只管走他的路，也不管他的大象会不会踩到脚底下那些可怜无助的人们。而大象却比主人善良多了，它左躲右闪，小心地越过那些可怜的人们。它有时用鼻子将他们托起，放到路边，有时将他们的脚往旁边挪一挪，小心翼翼地挪动着步子，唯恐伤着一个人。

The Elephant

The elephant is the largest of quadrupeds; his height is from eight to fourteen feet, and his length, from ten to fifteen feet. His form is that of a hog; his eyes are small and lively; his ears are long, broad and pendulous. He has two large tusks, which form the ivory of commerce, and a trunk, or proboscis, at the end of the nose, which he uses to take his food with, and for attack or defense. His color is a dark ash–brown.

Elephants often assemble in large troops; and, as they march in search of food, the forests seem to tremble under them. They eat the branches of trees, together with roots, herbs, leaves, grain, and fruit, but will not touch fish nor flesh. In a state of nature, they are peaceable, mild, and brave; exerting their power only for their own protection or in defense of their own species.

Elephants are found both in Asia and Africa, but they are of different species, the Asiatic elephant having five toes, and the African, three. These animals are caught by stratagem, and, when tamed, they are the most gentle, obedient, and patient, as well as the most docile and sagacious of all quadrupeds. They are used to carry burdens, and for traveling. Their attachment to their masters is remarkable; and they

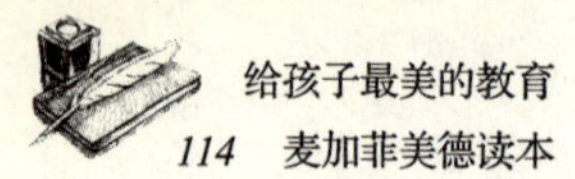

seem to live but to serve and obey them. They always kneel to receive their riders; or the loads they have to carry.

The anecdotes illustrating the character of the elephant are numerous. An elephant which was kept for exhibition at London, was often required, as is usual in such exhibitions, to pick up with his trunk a piece of money thrown upon the floor for this purpose. On one occasion a sixpence was thrown, which happened to roll a little out of his reach, not far from the wall. Being desired to pick it up, he stretched out his proboscis several times to reach it; failing in this, he stood motionless a few seconds, evidently considering how to act.

He then stretched his proboscis in a straight line as far as he could, a little distance above the coin, and blew with great force against the wall. The angle produced by the opposition of the wall, made the current of air act under the coin, as he evidently supposed it would, and it was curious to observe the sixpence traveling toward the animal till it came within his reach, when he picked it up.

A soldier in India, who had frequently carried an elephant some arrack, being one day intoxicated, and seeing himself pursued by the guard whose orders were to conduct him to prison, took refuge under the elephant. The guard soon finding his retreat, attempted in vain to take him from his asylum; for the elephant vigorously defended him with his trunk.

As soon as the soldier became sober, and saw himself placed under such an unwieldy animal, he was so terrified that he scarcely durst move either hand or foot; but the elephant soon caused his fears to subside by caressing him with his trunk, and thus tacitly saying, "Depart in peace."

A pleasing anecdote is related of an elephant which was the

property of the nabob of Lucknow. There was in that city an epidemic disorder, making dreadful havoc among the inhabitants. The road to the palace gate was covered with the sick and dying, lying on the ground at the moment the nabob was about to pass.

Regardless of the suffering he must cause, the nabob held on his way, not caring whether his beast trod upon the poor helpless creatures or not. But the animal, more kind-hearted than his master, carefully cleared the path of the poor, helpless wretches as he went along. Some he lifted with his trunk, entirely out of the road. Some he set upon their feet, and among the others he stepped so carefully that not an individual was injured.

Cats and Dogs

北欧神话中，神奇的猫能使天气发生变化；狗呢，则是风的使者。猫和狗形同水火，它们一见面，便是狂风暴雨，仿佛在打架。所以倾盆大雨就被描述为rain cats and dogs。像这样的俗语还有很多：

1. Let the cat out of the bag. 露出马脚。
2. A cat has nine lives. 猫有九条命。

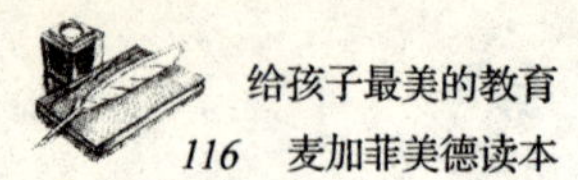

印第安玉米

那些看起来很普通的东西，身上也会有很多不为你知的东西，只是它们被我们选择性的忽视了。习以为常最容易蒙蔽我们的眼睛，普通人、普通的事物，其实只要你稍稍对他们多用一点心，你就可以挖掘出属于你的不平常。

对人类而言，很少有什么庄稼比玉米更为有用了。在除了水稻没有什么谷物的时候，玉米曾经一度是一种主要的食物。在有些国家，玉米几乎就是人们唯一的食物。

你知道为什么叫它们印第安玉米吗？这是因为美洲的印第安人是它们最早的种植者。当哥伦布发现新大陆时，他发现玉米已经在那里被广泛种植了。他们将玉米在石钵中轧碎，制成粗糙的面粉，用它们烤制面包。

玉米现在是美国首要的种植作物，无论我们住在什么地方，我们都会看到玉米在适合的季节里生长。但是几乎没有人能够告诉你，那些最简单也最重要的事情——种植玉米的方法。

玉米能够良好地生长，就必须有肥沃的土壤和温暖的气候。它是很脆弱的植物，很容易被冷空气所伤害。如果泥土寒冷而且潮湿，玉米种子是不会发芽的，而且会很快腐烂掉。

准备用于种植玉米的土地，必须是精心犁过，垄距要达到四英尺左右，在每个坑里大约放四到七粒种子，然后盖上大约两英寸的土，这样玉米就种完了。

在理想的气温下，十天到两周的时间内，嫩叶就会从泥土中钻出来；然后它的茎秆就会迅速生长。它那长长的流线型的叶子也开始一天天尽情地生长。当玉米苗还很小的时候，必须精心地耕作，等它能够遮蔽土地后，它们就不需要太多的锄整了。

水分和养料通过根被吸收，变成汁液，通过茎秆进入到叶子里，由此发生了很大的变化，这导致了玉米孕穗，小玉米也就开始生长。

玉米开两种花：雄花和雌花。两种花相距很远，雄花长在植株的顶端，雌花就是玉米穗外面散布着的丝一样的东西。玉米棒子上的每一粒果实都连着一根丝，除非那丝上落上了雄花的花粉，否则果实是不会生长的。

印第安玉米的用途十分广泛，它的绿茎和叶子是牛的很好的饲料，它成熟的果实可以被用作马、猪和家禽的饲料，没有比它更好的育肥饲料了。

嫩玉米、煮玉米、玉米粥、英格兰布丁和豆煮玉米是很受人们喜爱的美食，而烧玉米和爆米花则陪伴我们度过漫长的冬日。

淀粉具有很重要的商业价值，我们利用茎榨出的汁来做糖和糖浆，用成熟的果实榨油酿酒。玉米的外皮被用来填充床垫，编制成席子、篮子及其他有用的东西。

现在你知道印第安玉米多么有用了吧。除了以上这些用途，它们长在田里的样子也是一道漂亮的风景。夏末，大片的玉米地里，波浪般翻滚的绿色旗帜，漫天飞舞的红缨让人永世难忘。

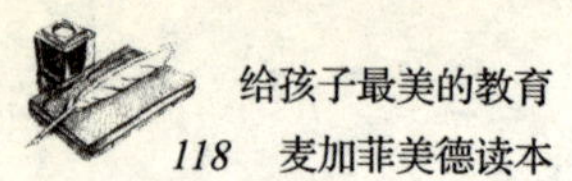

Indian Corn

Few plants are more useful to man than Indian corn, or maize. No grain, except rice, is used to so great an extent as an article of food. In some countries corn is almost the only food eaten by the people.

Do you know why it is called Indian corn? It is because the American Indians were the first corn growers. Columbus found this grain widely cultivated by them when he discovered the New World. They pounded it in rude, stone bowls, and thus made a coarse flour, which they mixed with water and baked.

Indian corn is now the leading crop in the United States. In whatever part of this land we live, we see corn growing every year in its proper season. Yet how few can tell the most simple and important facts about its planting and its growth!

Corn, to do well, must have a rich soil and a warm climate. It is a tender plant, and is easily injured by cold weather. The seed corn does not sprout, but rots, if the ground is cold and wet.

To prepare land properly for planting corn, the soil is made fine by plowing, and furrows are run across the field four feet apart each way. At every point where these furrows cross, the farmer drops from four to seven grains of seed corn. These are then covered with about two inches of earth, and thus form "hills" of corn.

In favorable weather, the tender blades push through the ground in ten days or two weeks; then the stalks mount up rapidly, and the long, streamer—like leaves unfold gracefully from day to day. Corn must be carefully cultivated while the plants are small. After they begin to shade the ground, they need but little hoeing or plowing.

The moisture and earthy matter, drawn through the roots, become sap. This passes through the stalk, and enters the leaves. There a great change takes place which results in the starting of the ears and the growth of the grain.

The maize plant bears two kinds of flowers—male and female. The two are widely separated. The male flowers are on the tassel; the fine silk threads which surround the ear, and peep out from the end of the husks, are the female flowers.

Each grain on the cob is the starting point for a thread of silk; and, unless the thread receives some particle of the dust which falls from the tassel flowers, the kernel with which it is connected will not grow.

The many uses of Indian corn and its products are worthy of note. The green stalks and leaves make excellent fodder for cattle. The ripe grain is used all over the earth as food for horses, pigs, and poultry. Nothing is better for fattening stock.

Green corn, or "roasting ears," hulled corn and hominy, New England hasty pudding, and succotash are favorite dishes with many persons. Then there are parched corn and pop corn—the delight of long winter evenings.

Cornstarch is an important article of commerce. Sirup and sugar are

made from the juice of the stalk, and oil and alcohol from the ripened grain. Corn husks are largely used for filling mattresses, and are braided into mats, baskets, and other useful articles.

Thus it will be seen how varied are the uses of Indian corn. And besides being so useful, the plant is very beautiful. The sight of a large cornfield in the latter part of summer, with all its green banners waving and its tasseled plumes nodding, is one to admire, and not to be forgotten.

猫咪的小知识

Fat cat 肥猫，指“为竞选出钱的富翁；享有特权或谋取特权的人；有钱有势的人，大亨”；

Cool cat 酷猫，指“时髦人（尤指嗜好冷爵士乐的人）；嗜好摇滚乐的人；做出孤傲冷漠的样子的人”；

Hepcat 迷恋爵士乐的猫，指“爵士或摇摆舞音乐迷，爵士或摇摆舞乐队乐师”；

Copy cat 好模仿的猫，指“盲目的模仿者（通常为儿童之间的用语）”；

Fraidy-cat 恐惧的猫，指“胆小鬼”；

Hell cat 好发脾气的猫，指“泼妇、巫婆”。迷信的人认为魔鬼撒旦常以黑猫的样子出现。巫婆也是抱着黑猫，骑着扫帚的形象。所以西方有一种说法：Don’t let a black cat across your path.（不要让黑猫从你面前走过）。

人与动物

人类与动物最大的区别就是不断尝试，不断犯错，然后不断的修正自己的错误。不要因为担心犯错而停住自己向前的脚步，人孰能无过，需要担心的只有两点：一是缺乏向前的勇气，二是错误得不到有效的纠正。

人与动物的区别主要在于前者有理性，而后者只有本能，但为了更好地理解这里所说的“理性”和“本能”，我们有必要说一说突出体现这两者区别的三个方面。

首先，让我们把两者放到一个最相似的程度上来看，想像人类还处于原始的野蛮状态，像田野里的野兽一样整日为了满足自己动物本性的需要而奔忙。这里就出现了两者间第一个区别：工具的使用。当野人搭起一处茅舍或小屋作为自己的栖身之地或开始储备物资时，他所做的与兔子、海狸、蜜蜂和各种各样的鸟儿没有什么不同。

但是在做这项工作时，如果没有工具人类不可能有任何进展。在砍倒一棵树以利用其木材之前，他必须为自己配备一把斧子。而那动物在构筑自己的洞穴、蜂巢或鸟窝时，所用的仅仅是大自然已经提供

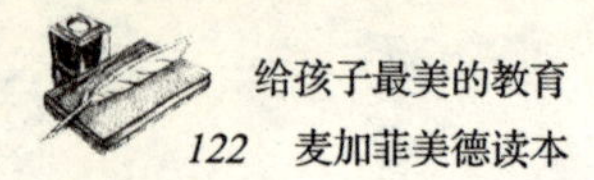

的一些工具而已。同样，如果没有铲子或犁头，人类将不能在土地上耕作；如果没有收割庄稼的工具，人类将不能收获自己播下的种子。但低等动物却没有为自己或后代准备任何类似的东西。

现在来看看第二个区别。人类在所有的活动中都会犯错误，而动物从不。你听说过类似一只鸟站在枝头为自己完成了一半的小窝悲叹，并费尽心思地思考如何继续完成这种事吗？你看过奇形怪状丑陋不堪的蜂窝吗？或是曾经留意在这些小群体中有任何类似人类讨论举动，好似这些建筑师们有什么不同的意见？

和我们相比较，低等动物是更高明的医生。如果生病了，许多动物都能找来特殊的草药。它们并不把这些草药作为食物，但找来的草药却的确可以治愈这些病症。然而，整个人类医学界却可能花上整整一个世纪去争论某种特定药物的效能。

人类在做任何事情时，都多多少少带有不肯定性，必须经过无数次实验才可能将其做得近乎完美。如果没有一定的经验，就算最简单的家庭生活，人也处理不好。当人类停止犯错误，开始从教训中受益时，他们的生命也已消耗大半。

第三个区别在于，动物永远不会有进步，而人类的知识、技能和成功却与日俱增。做任何事时，动物遵循的是它们首要的原始冲动或上帝赋予的本能天性，所以它们所做的工作总是要比人类的更完善，更有规律性。

但是上帝赋予了人类思考和推理自己所作所为的能力，这使得人类能够通过耐心和勤勉改正自己原先的错误，不断进步。鸟窝的结构的确堪称完美，但19世纪燕子筑的巢和诺亚方舟椽上的巢比较起来，几乎完全一样。但如果比较原始人的简陋的小屋和古希腊罗马的寺院宫殿，我们就能发现人类的错误，经过纠正和改进，是如何指引我们前进的。

当太阳掩盖了金色的光辉，
深深地沉入永恒的黑夜；
当狂野毁灭的火焰在天空中升腾，
当灭亡在放肆的狂笑，自然濒临灭绝，
人类将会独自存活于世界的遗骸中，
在这坠落的星球上，人类永存。

——简·泰勒

英语作文格式

1. 四边的距离

在书写时，上下左右要留有一定的空白距离。

2. 题目的写法

题目应写在第一行的中间，题目左右两边的空白距离大致相等。

题目的第一个单词的第一个字母必须大写。从第二个单词起，其中每个实义词的第一个字母大写，而冠词、介词和连词的第一个字母则一般小写。如：

Man and the Inferior Animals

写题目不要用括号或引号。题目后除了问号和感叹号之外，不加其他标点符号。

3. 文章本体

文章第一段的第一行应与题目隔一行或两行。每段的开头一般应该缩格，即向右缩进约四个字母的间隔；单词与单词之间需留一个字母的间隔，句与句之间需留两个字母的间隔。假若每行的最后一个单词写不下，最好不要轻易拆字移行，可将该单词移到后一行去书写。书写时，不要因为一行末尾还有一点空间就把一个词的前半截硬塞在那里，造成非移行不可的局面。实际上，移行过多是书写、打字或排印质量不高的表现。不必过分地去追求右边的整齐，宁可多空一些，每行长短错落，要比移行过多看上去更舒服。

Man and the Inferior Animals

The chief difference between man and the other animals consists in this, that the former has reason, whereas the latter have only instinct; but, in order to understand what we mean by the terms reason and instinct, it will be necessary to mention three things in which the difference very distinctly appears.

Let us first, to bring the parties as nearly on a level as possible, consider man in a savage state, wholly occupied, like the beasts of the field, in providing for the wants of his animal nature; and here the first distinction that appears between them is the use of implements. When the savage provides himself with a hut or a wigwam for shelter, or that he may store up his provisions, he does no more than is done by the rabbit, the beaver, the bee, and birds of every species.

But the man can not make any progress in this work without tools; he must provide himself with an ax even before he can cut down a tree for its timber; whereas these animals form their burrows, their cells, or their nests, with no other tools than those with which nature has provided them. In cultivating the ground, also, man can do nothing without a spade or a plow; nor can he reap what he has sown till he has shaped an implement with which to cut clown his harvest. But the inferior animals provide for themselves and their young without any of these things.

Now for the second distinction. Man, in all his operations, makes mistakes; animals make none. Did you ever hear of such a thing as a bird sitting on a twig lamenting over her half–finished nest and puzzling her little head to know how to complete it? Or did you ever see the cells of a beehive in clumsy, irregular shapes, or observe anything like a discussion in the little community, as if there were a difference of opinion among the architects?

The lower animals are even better physicians than we are; for when they are ill, they will, many of them, seek out some particular herb, which they do not, use as food, and which possesses a medicinal quality exactly suited to the complaint; whereas, the whole college of physicians will dispute for a century about the virtues of a single drug.

Man undertakes nothing in which he is not more or less puzzled; and must try numberless experiments before he can bring his undertakings to anything like perfection; even the simplest operations of domestic life are not well performed without some experience; and the term of man's life is half wasted before he has done with his mistakes and begins to profit by his lessons.

The third distinction is that animals make no improvements; while the knowledge, and skill, and the success of man are perpetually on the increase. Animals, in all their operations, follow the first impulse of nature or that instinct which God has implanted in them. In all they do undertake, therefore, their works are more perfect and regular than those of man.

But man, having been endowed with the faculty of thinking or reasoning about what he does, is enabled by patience and industry to correct the mistakes into which he at first falls, and to go on constantly improving. A bird's nest is, indeed, a perfect structure; yet the nest of a swallow of the nineteenth century is not at all more commodious or elegant than those that were built amid the rafters of Noah's ark. But if we compare the wigwam of the savage with the temples and palaces of ancient Greece and Rome, we then shall see to what man's mistakes, rectified and improved upon, conduct him.

"When the vast sun shall veil his golden light
Deep in the gloom of everlasting night;
When wild, destructive flames shall wrap the skies,
When ruin triumphs, and when nature dies;
Man shall alone the wreck of worlds survive;
'Mid falling spheres, immortal man shall live."

— *Jane Taylor*

CHAPTER 4

幸福的童年

童年原是一生最美妙的阶段，那时的孩子是一朵花，也是一颗果子，是一片朦朦胧胧的聪明，一种永远不息的活动，一股强烈的欲望。

——[法]巴尔扎克

小小战士

童年的幸福无法复制，那时的我们无忧无虑，充满幻想。伴随着成长，我们得到了许多，也丢弃了一些，但请保留下你的想像力，那是我们的翅膀，可以让我们飞得更高、更远，就如这些骄傲的小童子军一样。

假如你不曾是学童，
你肯定没有受到过如此的训练，
它让你热血沸腾，
而后再无这种感受。

你可曾遇到过，那些沿街走远的孩子，
他们插着鲜艳的羽毛，举着鲜明的旗帜，
以水壶作战鼓，
扮作军队，冲锋前进。

对我来说一切恍如昨日，
就在不久之前。

我们所有的战士端起步枪，
去突袭那些可怕的敌人。

我们的步枪用雪松制成，
推弹杆崭新而闪亮，
枪上永远上着刺刀，
枪管上更是有威武的图案。

我们袭击了一群鹅，
将它们一举击溃，
唯有一只强健的雄鹅，
还想与我们抗争。

但是我们精明又强干，
我们的队长冲锋在前，
我们紧随其后，
不曾让一人落单。

队长是个勇敢的少年，
不由地让人心生喜爱，
他的锡剑闪闪发亮，
一顶纸帽顶在头上。

他带领我们到陡峭的山边，
迎着西风，
雄鸡的羽毛装点在他的头上，
英武地随风飘扬。

我们把步枪扛在肩上，握在手中，
一律上好刺刀，
途中遇到的毛芯花秆，
都会好运不长。

两点钟我们点名出发，
直到日落前夕，
虽四肢疲惫，却勇敢无畏。
我们进行着模拟大战，
直到晚餐的钟声响起，我们才从山谷撤退，
命令我们的军队，凯旋而归。

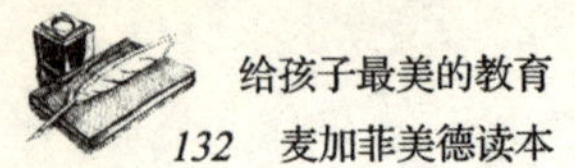

Young Soldiers

Oh, were you ne'er a schoolboy,
And did you never train,
And feel that swelling of the heart
You ne'er can feel again?

Did you never meet, far down the street,
With plumes and banners gay,
While the kettle, for the kettledrum,
Played your march, march away?

It seems to me but yesterday,
Nor scarce so long ago,
Since all our school their muskets took,
To charge the fearful foe.

Our muskets were of cedar wood,
With ramrods bright and new;

With bayonets forever set,
And painted barrels, too.

We charged upon a flock of geese,
And put them all to flight—
Except one sturdy gander
That thought to show us fight.

But, ah! we knew a thing or two;
Our captain wheeled the van;
We routed him, we scouted him,
Nor lost a single man!

Our captain was as brave a lad
As e'er commission bore;
And brightly shone his new tin sword;
A paper cap he wore.

He led us up the steep hillside,
Against the western wind,
While the cockerel plume that decked his head
Streamed bravely out behind.

We shouldered arms, we carried arms,
We charged the bayonet;
And woe unto the mullein stalk
That in our course we met!

At two o'clock the roll we called,
And till the close of day,
With fearless hearts, though tired limbs,
We fought the mimic fray,
Till the supper bell, from out the dell,
Bade us march, march away.

童子军

童子军（Boy Scout）是一种野外活动的训练方式，这种方法用以培养青少年成为快乐健康有用的公民。目前全世界约有两亿五千多万名童子军。

童子军的创始人是英国罗伯特·贝登堡爵士，贝登堡鉴于当时英国青年道德堕落，体格衰弱，恐遭古代罗马帝国亡国的覆辙，因此研发出一套可行的训练方法试图挽救这种危机。

贝登堡于1907年在英国南部的白浪岛组织了一次野营。之后他写了一本名为《少年警探》的手册并于1908年出版。正是这本书的指导下，一支童子军很快建立起来了，并很快被推广至世界各国。

稚龄童军(Pre Cub Scouts) ⟶六岁半至十岁半
幼童军(Cub Scouts) ⟶八岁至十二岁
童子军(Boy Scout) ⟶十一岁以上
行义童子军(Senior Scout) ⟶十四岁以上
海童军(Sea Scout)及空童军(Air Scout) ⟶十五岁以上
罗浮童军(Rover Scout) ⟶十七岁以上

七彩的泡泡

你知道肥皂泡为何是彩色的吗？其实，肥皂膜本身是无色的，就像一张透明的玻璃纸一样，但阳光在肥皂膜的正面和背面都会产生反射。我们知道，阳光是由红、橙、黄、绿、青、蓝、紫七种颜色组成的。当它在肥皂膜的正反两面来回反射时，由于这两个面之间的距离极微小，分别从正面和背面反射出来的两束光线，就可能重叠起来。这样一来，阳光中的七种颜色光，在不同厚度的地方，有的会得到加强，有的却会减弱，甚至相互抵消。于是，膜上有的地方显得红一些，有些地方显得蓝一些，有些地方又显出别的颜色，于是就呈现出五颜六色。这样的现象，物理学上叫做光的干涉。

男孩子们来到门廊上吹起了泡泡。门旁的垫子上，一只老猫正趴在上面熟睡。

看到一个泡泡轻轻落在老猫的背上还没有破时，罗伯特“哈哈”大笑起来。威利也想照样来一个。不过，这次泡泡落在了猫的脸上，让它打了个喷嚏。

“呵呵，它可不想用肥皂洗脸，”哈瑞说，“来吧，现在让我们看

看谁吹的泡泡最大。”

男孩们争先恐后地吹起泡泡来。“我的是最大的！”罗伯特喊道，“看，它在空中飞得多高啊！啊呀！它破掉了！”

“我能从我的泡泡中看到大树、森林、房子与天空，”威利说，“真漂亮啊！”

“有多少种颜色呢，威利？”

“红的是一种；还有一种是蓝色；第三种是……哎，它们全破了。我们再吹几个来数数吧。”

“我知道有多少种颜色，”哈瑞跳着脚说，“就和彩虹的颜色一样多。”

孩子们，你们知道彩虹有多少种颜色吗？

彩虹

彩虹，又称天虹，简称虹，是气象中的一种光学现象。当太阳光照射到空气中的水滴时，光线被折射及反射，在天空上形成拱形的七彩光谱，形状弯曲，色彩艳丽，尤其在雨后较为常见。东亚和中国对于七色光的最普遍说法是（从外至内）：红、橙、黄、绿、青、蓝、紫。

很多时候会见到两条彩虹同时出现，在平常的彩虹外边出现同心，但较暗的副虹(又称霓)。副虹是阳光在水滴中经两次反射而成。

Bubbles

The boys have come out on the porch to blow bubbles. The old cat is asleep on the mat by the door.

"Ha! ha!" laughs Robert, as a bubble comes down softly on the old cat's back, and does not burst.

Willie tries to make his bubble do the same. This time it comes down on the cat's face, and makes her sneeze.

"She would rather wash her face without soap," says Harry. "Now let us see who can make the biggest bubble."

"Mine is the biggest," says Robert. "See how high it floats in the air! I can see—ah! it has burst."

"I can see the house and the trees and the sky in mine," says Willie; "and such beautiful colors."

"How many, Willie?"

"Red, one; blue, two; there—they are all out. Let us try again."

"I know how many colors there are," says Harry. "Just as many as there are in the rainbow."

"Do you know how many that is?"

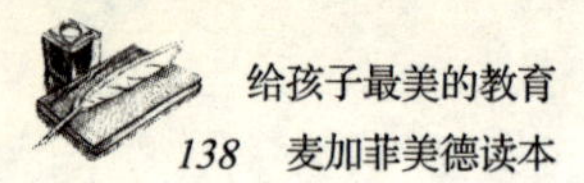

小古斯塔娃

小古斯塔娃告诉了我们如何和这个世界相处：一、善待身边的小动物；二、懂得分享，和朋友们一起分享自己的好东西；三、自在的享受美好时光。

一个阳光普照的早晨，小古斯塔娃坐在门廊上，旁边屋檐下的冰柱在不停地往下滴水，春日的阳光暖洋洋的，小古斯塔娃的心情也和这阳光一样。

她戴着一顶有趣的小红帽，膝盖上放着一个绿色的碗，碗边上镶着金黄的花纹，漂亮极了，里面盛满了牛奶和面包等一些食物。看着丰盛的早餐，小古斯塔娃开心地哈哈笑。

她把她那灰色的小猫引到面前。可爱的小猫用它那粉红色的鼻子小心地嗅了嗅，好像在说："这是什么呀？"小古斯塔娃喂了它一点，小馋猫却想要更多。这时，棕色的小母鸡也跑到门边。"你好啊！"小古斯塔娃冲它喊道。

她把面包捏碎了给小母鸡吃，一群小白鸽拍着翅膀冲了过来，洁白的羽翼和深红色的小脚，显得可爱极了。"欢迎你们！"小古斯塔娃笑着说。

它们急匆匆地啄着面包屑，动作却不失优雅。突然不知是谁从外面回来了。哦，原来是小瑞格斯——一只苏格兰犬，眼巴巴地看着主人，尾巴讨好地摇个不停，“哈！哈！”小古斯塔娃不禁又乐起来。

“你也想吃点吗？”她把碗放在灰褐色的砖地上，小狗不一会儿便喝光了她的牛奶。小古斯塔娃轻抚着小狗如丝般顺滑的毛发，轻声说，“瑞格斯，我亲爱的。”

几只麻雀和乌鸦远远地站在冰冷的雪地里，却不敢过来。“你们不过来吗，朋友们？”她问。可是它们实在是太害羞了，尽管小古斯塔娃一再说“请你们过来呀！”它们还是在外面待着。

小古斯塔娃只好将面包屑丢给它们，然后跪坐在垫子上，和鸽子、小鸟、小狗、猫咪挤做一团。妈妈从屋子里走了出来，笑着说：“我亲爱的女儿呀，让我再给你多拿些吧，快乐的小古斯塔娃，你真是太淘气了。”

无论是猫还是狗，小鸡还是小鸟，小古斯塔娃都很喜欢，她喜欢喂养这些可爱腼腆的小动物。哦，小古斯塔娃的早餐吃的实在是太香了，祝她永远这么快乐。

有趣的城市名

美国的每个城市的命名方式不同。怀俄明州的一个城市叫“十眠城(Ten Sleep)”。当地的人用自己的方式来诉说一个地方距离有多远：他们会用旅途中要经过多少个夜晚来表示行程的距离。

新泽西州的盎斯海特（Ong's Hat），它的名字由来非常有趣。从前有一个名叫雅各布·昂（Jacob Ong）的人住在这里，他有三大喜好：跳舞、女人和高档的帽子。一天晚上，他出席一个大型舞会。舞会上有一个女人认为雅各布应该和自己多跳一会儿舞。后来她抓起他高档的帽子，随手把它扔到地板上，然后在他的帽子上跳起舞来。小城也就有了一个名字叫“盎斯海特”。

Little Gustava

Little Gustava sits in the sun,
Safe in the porch, and the little drops run
From the icicles under the eaves so fast,
For the bright spring sun shines warm at last,
And glad is little Gustava.

She wears a quaint little scarlet cap,
And a little green bowl she holds in her lap,
Filled with bread and milk to the brim,
And a wreath of marigolds round the rim:
"Ha! ha!" laughs little Gustava.

Up comes her little gray, coaxing cat,
With her little pink nose, and she mews, "What's that ?"
Gustava feeds her,—she begs for more,
And a little brown hen walks in at the door:
"Good day!" cries little Gustava.

She scatters crumbs for the little brown hen,
There comes a rush and a flutter, and then
Down fly her little white doves so sweet,
With their snowy wings and their crimson feet:
"Welcome!" cries little Gustava.

So dainty and eager they pick up the crumbs.
But who is this through the doorway comes?
Little Scotch terrier, little dog Rags,
Looks in her face, and his funny tail wags:
"Ha! ha!" laughs little Gustava.

"You want some breakfast, too?" and down
She sets her bowl on the brick floor brown,
And little dog Rags drinks up her milk,
While she strokes his shaggy locks, like silk:
"Dear Rags!" says little Gustava.

Waiting without stood sparrow and crow,
Cooling their feet in the melting snow.
"Won't you come in, good folk?" she cried,
But they were too bashful, and staid outside,
Though "Pray come in!" cried Gustava.

So the last she threw them, and knelt on the mat,
With doves, and biddy, and dog, and cat.
And her mother came to the open house door:

"Dear little daughter, I bring you some more,
My merry little Gustava."

Kitty and terrier, biddy and doves,
All things harmless Gustava loves,
The shy, kind creatures't is joy to feed,
And, oh! her breakfast is sweet indeed
To happy little Gustava!

国际儿童节

国际儿童节的设立和发生在二战期间一次著名的屠杀有关。1942年6月，德国法西斯枪杀了捷克利迪策村16岁以上的男性公民140余人和全部婴儿，并把妇女和90名儿童押往集中营。村里的房舍、建筑物均被烧毁，好端端的一个村庄就这样被德国法西斯给毁了。为了悼念利迪策村和全世界所有在法西斯侵略战争中死难的儿童，1949年11月，国际民主妇女联合会在莫斯科举行理事会议。为了保障世界各国儿童的生存权、保健权和受教育权，为了改善儿童的生活，会议决定以利迪策村屠杀时的6月的第一天作为国际儿童节。

大多数伊斯兰国家都将斋月后第14天定为“糖果节”，对孩子们来说，这也是最快乐的儿童节。“糖果节”一般为期三天，小朋友们三五成群，到附近的各家各户索要糖果。按照当地民俗，大人们不能拒绝儿童的要求，所以孩子们这一天总是能欢天喜地地满载而归。

非洲西部的儿童节是疯狂的，那里的国家大都有专门的“儿童狂欢节”，而且往往持续一个月。

回声的故事

人生就好比一个大山谷，也会产生回声。你用什么样的态度去对待生活，对待他人，他们就会用什么样的态度来对待你。你的付出会得到回报，你犯了错误也会受到惩罚。

所以，你的人生将会是什么样子，完全取决于你自己。

一天，罗伯特在山中漫步，突然兴致来了他放声高喊起来："啊！啊！"。几乎同时，他听到附近的山里也传回来一样的声音"啊！啊"。

他吃了一惊，提高嗓门问道："你是谁？"同样的声音又一次传来："你是谁？"

罗伯特扯着嗓子喊："你一定是个愚蠢的家伙！""愚蠢的家伙！"山那边又传回同样的声音。

罗伯特火冒三丈，他大声而猛烈地冲着声音传来的地方喊着，山里也同样传来一样生气地语句。

罗伯特躲进灌木丛，想看看是谁在愚弄他，可是一个人影也没有。

他回到家，告诉妈妈，有一个男孩故意躲在树林里愚弄他。

"罗伯特，"妈妈说，"你是在生自己的气呀。你听到的不是别人的捉弄，而是你自己的声音呢！"

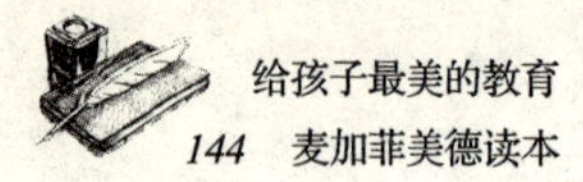

“不会吧！妈妈，那怎么可能呢？”罗伯特说。

“难道你没有听说过回声吗？”妈妈问。

“回声？妈妈，那是什么东西呀？我从来没有听说过。”

“让我来告诉你吧，”妈妈说，“你知道当你打球时，把球扔到墙壁上它会弹回来吗？”

“是的，妈妈，”他说，“等它弹回来时，我便又把它抓住了。”

“同样的道理，”妈妈说，“如果我在一个空旷的地方，比如山边或一座高大的建筑物旁，这时我大声呼喊，我的声音就会被反弹回来。就这样，我又听到了我喊出的话。”

“那就是回声，儿子。当你觉得仿佛有人在捉弄你时，那就是你面前的山了，它把你的声音反弹了回来，于是就产生了回声。”

“你所谓的那个坏男孩不会比你更加生气的。如果你说话温和一点，你也会听到温和的回声。如果你用轻柔甜美的声音说话，你也会听到同样动听的回音。《圣经》上说‘温和能驱走愤怒’，当你和你的同学玩耍的时候，你也要记住这句话。”

“如果有人对你不礼貌地大声说话，你要记着回声的故事，说话尽量和气一点。当你放学回家，发现你弟弟在生气时，如果你温和地和他说话，他的嘴角会慢慢露出笑容，说话也会变得和气起来。”

妈妈最后说：“不管你在田野里，还是树林里，在学校还是在玩耍，在家或是在外边，无论在什么地方，都要记住：

The good and the kind,
By kindness their love ever proving,
Will dwell with the pure and the loving.

和蔼可亲本身就是美好和善良的，
它能产生纯洁和爱。”

The Echo

As Robert was one day rambling about, he happened to cry out, "Ho, ho!" He instantly heard coming back from a hill near by, the same words, "Ho, ho!"

In great surprise, he said with a loud voice, "Who are you?" Upon this, the same words came back, "Who are you?"

Robert now cried out harshly, "You must be a very foolish fellow." "Foolish fellow!" came back from the hill.

Robert became angry, and with loud and fierce words went toward the spot whence the sounds came. The words all came back to him in the same angry tone.

He then went into the thicket, and looked for the boy who, as he thought, was mocking him; but he could find nobody anywhere.

When he went home, he told his mother that some boy had hid himself in the wood, for the purpose of mocking him.

"Robert," said his mother, "you are angry with yourself alone. You heard nothing but your own words."

"Why, mother, how can that be?" said Robert. "Did you never hear an echo?" asked his mother. "An echo, dear mother? No, ma'am. What is it?"

"I will tell you," said his mother. "You know, when you play with your ball, and throw it against the side of a house, it bounds back to you." "Yes, mother," said he, "and I catch it again."

"Well," said his mother, "if I were in the open air, by the side of a hill or a large barn, and should speak very loud, my voice would be sent back, so that I could hear again the very words which I spoke.

"That, my son, is an echo. When you thought some one was mocking you, it was only the hill before you, echoing, or sending back, your own voice.

"The bad boy, as you thought it was, spoke no more angrily than yourself. If you had spoken kindly, you would have heard a kind reply.

"Had you spoken in a low, sweet, gentle tone, the voice that came back would have been as low, sweet, and gentle as your own.

"The Bible says, 'A soft answer turneth away wrath.' Remember this when you are at play with your school mates.

"If any of them should be offended, and speak in a loud, angry tone, remember the echo, and let your words be soft and kind."

"When you come home from school, and find your little brother cross and peevish, speak mildly to him. You will soon see a smile on his lips, and find that his tones will become mild and sweet.

"Whether you are in the fields or in the woods, at school or at play, at home or abroad, remember,

The good and the kind,
By kindness their love ever proving,
Will dwell with the pure and the loving."

懂事的贝茜

很多时候我们都会面临抉择，既然是抉择，就意味着我们必然会得到一些而舍弃另外的一些。想清楚什么对于自己更为重要，你就能做出正确的选择。相比于篮子，家人对于贝茜无疑更为重要。

有一天，贝茜突然想，如果能拥有一处野花在其中盛开的花园该有多好。于是，她跑进屋里找到安妮阿姨，问她是否可以穿过淙淙的溪水，到山坡的密林中去——那里开满了繁茂的野花。

“当然，你可以去的，”安妮姑妈说，“但是，你修建花园时，想把花儿和土装在哪儿呢？”

“哦，”贝茜说，“我可以用我的围裙。”

安妮姑妈笑了，说，“我想一个篮子可能更好一点。”于是，她们走进储藏室，爬上阁楼，找遍了每一个角落。可是一些篮子装满了东西，一些篮子破旧不堪，她们没有找到一个可以用的篮子。

后来，安妮姑妈用袋子和线将一个大针线筐改装成了漂亮的篮子。“给你这个，”她说，“可以用它装土，还有花啊，喜欢装什么你就用它装什么吧。”

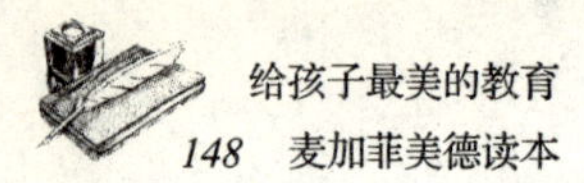

“哦！我真不知道该怎么感谢您。”贝茜雀跃着说。一转眼，她就蹦蹦跳跳地穿过花园，像一只蝴蝶一样飞出大门，来到满是蒲公英的田野里。不一会，贝茜就涉过山谷的小溪，爬上山坡，消失在茂密的树阴当中。

那个午后，贝茜是多么快乐！她捧起肥沃的黑土，用手把它们变平整，之后她四处去找寻漂亮的花朵——让紫罗兰、迎春花和其他一些鲜艳的花在她平整好的土壤上安家。她哼着歌儿，不曾有一时地停歇。

松鼠跑出洞外好奇地看着贝茜，小鸟在枝头鸣唱。突然，“砰”，不知是什么砸在了河床中。贝茜吓得跳了起来，慌乱中篮子被碰翻了，沿着山坡一溜烟滚到山下去了。当贝茜看到一只大癞蛤蟆瞪着它那亮亮的眼睛看着她，仿佛在说“我是无意的”，禁不住哈哈大笑起来。

这时贝茜听到钟声响亮地响起来，她知道那是在叫她回家。但是她怎么能丢下她的篮子呢？那可是安妮姑妈做给她的，她必须首先找到它。

“留下吧，留下吧，留下吧，”一只躲在树叶间的小鸟唱了起来：“留下吧，贝茜。”

“对呀，”贝茜说，“我怎么能让亲爱的妈妈或是姑妈等我呢，她们对我是那样的好。我不及时赶回去，她们会着急的。我最好先把篮子留在这。好好照顾它，小鸟；还有你，癞蛤蟆先生，可不要跳到我的花上哦。”

不一会，贝茜就跑回家了。她一回到家就喊道：“妈妈，妈妈！姑妈！你们谁找我？”

“是我，宝贝，”妈妈说，“我就要动身去远方旅行，如果你没有立刻赶回来，我就不能和我的小姑娘说再见了。”然后妈妈吻了她，告诉贝茜在她外出的时候要听安妮姑妈的话。当然，贝茜很乐意这么做。

第二天早上，贝茜醒来时发现，外边下起了大雨。她一脸沮丧地跑到姑妈的房间。“哦，姑妈！这么大的雨！”

“多么好的一场雨啊！贝茜！它会让我们的花儿生长，而且，我们可以一起在家里度过一段快乐的时光！”

“我知道的，姑妈，但你会认为我太粗心了！”贝茜还是高兴不起来。

“粗心得让天下了雨吗？”安妮姑妈愉快地笑了起来。

“不，不要笑，安妮姑妈。我把你漂亮的篮子留在外面过了整整一夜。现在它肯定被浸泡坏了，被这，这，这场雨。”看起来，这场雨显然不能让贝茜高兴起来。

“你会变得越来越细心的，亲爱的，”安妮姑妈轻轻地说，“过来，宝贝，告诉我一切，好吗？”

贝茜慢慢地走到姑妈身边，告诉姑妈她昨天所度过的快乐时光：那只松鼠和癞蛤蟆先生，篮子为什么会滚下山去？还有，因为听到了召唤的钟声，她根本没有时间去找篮子。

“你做得很对，”安妮姑妈说，“如果你留下来去找篮子的话，你的妈妈可能要一整天都等着你，或是看不到你就走了。我会写信告诉她你是这样的听话，还有什么比这更令她高兴呢！”

Bessie

One day, Bessie thought how nice it would be to have a garden with only wild flowers in it. So into the house she ran to find her Aunt Annie, and ask her leave to go over on the shady hillside, across the brook, where the wild flowers grew thickest.

" Yes, indeed, you may go," said Aunt Annie; "but what will you put the roots and earth in while you are making the garden?"

"Oh," said Bessie, "I can take my apron."

Her aunt laughed, and said, "A basket will be better, I think." So they looked in the closets and the attic, everywhere; but some of the baskets were full, and some broken; not one could they find that would do.

Then Aunt Annie turned out the spools and the bags from a nice large workbasket, and gave that to Bessie. "You may have this for your own," she said, "to fill with earth, or flowers, or anything you like."

"Oh I thank you," said Bessie, and she danced away through the garden. She slipped through the gate, out into the field all starred with dandelions, down in the hollow by the brook, then up on the hillside out of sight among the shady trees.

How she worked that afternoon! She heaped up the dark, rich earth, and smoothed it over with her hands. Then she dug up violets, and spring–beauties, and other flowers,—running back and forth, singing all the while.

The squirrels peeped out of their holes at Bessie. The birds sang in the branches overhead. Thump, came something all at once into the middle of the bed. Bessie jumped and upset the basket, and away it rolled down the hill.

How Bessie laughed when she saw a big, brown toad winking his bright eyes at her, as if he would say, "No offense, I hope."

Just then Bessie heard a bell ringing loudly. She knew it was calling her home; but how could she leave her basket? She must look for that first.

"Waiting, waiting, waiting," all at once sang a bird out of sight among the branches; "waiting, Bessie."

"Sure enough," said Bessie; "perhaps I'm making dear mother or auntie wait; and they are so good to me. I'd better let the basket wait. Take care of it, birdie; and don't jump on my flowers, Mr. Toad."

She was back at the house in a few minutes, calling, "Mother! mother! auntie! Who wants me?"

"I, dear," said her mother. "I am going away for a long visit, and if you had not come at once, I could not have said good–by to my little girl."

Then Bessie's mother kissed her, and told her to obey her kind aunt while she was gone.

The next morning, Bessie waked to find it raining hard. She went into her aunt's room with a very sad face. "O auntie! this old rain!"

"This new, fresh, beautiful rain, Bessie! How it will make our flowers grow, and what a good time we can have together in the house!"

"I know it, auntie; but you will think me so careless!"

"To let it rain?"

"No; don't laugh, Aunt Annie; to leave your nice basket out of doors all night; and now it will be soaked and ruined in this—this—beautiful rain." Bessie did not look as if the beautiful rain made her very happy.

"You must be more careful, dear, another time," said her aunt, gently. "But come, tell me all about it."

So Bessie crept very close to her auntie's side, and told her of her happy time the day before; of the squirrel, and the toad, and how the basket rolled away down the hill; and then how the bell rang, and she could not stop to find the basket.

"And you did quite right," said her aunt. "If you had stopped, your mother must have waited a whole day, or else gone without seeing you. When I write, I will tell her how obedient you were, and that will please her more than anything else I can say."

风筝事件

孩子们总会有些异想天开的念头，爱迪生小时候也曾尝试孵化小鸡。天知道，这些奇思妙想日后很有可能就会孵化成世界的推动力。

所以，我们努力要做的不是去嘲笑，而是为孩子们的想像力插上翅膀。

在人们眼里，雷是个奇怪的孩子。等你读过这则故事，你也会这样认为的。

雷也喜欢与同学们在学校里玩耍，但他更喜欢独自一人待在树阴下读童话故事或是做白日梦。不过，他与他的小伙伴都喜欢一样游戏，那就是放风筝。

有一天，他在放风筝时突然想："不知道有没有人在夜里放风筝，我想那一定棒极了。只是如果天太黑的话，会看不到风筝的方位吧。有了，我在上面绑盏灯怎么样？那就能看到风筝了。嗯，今晚我就要尝试一下。"

天刚刚黑，雷没有跟任何人打招呼，就带着风筝和灯出去了。他来到一块很大的开阔地上，那离家大约有四分之一英里远。"这种感觉真有点奇怪，竟然周围没有一个人！但既然来了，还是开始放风筝吧。”雷想。

于是，雷将灯绑在了风筝的尾巴上，那灯是他用一只打满了小孔的罐头盒做成的。然后他拉着绳子开始跑起来，经过好几次尝试之后，风筝终于升起来了。风筝越飞越高，线一会就放光了。雷将风筝线系在了篱笆上，然后站在那里注视着高高地飘在空中的风筝。

就在雷享受着他的创举时，街上的行人发现了天空中那奇怪的亮光，他们聚在一起观察着那光。有时，发光物会停留在一个地方几秒钟，有时，那光会上下跳动，或者在天空中前后平稳地移动。

“那能是什么呢？”一个人问。

“太奇怪了！”又一个人叫道。

“那不像是彗星，因为彗星应该有尾巴。”第三个人判断说。

“也许是一只大萤火虫。”又有人推测。

好奇的人们最终决定去看看那奇怪的光到底是什么。是在空中跳舞的精灵，或是从天上掉下来的什么东西？于是他们开始尽可能地接近那光亮。

这时，雷已经站累了，他坐在了篱笆边上的一棵树后，他能看见走近的人群，但人们却看不到他。

当人们来到光的正下方时，终于看清那是什么了。人们互相看看，大笑起来，说道：“这是哪个孩子的恶作剧，把我们都给捉弄了。我们不要说出去，看看还有谁会上当吧！”大家嘻嘻哈哈地笑着，往镇子里走去了。可是还有一些人仍然没有发现那奇怪的光到底是什么。

当人们都离开之后，雷想该是回家的时候了。于是他收起线，带着风筝和灯回到了家，而此时他妈妈正在担心，以为他出了什么事呢。

当妈妈知道一切后，被他的举动弄得哭笑不得。但我想，最后她一定是哈哈笑着打发雷去上床睡觉。

Ray and His Kite

Ray was thought to be an odd boy. You will think him so, too, when you have read this story.

Ray liked well enough to play with the boys at school; yet he liked better to be alone under the shade of some tree, reading a fairy tale or dreaming daydreams. But there was one sport that he liked as well as his companions; that was kiteflying.

One day when he was flying his kite, he said to himself, "I wonder if anybody ever tried to fly a kite at night. It seems to me it would be nice. But then, if it were very dark, the kite could not be seen. What if I should fasten a light to it, though? That would make it show. I'll try it this very night."

As soon as it was dark, without saying a word to anybody, he took his kite and lantern, and went to a large, open lot, about a quarter of a mile from his home. "Well," thought he, "this is queer. How lonely and still it seems without any other boys around! But I am going to fly my kite, anyway."

So he tied the lantern, which was made of tin punched full of small holes, to the tail of his kite. Then he pitched the kite, and, after several attempts, succeeded in making it rise. Up it went, higher and higher, as Ray let out the string. When the string was all unwound, he tied it to a fence; and then he stood and gazed at his kite as it floated high up in the air.

While Ray was enjoying his sport, some people who were out on the street in the village, saw a strange light in the sky. They gathered in groups to watch it. Now it was still for a few seconds, then it seemed to be jumping up and down; then it made long sweeps back and forth through the air.

"What can it be?" said one person. "How strange!" said another. "It can not be a comet; for comets have tails," said a third. "Perhaps it's a big firefly," said another.

At last some of the men determined to find out what this strange light was—whether it was a hobgoblin dancing in the air, or something dropped from the sky. So off they started to get as near it as they could.

While this was taking place, Ray, who had got tired of standing, was seated in a fence corner, behind a tree. He could see the men as they approached; but they did not see him.

When they were directly under the light, and saw what it was, they looked at each other, laughing, and said, "This is some boy's trick; and it has fooled us nicely. Let us keep the secret, and have our share of the joke."

Then they laughed again, and went back to the village; and some of the simple people there have not yet found out what that strange light was.

When thc men had gone, Ray thought it was time for him to go; so he wound up his string, picked up his kite and lantern, and went home. His mother had been wondering what had become of him.

When she heard what he had been doing, she hardly knew whether to laugh or scold; but I think she laughed, and told him that it was time for him to go to bed.

安妮的梦

相信安妮一定在梦中了解了水的形态变化。如果知识都能以这样诱人的面目出现，何愁还引不起人们的兴趣？但反过来讲，即便是高深难懂的自然科学也能孕育出这么精彩的世界，为什么我们不去潜心钻研呢？

在一个寒冷冬天的晚上，辛克莱一家除了安妮都到邻居家串门去了，她决定在家学习自然哲学，那一课又长又难。

一个人在家，感觉时间过得飞快，但安妮学习完后，家人还有足足半个小时才能回来。

合上书本，安妮顺势往软软的扶手椅上一靠，很快就进入了梦乡。她梦见在一个非常寒冷的早晨，自己站在饭厅的火炉旁，一只玻璃盆里面盛满了水，每天放在那里为房间增加湿度。

“哎呀，”她叹了一口气，“快到上学时间了。今天早晨这么冷，我真不想去上学了，而且这一篇课文太长了，不知道我能不能记下来。让我想想，呃……，我想，水在100℃时才能蒸发……”

“胡说什么呀！”“真滑稽啊！”旁边一些奇怪的声音异口同声地叫着。“看哪！难道这是水沸腾吗？多么荒谬呀！100℃之后，我们才能飞起来吗？哈！哈！哈！”

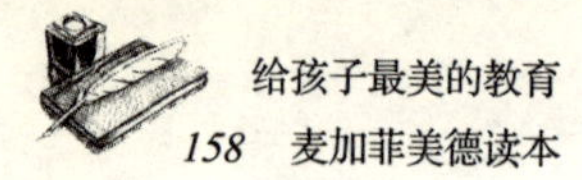

“你们是谁？”安妮惊奇地问道。“我在哪儿能看到你们？”

“当然是看盆里。”

安妮照着做了。于是，她看到了许许多多的小东西在快速地到处跑动。她发现随着火的温度上升，它们的数量也随之增加。“哎呀，可爱的小东西们！”她问道，“你们在做什么呀？”

“我们是水精灵，”其中一个脆生生地答道，“正如你所看到的，当惬意的温暖扑面而来时，我们就会变轻飞起来。”

一会儿，他展开翅膀飞了起来，加入了同伴的行列，他们就像卷曲的白色的云彩，在安妮的头顶上飞舞着。他们是那么轻盈，那么小巧，一会儿就消失在了空气中。

安妮看不到它们飞到哪儿去了，于是又向盆里看去。“这么热，不会弄伤你吧？”安妮问其中一个道。“还没有达到100℃呢，”小精灵不无讽刺地说。

安妮气呼呼地回答道，“我记得100℃是水的沸点。但我的意思是说，你们在受热之后，才在这么寒冷的天气飞走？”

“不，不，”小精灵哈哈大笑，“我们喜欢这样。这是英明的上帝制定的规则，所以那样不会伤害到我们。我们无时无刻不在用我们的方式工作，也就是说，变成不同的形态就是我们的工作。如果愿意的话，请你走到窗户旁，你会看到我的一些兄弟姐妹们都附在玻璃上。”

安妮走到窗户旁，刚开始只看到了一些美丽的霜花。然而，很快，她就发现玻璃上聚集了许许多多的小精灵，他们的翅膀像雪一样白，如冰晶般闪耀发光。

“天哪，”安妮快乐地叫道，“这是我所看到的最美丽的景致。亲爱的，你叫什么名字呀？”她向一个头戴冰玫瑰花冠的精灵问道。小精灵回答的声音又尖又细，就像针尖一样，把安妮给逗乐了。

“Fine Frost是我们的姓，”小精灵说，“我自己有名字，但我不想告诉你，因为你取笑我，太不礼貌了。”

“亲爱的，对不起，”安妮抱歉地说，“我是忍俊不禁。我不会再嘲笑你了，请你告诉我你是怎么来到这儿的，我刚才与那边水盆里你的一个兄弟聊得很好。”

于是，小精灵高贵地叠起翅膀，说，“既然你发誓不再无礼，我就把我所知道的都告诉你吧！尽管故事非常简短。”

“昨天晚上，我们就从玻璃盆里逃了出来，就像你今天早晨看到我们的伙伴所做的那样。哎呀，逃出来是多么轻松，多么自由啊！因为我们长得小巧玲珑，我们在房间里飞来飞去，没有人看得见我们。”

“过了一会儿，我就跟伙伴飞到了这扇窗户上并降落到玻璃上，因为天冷，就由水精灵变成了现在Fine Frost家族的精灵。”“太奇妙了，”安妮说。“做一个精灵好吗？”

“哦，当然了，做一个精灵非常快乐。一整个晚上在月光下熠熠发光，可把我们高兴坏了。当时，我戴了一个长长的花环，镶嵌着冰珍珠和冰钻石。你看，这里就有一颗，不久，我们又要变成水精灵了，我看到阳光已经照到这边来了。”

“你害怕被融化吗？”安妮问道。“不，不怕。”精灵肯定地回答道，“我喜欢经常地变来变去。”

突然，一个想法在安妮的脑子里一闪，如果赶在太阳融化他之前对着他吹气，会怎么样呢？她想到就做到。这时，许许多多的霜精灵降落到窗台上，汇聚成了一颗水滴。

“哎呀，我是不是伤到他们了？”她惊呼了起来。“没有，没有。”许多个声音异口同声地答道，“我们只是又变成了水精灵而已。我们哪儿也没有受伤，只是形态发生了变化。”“你们永远是美丽、可爱的小精灵，”安妮说，“我希望……”

这时，门铃响了，吵醒了安妮。她从椅子上跳了起来，原来家里人回来了。他们都说聚会很愉快，可是安妮说她不相信他们的聚会能好过她这半小时里所做的梦。

Annie's Dream

It was a clear, cold, winter evening, and all the Sinclairs but Annie had gone out for a neighborly visit. She had resolved to stay at home and study a long, difficult lesson in Natural Philosophy.

Left to herself, the evening passed quickly, but the lesson was learned a full half hour before the time set for the family to come home.

Closing her book, she leaned back in the soft armchair in which she was sitting, soon fell asleep, and began to dream. She dreamed that it was a very cold morning, and that she was standing by the dining–room stove, looking into the glass basin which was every day filled with water for evaporation.

"Oh, dear," she sighed, "it is nearly school time. I don't want to go out in the cold this morning. Then there is that long lesson. I wonder if I can say it. Let me see—it takes two hundred and twelve degrees of heat, I believe, for water to evaporate—"

"Nonsense!" "Ridiculous!" shouted a chorus of strange little voices near by; "Look here! Is this water boiling? What an idea, two hundred and twelve degrees before we can fly, ha, ha!"

"Who are you?" asked Annie, in amazement. "Where must I look?"

"In the basin, of course."

Annie looked, and saw a multitude of tiny forms moving swiftly around, their numbers increasing as the heat of the fire increased. "Why you dear little things!" said she, "what are you doing down there?"

"We are water sprites," answered one, in the clearest voice that can be imagined, "and when this delightful warmth comes all about us, we become so light that we fly off, as you see."

In another moment he had joined a crowd of his companions that were spreading their wings and flying off in curling, white clouds over Annie's head. But they were so light and thin that they soon disappeared in the air.

She could not see where they went, so she again turned to the basin. "Doesn't it hurt you," she asked one, "to be heated—?" "Not always to two hundred and twelve," said the sprite, mischievously.

"No, no," replied Annie, half-vexed; "I remember, that is boiling point—but I mean, to be heated as you all are, and then to fly off in the cold?"

"Oh, no," laughed the little sprite; "we like it. We are made to change by God's wise laws, and so it can't hurt us. We are all the time at work, in our way, taking different shapes. It is good for us. If you will go to the window, you will find some of my brothers and sisters on the glass."

Annie went to the window, and at first could see nothing but some beautiful frostwork on it. Soon, however, the panes seemed to swarm with little folks. Their wings were as white as snow, and sparked with ice jewels.

"Oh," cried Annie, "this is the prettiest sight I ever saw. What is

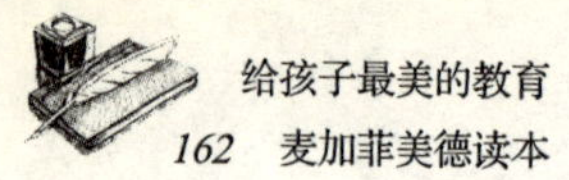

your name, darling?" she asked one that wore a crown of snow roses. The little voice that replied was so sharp and fine that Annie thought it seemed like a needle point of sound, and she began to laugh.

"Fine Frost is our family name," it said. "I have a first name of my own, but I shall not tell you what it is, for you are so impolite as to laugh at me."

"I beg your pardon, dear," said Annie; "I could not help it. I will not laugh at you any more if you will tell me how you came here. I have been talking with one of your brothers over there in the basin."

The little sprite then folded her wings in a dignified manner, and said, "I will tell you all I know about it, since you promise to be polite. It is a very short story, however.

"Last evening we all escaped from the glass basin, as you have seen our companions do this morning. Oh, how light and free we felt! But we were so very delicate and thin that no one saw us as we flew about in the air of the room.

"After a while I flew with these others to this window, and, as we alighted on the glass, the cold changed us from water sprites into sprites of the Fine Frost family." "It is very wonderful," said Annie. "Is it nice to be a sprite?"

"Oh, yes, we are very gay. All last night we had a fine time sparkling in the moonlight. I wore a long wreath full of ice pearls and diamonds. Here is a piece of it. Before long we shall be water sprites again. I see the sun is coming this way."

"Shall you dread to be melted?" inquired Annie. "No, indeed," answered the sprite. "I like to change my form now and then."

A thought flashed across Annie's brain. What if she should breathe on the frost and not wait for the sun to melt it. In a moment more she had done so. Down fell a great number of the tiny mountains and castles, carrying with them a multitude of frost sprites, and all that could be seen was a drop of water on the window sill.

"Oh, dear! have I hurt them?" she exclaimed. "No, no," replied a chorus of many small voices from the drop of water, "we are only water sprites again. Nothing hurts us; we merely change." "But you are always pretty little things," said Annie. "I wish—"

Here a ring at the doorbell woke Annie. She started up to find the family had returned from their visit, which all declared was a delightful one. But Annie said she did not believe they had enjoyed their visit better than she had her half hour's dream.

华氏温标

1714年，德国物理学家华伦海特（1686~1736）用水银代替酒精作为测温物质，制定了华氏温标（Fahrenheit temperature scale），符号℉。他把一定浓度的盐水凝固时的温度定为0℉,把纯水凝固时的温度定为32 ℉，把标准大气压下水沸腾的温度定为212℉。中间分为180等份，每一等份代表1度，这就是华氏温标。华氏温标中，人体的正常体温为98.6度。至今，英国和美国等英语国家仍在使用华氏温标。

1742年，瑞典天文学家摄尔修斯（1707~1744）提出一个新的测温系统。他以水银为测温物质，将水的沸点定为0度，冰的溶点定为100度，八年以后，摄尔修斯的同事建议把标度倒过来，于是形成了今日广为采用的摄氏温标。

摄氏温度与华氏温度的换算公式是：摄氏度 =（华氏度− 32）×5÷9。

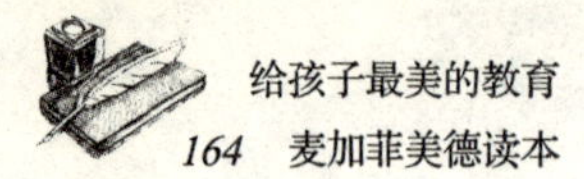

河口剧院

选自托马斯.贝利·奥尔得里奇的《坏男孩的故事》。作者于1836年生于新罕布什尔州的朴茨茅斯，在他很小的时候全家迁往路易斯安那州，但他被送回新英格兰接受教育，后来定居纽约。他是一位著名的散文家和诗人。

“伙伴们，现在我们该干什么？”在一个阴沉得快要下雨的下午，我向聚集在我们的谷仓中开秘密会议的七个伙伴问道。“让我们建一个剧院吧！”宾尼·华莱士建议道。

太好了！但是建在哪里呢？马厩的草料棚将要堆满提供给吉普赛人的干草，但是马车房那边的长房间还是空的，就这个地方！以我的专业眼光一眼便看出它是适合做剧院的。

我在新奥尔良的时候参加过很多次的演出，十分精通戏剧方面的东西。在这儿，我在适当时候会布置一些自己画的独特布景。而帷幕尽管在我记忆中其他时候它拉起来十分顺利，但在演出时总是会被哪儿钩住。

到目前为止，剧院还是成功的。当我走下舞台时，我至少得到了 一千五百个大头针，这还不包括那些没针帽、没针尖和弯曲的大头针——这种大头针经常让我们的守门人不知怎么办好。从头至尾，我们一直都是拿大量的大头针当作钱。“河口剧院”的门票是二十个大头针。我自己扮演所有的主要角色——不是因为我比其他伙伴演得好，而是因为我是创建人。

在第十次演出时，我的演出生涯不幸被迫结束。当时我们正在演出戏剧《威廉·特尔，瑞士的英雄》。当然是我演威廉·特尔，尽管弗雷德·兰登也想扮演这个角色，但我是不会让给他的，因此他宣布退出，带走了我们拥有的唯一的弓和箭。

我用鲸鱼骨做了一个弓，没有他我也能做得很好。我们已经到达了最高潮的一幕，哥士勒，奥地利的暴君，要求特尔射向摆在他儿子头上的苹果。一向包揽少年和妇女角色的佩皮斯·惠特克姆，在其中扮演我的儿子。

为了防止出错，惠特克姆的上半部脸用手帕绑了一块木板，要用的箭头上则缝了一块绒布。我是一名神箭手，离那个只有两码远的黄色的大苹果简直是面对面。

现在我可以看见可怜的小佩皮斯正毫无畏惧地站在那里，等着我表演我的高超技艺。我举起了我的弓开始瞄准，所有的观众都屏住了呼吸，一共有七名男孩和三名女孩，其中包括凯蒂·科林斯，她坚持用缝衣针付门票。我再次举起了我的弓。咣！弓弦弹了出来。但，糟糕！箭没有射中苹果，而是正好射进了佩皮斯·惠特克姆的嘴里，他的嘴恰好在那时张开，扰乱了我的瞄准。

我将永远不会忘记这个可怕的时刻，佩皮斯那惊恐、愤怒和痛苦的嚎叫声仍然回响在我耳边。我以为他会死去，灰暗的未来在向北招手，想像自己不要多久就会在同样的观众面前被处死。

幸运的是，可怜的佩皮斯伤的并不严重，但纳特爷爷对此情状却显得很慌乱（他是被小特尔的嚎叫声引过来的）。他宣布今后禁止玩所有有关戏剧的东西，这个剧场要被关闭了。不过，我还可以作个告别演说。我说道，如果没有射中佩皮斯·惠特克姆的嘴巴，这一刻将是我生命中最骄傲的时刻。所有的观众（我很高兴地指出，因为有佩皮斯在一旁协助）都在大喊：“听！听！”

然后我将事故的责任推到了佩皮斯自己的身上，他的嘴巴在我射箭的那一刻刚好张开，就像一个漩涡那样，把那支不幸的箭吸了过去。我正要解释一个相当小的漩涡如何能粘住巨大的轮船的时候，幕布在观众的叫喊声中自己掉了下来。

这是我最后一次出现在舞台上。尽管很长一段时间之后威廉·特尔事件才告平息。曾经不允许买票进我的剧院的小男孩经常跟在我后面在街上恶意地大叫：“谁杀死了知更鸟？”

玩　具

孩子，你真是快活呀，
整个早晨坐在尘土里，玩着一根嫩绿的树枝
我微笑着，看你玩着那根折断的小树枝
我呢，正忙着算账，一小时一小时在那里加叠着数字。
也许你在看我，想道：
这种好没趣的游戏，竟把你的一早晨的好时间浪费掉了！
孩子，我已经忘了聚精会神玩耍树枝与泥饼的本领了。
我寻找着昂贵的玩具，收集一块儿一块儿的金银。
而你，无论找着什么，都能发明出一个开心的游戏 。
我却把我的时间与气力都浪费在那些我永远不能得到的东西上。
我在脆弱的独木舟里挣扎着要渡过欲望之海，
忘却了自己也是在玩一个游戏。

——[印]泰戈尔

Rivermouth Theater

From "The Story of a Bad Boy," by Thomas Bailey Aldrich. The author was born at Portsmouth, N. H., in 1836. When quite young his family moved to Louisiana, but he was sent back to New England to be educated, and later he located at New York. He is a well–known writer of both prose and poetry.

"Now, boys, what shall we do?" I asked, addressing a thoughtful conclave of seven, assembled in our barn one dismal, rainy afternoon. "Let's have a theater," suggested Binny Wallace.

The very thing! But where? The loft of the stable was ready to burst with hay provided for Gypsy, but the long room over the carriage house was unoccupied. The place of all places! My managerial eye saw at a glance its capabilities for a theater.

I had been to the play a great many times in New Orleans, and was wise in matters pertaining to the drama. So here, in due time, was set up some extraordinary scenery of my own painting. The curtain, I recollect, though it worked smoothly enough on other occasions, invariably hitched during the performances.

The theater, however, was a success, as far as it went. I retired from the business with no fewer than fifteen hundred pins, after deducting the headless, the pointless, and the crooked pins with which our doorkeeper frequently got "stuck." From first to last we took in a great deal of this counterfeit money. The price of admission to the "Rivermouth Theater" was twenty pins. I played all the principal characters myself—not that I was a finer actor than the other boys, but because I owned the establishment.

At the tenth representation, my dramatic career was brought to a close by an unfortunate circumstance. We were playing the drama of "William Tell, the Hero of Switzerland." Of course I was William Tell, in spite of Fred Langdon, who wanted to act that character himself. I wouldn't let him, so he withdrew from the company, taking the only bow and arrow we had.

I made a crossbow out of a piece of whalebone, and did very well without him. We had reached that exciting scene where Gesler, the Austrian tyrant, commands Tell to shoot the apple from his son's head. Pepper Whitcomb, who played all the juvenile and women parts, was my son.

To guard against mischance, a piece of pasteboard was fastened by a handkerchief over the upper portion of Whitcomb's face, while the arrow to be used was sewed up in a strip of flannel. I was a capital marksman, and the big apple, only two yards distant, turned its russet cheek fairly towards me.

I can see poor little Pepper now, as he stood without flinching, waiting for me to perform my great feat. I raised the crossbow amid the breathless silence of the crowded audience—consisting of seven boys and three girls, exclusive of Kitty Collins, who insisted on paying her way in with a clothespin. I raised the crossbow, I repeat. Twang! went the whipcord; but, alas! instead of hitting the apple, the arrow flew right into Pepper Whitcomb's mouth, which happened to be open at the time, and destroyed my aim.

I shall never be able to banish that awful moment from my memory. Pepper's roar, expressive of astonishment, indignation, and pain, is still ringing in my ears. I looked upon him as a corpse, and, glancing not far into the dreary future, pictured myself led forth to execution in the presence of the very same spectators then assembled.

Luckily, poor Pepper was not seriously hurt; but Grandfather Nutter, appearing in the midst of the confusion (attracted by the howls of young Tell), issued an injunction against all theatricals thereafter, and the place was closed; not, however, without a farewell speech from me, in which I said that this would have been the proudest moment of my life if I hadn't hit Pepper Whitcomb in the mouth. Whereupon the audience (assisted, I am glad to state, by Pepper) cried, "Hear! hear!"

I then attributed the accident to Pepper himself, whose mouth, being open at the instant I fired, acted upon the arrow much after the fashion of a whirlpool, and drew in the fatal shaft. I was about to explain how a comparatively small maelstrom could suck in the largest ship, when the curtain fell of its own accord, amid the shouts of the audience.

This was my last appearance on any stage. It was some time, though, before I heard the end of the William Tell business. Malicious little boys who hadn't been allowed to buy tickets to my theater used to cry out after me in the street,–"'Who killed Cock Robin?'"

CHAPTER 5

美好的品德

当良心、羞耻心、责任心和事业心在你的心灵中永远扎下根来的时候，你就会形成一种有道德的个性。

——[苏]苏霍姆林斯基

一块小面包

谦让是一种美德，一种修养，更是一种做人的境界。谦让的人虽然总是习惯于排在别人的后面，但上帝不会忘记他，总会有一些意想不到的惊喜等着他。

有一次闹饥荒，一位富有的面包师把镇子上最穷的二十个孩子叫来，对他们说："篮子里有二十块面包，你们每人可以拿上一块，以后每天这个时候来这里，直到我们平安地度过饥荒。"

那些饥饿的孩子争着去抢篮子里的面包，还吵了起来，因为他们都想要最大的那一块。最后，他们连感谢都没感谢这位好心人就跑掉了。

可是格雷奇，一个衣服破旧的小姑娘，没有和别人争抢，只是远远地站在一旁。当那些表现糟糕的女孩子们离去后她才拿起最小的那一块面包，亲吻了一下面包师的手之后才转身回家。第二天，那些孩子表现得和昨天一样差劲，可怜的小格雷奇只拿到有第一天一半大的面包。回到家后，她的妈妈把面包切开。却意外地发现里面有许多闪闪发光的银币。

她的妈妈惊呆了，对她说："赶快把这些钱送回去吧，肯定是面

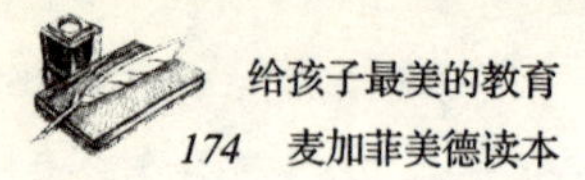

包师不小心掉进来的。快点，格雷奇！快去！”

可是当小姑娘把她妈妈的话告诉面包师时，他却回答：“不是的，孩子，不是的。我故意把银币放进来的，这是对你的奖赏的。希望你能像现在这样，怀着一颗感恩的心，永远都知足地、文雅地生活。回去吧，孩子，告诉你妈妈，这是属于你的钱。”

人生格言

诚者，天之道也；思诚者，人之道也。

——孟子

失去了诚信，就等同于敌人毁灭了自己。

——[英]莎士比亚

诚实和勤勉，应该成为你永久的伴侣。

——[美]富兰克林

走正直诚实的生活道路，定会有一个问心无愧的归宿。

——[苏]高尔基

自以为聪明的人，往往是没有好下场的，世界上最聪明的人是老实的人，因为只有老实人才能经得起事实和历史的考验。

——周恩来

诚实是力量的一种象征，它显示着一个人的高度自重和内心的安全感与尊严感。

——[美]艾琳·卡瑟

The Little Loaf

Once when there was a famine, a rich baker sent for twenty of the poorest children in the town, and said to them, "In this basket there is a loaf for each of you. Take it, and come back to me every day at this hour till God sends us better times."

The hungry children gathered eagerly about the basket, and quarreled for the bread, because each wished to have the largest loaf. At last they went away without even thanking the good gentleman.

But Gretchen, a poorly-dressed little girl, did not quarrel or struggle with the rest,but remained standing modestly in the distance. When the ill-behaved girls had left, she took the smallest loaf, which alone was left in the basket, kissed the gentleman's hand, and went home.

The next day the children were as ill behaved as before, and poor, timid Gretchen received a loaf scarcely half the size of the one she got the first day. When she came home, and her mother cut the loaf open, many new, shining pieces of silver fell out of it.

Her mother was very much alarmed, and said, "Take the money back to the good gentleman at once, for it must have got into the dough by accident. Be quick, Gretchen! be quick!"

But when the little girl gave the rich man her mother's message, he said, "No, no, my child, it was no mistake. I had the silver pieces put into the smallest loaf to reward you. Always be as contented, peaceable, and grateful as you now are. Go home now, and tell your mother that the money is your own."

星期的英文名称语意（一）

一星期七天的不同名称起源于古代罗马神话，后来被德国人用自己的语言和文化习俗进行了改造，把其中代表周二至周五的四个神换成了相应的德国人的神。最后这些名称流传到英国，才成为今天的样子。在17世纪以前，一星期七天的首字母都无须大写。

在古罗马神话中，Sunday的寓意是太阳，罗马人把星期天叫做Dies Solis（Day of the Sun）。当然了，有Sun Day就会有Moon Day，月亮神是太阳神之妻，因此她紧跟在Sunday后面作了Monday。

罗马人把星期二叫做Dies Martis，这是罗马战神Mars（火星）的日子。但是，今天的Tuesday源自Tiu's day，和德国战神和天空之神泰尔（Tiu/Tiw）有关，Tiu即古希腊诸神中的火神Zeus（Tiu和Zeus音同）。

值得一提的是，星期二Mars在法语中作Mardi。Mardi Gras表示四旬斋前的狂欢节（星期二），是天主教徒在复活节之前必需的斋戒仪式。斋戒之前当然要大吃大喝一番了，因此这一天又叫Fat Tuesday。Mardi Gras Day是美国最大的嘉年华会，这一持续两周的盛会每年都会在新奥尔良举行，有数百万人参加。

美丽的手

判断一个人、一样东西的价值并不能仅仅看他是否美丽。美丽的外表、漂亮的话语，都不如行动来的更为实在。况且，说到美丽，没有什么比得上善良的心灵——容颜总会老去，而心灵却始终常青。

“哦，罗伯特小姐，玛丽·杰萨普的手看起来好粗糙啊！”黛西·马文在与老师一起回家的路感叹道。

“可是黛西，在我看来，玛丽的手是我们班上最漂亮的了。”老师这样回答说。

“为什么？罗伯特小姐，”黛西感到很吃惊，“她那双手红肿粗笨，如果她用它来弹钢琴，不知道会弹成什么样子！”

罗伯特小姐拉起黛西的双手说：“你的手柔软白皙，但是它只是在弹钢琴的时候好看，它们仍缺少玛丽的手所具有的那种美。我能告诉你差别在哪里吗？”

“好的，请说吧，罗伯特小姐。”

“是这样的，黛西，玛丽的双手总是很忙碌，她要洗盘子，生火做饭，洗晒衣物，还有许多繁重的家务，她总是用这双手去努力帮助自己辛劳的母亲。”

“还有，她还用这双手为孩子们洗衣穿衣，修理他们的玩具，给洋娃娃做衣服，有时候还为邻居生病的小女孩洗头。”

“她对待一切有生命的东西都有爱心。我曾看到她用那双手在街上轻轻抚摩疲劳的马匹和瘸腿的狗。她时刻准备着去帮助需要帮助的人。”老师赞许地说。

“我不再认为玛丽的手难看了，罗伯特小姐。”黛西小声说。

“我很高兴听到你这样说，黛西。我必须告诉你，她的手之所以美丽，是因为这双手总是欣然地接受并且高兴地做她的工作。”

“哦，罗伯特小姐！我对我之前说的话感到十分羞愧，我真抱歉。”黛西眼含泪水看着老师说。

“那么，亲爱的，就请用你的善行来表达你的懊悔吧。善良才是真正的美丽。”

Beautiful Hands

"O Miss Roberts! what coarse-looking hands Mary Jessup has!" said Daisy Marvin, as she walked home from school with her teacher.

"In my opinion, Daisy, Mary's hands are the prettiest in he class."

"Why, Miss Roberts, they are as red and hard as they can be. How they would look if she were to try to play on a piano!" exclaimed Daisy.

Miss Roberts took Daisy's hands in hers, and said, "Your hands are very soft and white, Daisy—just the hands to look beautiful on a piano; yet they lack one beauty that Mary's hands have. Shall I tell you what the difference is? "

"Yes, please, Miss Roberts."

"Well, Daisy, Mary's hands are always busy. They wash dishes; they make fires; they hang out clothes, and help to wash them, too; they sweep, and dust, and sew; they are always trying to help her poor, hard-working mother.

"Besides, they wash and dress the children; they mend their toys and dress their dolls; yet, they find time to bathe the head of the little girl who is so sick in the next house to theirs.

"They are full of good deeds to every living thing. I have seen them patting the tired horse and the lame dog in the street. They are always ready to help those who need help."

"I shall never think Mary's hands are ugly any more, Miss Roberts."

"I am glad to hear you say that, Daisy; and I must tell you that they are beautiful because they do their work gladly and cheerfully."

"O Miss Roberts! I feel so ashamed of myself, and so sorry," said Daisy, looking into her teacher's face with tearful eyes.

"Then, my dear, show your sorrow by deeds of kindness. The good alone are really beautiful."

星期的英文名称语意（二）

星期三是Dies Mercurii，是众神信使墨丘利神Mercury（水星）的日子，Mercury不但是各路神灵的使者，还是商业、旅行及盗窃的守护神。后来，日耳曼民族用他们自己的神Woden（挪威神话里的Odin）取代了墨丘里神，这就是Wednesday的起源。现在知道星期三的拼写为什么怪怪的了吧，很多英美成年人都拼不好这个单词呢。

星期四是Dies Iovis，代表朱庇特主神、雷神Jove（木星）。后来这些罗马神话流传到德国，德国人就用他们自己的雷神Thor来代替Jove，这就是Thursday的起源。

星期五是Dies Veneris，代表爱神维纳斯Venus（金星）。后来挪威人用他们自己的爱神Frigg（Odin的妻子）取代了维纳斯的地位，所以今天的星期五就是Friday了。

星期六代表的是罗马神话里的萨杜恩农神Saturn（土星），这个词没被德国人"动手脚"，所以Saturday还是原汁原味。

真正的勇敢

胆大并不等同于勇敢，勇敢来自于对真理、对自我的坚持，尤其是在得不到周围的人认同的情况下，能够做到勇敢的坚持，才是真正的勇敢。

也许我们都曾有过类似于乔治的经历，希望下次遇到相似的情况时，我们能勇敢的说一声“不”。

一个寒冷的冬天，三个小男孩经过一所学校。最大的那个是一个品行不端的孩子，不仅自己经常麻烦不断，还总想让别的孩子去做坏事。最小的男孩叫乔治，他是个安分守己的孩子。

乔治不想做错事，但他想让自己更大胆一些。另外两个孩子一个叫亨利，一个叫詹姆斯。他们一边走路，一边说着话。

亨利：要是用雪球砸一下教室的门，一定会把老师和学生吓一跳，我想一定很好玩。

詹姆斯：如果你真砸的话，你才会跳起来呢。即使老师抓不到你，他也会告诉你的父亲是你干的，你就会挨一顿鞭子，我想你会比那些学生跳得更高的。

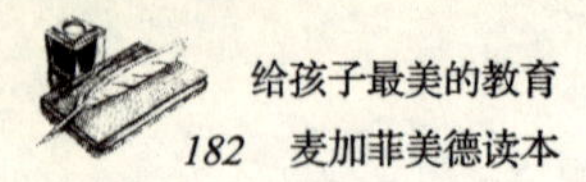

亨利：不会的，在老师打开门之前，我们就跑远了，他根本不知道是谁干的。这儿有一个结实的雪球，乔治就可以干这事，当他砸门后也不会被捉住。

詹姆斯：你让他试试，他根本不敢扔出去的。

亨利：来，乔治，拿着这个雪球，让詹姆斯瞧瞧你不是胆小鬼。

乔治：我不是不敢，只是我不想，我觉得这不是什么好事，更没有什么乐趣可言。

詹姆斯：瞧，我跟你说过他不敢扔的。

亨利：不会吧，乔治，你怎么变胆小了。我觉得你什么都不会怕的。来，别让人看扁了，就扔一下，我知道你不会害怕的。

乔治：好吧，我不害怕，给我雪球，我可以砸一下门而不被捉住的。

砰！雪球重重地砸在了门上，几个小男孩拔腿就跑。亨利尽情嘲笑着乔治，说乔治像个傻子般被他给耍了。

乔治为他的愚蠢挨了一顿鞭子，这是他应得的。他才是个胆小鬼呢，因为他害怕别人说他胆小。他不敢拒绝亨利让他做的坏事，只因为他怕被人嘲笑。

如果他是一个真正勇敢的男孩，他会说："亨利，你以为我会因为你让我去做，我就傻傻的去扔雪球吗？如果你想扔，你可以自己扔呀！"

亨利也许还会嘲笑他是个胆小鬼，但是乔治可以对他说："你想我会在乎你的话吗？我觉得用雪球砸门是不对的，我不做我觉得不对的事，即使全城的人都来笑我也不会。"

这才是真正的勇气。如果亨利看到的是这样的情形，他就不会笑乔治了，因为乔治拥有一颗坚强的心。这个故事告诉我们，即便你身陷困境，你都要有一种无畏的勇气，你应该而且必须坚持自我，不去做那些你不喜欢做的事情。

True Courage

One cold winter's day, three boys were passing by a schoolhouse. The oldest was a bad boy. always in trouble himself, and trying to get others into trouble. The youngest, whose name was George, was a very good boy.

George wished to do right, but was very much wanting in courage. The other boys were named Henry and James. As they walked along, they talked as follows:

Henry: What fun it would be to throw a snowball against the schoolroom door, and make the teacher and scholars all jump!

James: You would jump, if you should. If the teacher did not catch you and whip you, he would tell your father, and you would get a whipping then; and that would make you jump higher than the scholars, I think.

Henry: Why, we would get so far off, before the teacher could come to the door, that he could not tell who we are. Here is a snowball just as hard as ice, and George would as soon throw it against the door as not.

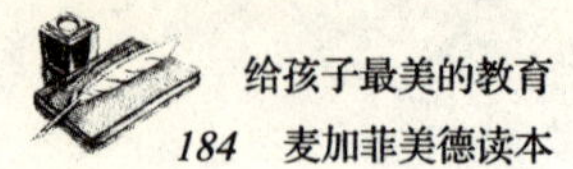

James: Give it to him, and see. He would not dare to throw it.

Henry: Do you think George is a coward? You do not know him as well as I do.

Henry: George, take this snowball, and show James that you are not such a coward as he thinks you are.

George: I am not afraid to throw it; but I do not want to. I do not see that it will do any good, or that there will be any fun in it.

James: There! I told you he would not dare to throw it.

Henry: Why, George, are you turning coward? I thought you did not fear anything. Come, save your credit, and throw it. I know you are not afraid.

George: Well, I am not afraid to throw. Give me the snowball. I would as soon throw it as not.

Whack! went the snowball against the door; and the boys took to their heels. Henry was laughing as heartily as he could, to think what a fool he had made of George.

George had a whipping for his folly, as he ought to have had. He was such a coward, that he was afraid of being called a coward. He did not dare refuse to do as Henry told him, for fear that he would be laughed at.

If he had been really a brave boy, he would have said, "Henry, do you suppose that I am so foolish as to throw that snowball, just because you want to have me? You may throw your own snowballs, if you please!"

Henry would, perhaps, have laughed at him, and called him a coward.

But George would have said, "Do you think that 1 care for your laughing? I do not think it right to throw the snowball. I will not do that which 1 think to be wrong, if the whole town should join with you in laughing."

This would have been real courage. Henry would have seen, at once, that it would do no good to laugh at a boy who had so bold a heart. You must have this fearless spirit, or you will get into trouble, and will be, and ought to be, disliked by all.

勇 敢

bold, brave, courageous都含有“勇敢的”意思

bold侧重指面对困难或危险时勇往直前、勇于进取的勇敢精神。

Mr. Brown made a bold speech. 布朗先生进行了一次大胆的演讲。

brave含义广泛，指天生的勇敢，无所畏惧地面对困难与危险，侧重胆识与果断。

The business folded up despite its barve start.生意开始时虽然很成功，但终究失败了。

courageous是正式用词，侧重指在一切情况下都有胆量、无所畏惧，强调基于道德信念，经深思熟虑后所产生的勇敢。

It was courageous of him to oppose his chief.他敢发对他的上司，真是勇敢。

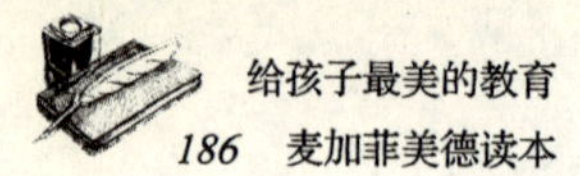

善良的行为

诸葛亮曾说：“勿以恶小而为之，勿以善小而不为”，任何事物都是由小的东西汇聚而成的，善良的习惯也需要从点滴做起。一个善举，只是一滴水，许多的善举汇聚起来，却能成就江河海洋。

为他人提供力所能及的帮助，向对面的行人露出笑脸，享受善良带给你的快乐吧！

一天，两个小男孩正走在路上，他们看到一个女人正吃力地提着一大篮子的苹果。

男孩们看到那个女人脸色苍白显出很疲惫的样子，就走上前去问：“你是往城里去吗？顺路的话，我们可以帮你提篮子。”

“谢谢你们，”那个女人回答，“你们真是太好了。我病了，浑身没劲。”她还告诉他们，她是一个寡妇，家里还有一个残疾的儿子。

她住在三英里外的一个小屋里，现在是去集市上卖苹果，那可是她们家唯一的一棵苹果树上结的。她需要钱去交房租。

“我们刚好顺路，”两个男孩说，“让我们帮你提篮子吧。”他们两人接过篮子，一人抬一边，吃力地向前走着，心情却很好。

可怜的寡妇高兴极了，但担心他们的妈妈会责怪他们。

“哦，不会的。”他们回答，“我们的妈妈常教育我们要乐于助人，只要我们能做得到的事，我们一定帮忙。”

为了表示感谢，老妇人拿出几个熟透了的苹果给两个男孩。“不用了，谢谢。”他们说，“我们做这样的事不需要任何报酬。”

当寡妇回家后，她告诉了她的那个残疾儿子发生在路上的事。一整天，他们都因为得到了两个小男孩的帮助而变得快乐起来。

另外有一天，我曾看到一个小女孩从地上拾起一块橘子皮扔到路边的水沟里。“但愿不会再有人把橘子皮扔到人行道上了。”她说，“没准有人踩到后会摔跤的。”

“是的，孩子，”我说，“你做的这件事虽说看起来是小事，但它却体现出你是一个热心肠和善良的人。”

或许有人会说这都是些小事情，也许是吧，但是我们不能一直因为等待做大事的机会而什么都不去做。请记住：点滴有爱。

Deeds of Kindness

One day, as two little boys were walking along the road, they overtook a woman carrying a large basket of apples.

The boys thought the woman looked very pale and tired; so they said, "Are you going to town? If you are, we will carry your basket."

"Thank you," replied the woman, "you are very kind: you see I am weak and ill." Then she told them that she was a widow, and had a lame son to support.

She lived in a cottage three miles away, and was now going to market to sell the apples which grew on the only tree in her little garden. She wanted the money to pay her rent.

"We are going the same way you are," said the boys. "Let us have the basket;" and they took hold of it, one on each side, and trudged along with merry hearts.

The poor widow looked glad, and said that she hoped their mother would not be angry with them. "Oh, no," they replied;"our mother has taught us to be kind to everybody, and to be useful in any way that we can."

She then offered to give them a few of the ripest apples for their trouble. "No,thank you," said they; "we do not want any pay for what we have done."

When the widow got home, she told her lame son what had happened on the road, and they were both made happier that day by the kindness of the two boys.

The other day, I saw a little girl stop and pick up a piece of orange peel, which she threw into the gutter. "I wish the boys would not throw orange peel on the sidewalk," said she. "Some one may tread upon it, and fall."

"That is right, my dear," I said. "It is a little thing for you to do what you have done, but it shows that you have a thoughtful mind and a feeling heart."

Perhaps some may say that these are little things. So they are; but we must not wait for occasions to do great things. We must begin with little labors of love.

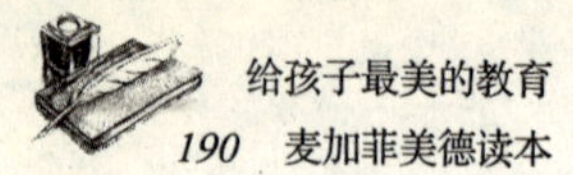

通往快乐的道路

人生路上，爱是最好的通行证。如果大家能够感受到你的爱，他们一定非常乐于接受你，爱会让你如鱼得水。因为爱可以传递，在这个过程中，每个人都可以得到快乐。

不过，爱只能通过给予才能获得，而没有爱，就没有快乐的心灵。所以，在你准备上路的时候，请给自己的行囊里装上满满的爱。

每个孩子都一定注意到了，有些孩子要比别的孩子快乐和可爱得多。有些孩子人人都爱和他做伴。他们不仅自得其乐，还能使你开心。

而有的孩子你则想离他远远的。他们似乎一个朋友都没有。没有朋友的人是不会快乐的。心灵是为爱而长的，没有爱，就没有快乐的心灵。

不是头衔也不是身份，
更不是伦敦银行里的财富，
会带给你真诚的祝福。
如果在我们心中，

没有幸福的位置，

我们或许睿智，或许富有，或许伟大

但永不会被祝福。

但你不会获得情感除非你先行付出，如果你不爱别人，别人也不会爱你。爱只能通过给予才能获得。因此，培养好的性格是非常重要的。缺少了它，你就不会快乐。

我曾经听过一个女孩说，“我知道我在学校非常不受欢迎”，这明显表明是她自己不够友善。

如果你的同伴不喜欢你，这是你自己的过错。假设你友善待人，他们就会不由自主地喜欢你。如果你得不到别人的爱，那是因为你不值得被爱。确实，有时责任感要求你不得不做一些使你的同伴不高兴的事情。但是如果你心灵高尚，大公无私，并且愿意为别人的幸福而作出牺牲，你就永远不会缺少朋友。

不要把无人喜欢你当作自己的不幸，而应该认识到这是你自己的过错。美貌和财富并不能带来朋友。如果你想赢得周围人的尊敬和喜爱，你的心灵就必须洋溢着仁慈。

你还没有意识到，你一生的幸福其实就取决于你有无良好的性格。如果你决心尽力帮助别人，你的周围就一定会有许多热心的朋友。倘若你从小就以此为原则，并一生遵守，那么你就能获得幸福，并使所有在你影响范围之内的人更加幸福。

寒冬的清晨，你去上学。炉子里的火生得很旺，大家都围着火炉，使劲地挤上前去烤火。在你身上稍微暖和时，一名冻得发抖的同学走了进来。“这儿，詹姆斯”，你朝他热情地打着招呼，说，“我烤得差不多了，你来我这吧。”

在你起身让他过来烤火时，难道他感觉不到你的好意吗？世上最坏的孩子也会情不自禁地佩服起你的这种慷慨行为。即便他不领情，

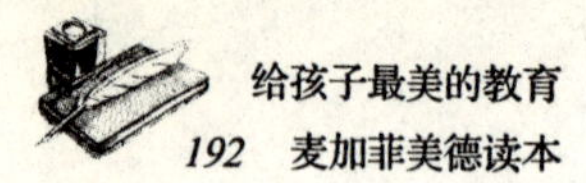

你也可以确信只要他想交朋友时，他一定会成为你的朋友。倘若你总是按照这个原则行事，你的身边就会永远有朋友。

假设某天你和同伴去打球。你打了一段时间后，另一个男孩来了。他无法加入任何一方，因为这样都会多出一个人。“亨利，”你说，“你顶我一下，我想歇会儿。”

你躺倒在草地上，而新上场的亨利拿起了你的球拍，精神抖擞地投入了比赛。他心里自然会明白，你放弃是为了让他加入，他怎么会不因此而喜欢你呢？事实上，像这样慷慨善良的人，无论成人还是孩子，没有一个不会赢得旁人的尊敬和喜爱的。

看看你的那些拥有最多朋友的同伴就会发现，他们都是这种品格高尚的人。为了使别人快乐，他们愿意牺牲自己的享受。友善待人，这才是交朋友的唯一途径。

也许有的小读者觉察到了自己不受欢迎，却很渴望得到同伴的友谊。你问我你该怎么做。我会告诉你一条屡试不爽的法则：尽自己最大的力量使别人快乐。为了别人的快乐，要甘于牺牲自己的利益。

这是交朋友的唯一的办法。在家里要尽量让着你的兄弟姐妹，展示你乐于助人的性情，你就能得到他们的爱。在外面与人交往时，如果你按这条规则行事，你也一定会得到丰厚的回报。

The Way to be Happy

Every child must observe how much more happy and beloved some children are than others. There are some children you always love to be with. They are happy themselves, and they make you happy.

There are others whom you always avoid. They seem to have no friends. No person can be happy without friends. The heart is formed for love, and can not be happy without it.

"*'Tis not in titles nor in rank,*
'Tis not in wealth like London bank,
To make us truly blest.
If happiness have not her seat
And center in the breast,
We may be wise, or rich, or great,
But never can be blest."

But you can not receive affection unless you will also give it. You can not find others to love you unless you will also love them. Love is only to be obtained by giving love in return. Hence the importance of cultivating a good disposition. You can not be happy without it.

I have sometimes heard a girl say, "I know that I am very unpopular at school." Now, this plainly shows that she is not amiable.

If your companions do not love you, it is your own fault. They can not help loving you if you will be kind and friendly. If you are not loved, it is a good proof that you do not deserve to be loved. It is true that a sense of duty may, at times, render it necessary for you to do that which will displease your companions.

But if it is seen that you have a noble spirit, that you arc above selfishness, that you are willing to make sacrifices to promote the happiness of others, you will never be in want of friends.

You must not regard it as your misfortune that others do not love you, but your fault. It is not beauty, it is not wealth, that will give you friends. Your heart must glow with kindness, if you would attract to yourself the esteem and affection of those around you.

You are little aware how much the happiness of your whole life depends upon the cultivation of a good disposition. If you will adopt the resolution that you will confer favors whenever you can, you will certainly be surrounded by ardent friends. Begin upon this principle in childhood, and act upon it through life, and you will make yourself happy, and promote the happiness of all within your influence.

You go to school on a cold winter morning. A bright fire is blazing in the stove, surrounded with boys struggling to get near it to warm themselves. After you are slightly warmed, a schoolmate comes in suffering with cold. "Here, James," you pleasantly call out to him, "I am almost warm; you may have my place."

As you slip aside to allow him to take your place at the fire, will he not feel that you are kind? The worst boy in the world can not help admiring such generosity; and, even though he be so ungrateful as not to return the favor, you may depend upon it that he will be your friend as far as he is capable of friendship. If you will always act upon this principle, you will never want for friends.

Suppose, some day, you are out with your companions playing ball. After you have been playing for some time, another boy comes along. He can not be chosen upon either side, for there is no one to match him. "Henry," you say, "you may take my place a little while, and I will rest."

You throw yourself down upon the grass, while Henry, fresh and vigorous, takes your bat and engages in the game. He knows that you give up to oblige him, and how can he help liking you for it? The fact is, that neither man nor child can cultivate such a spirit of generosity and kindness without attracting affection and esteem.

Look and see which of your companions have the most friends, and you will find that they are those who have this noble spirit; who are willing to deny themselves, that they may make others happy. There is but one way to make friends; and that is, by being friendly to others.

Perhaps some child who reads this feels conscious of being disliked, and yet desires to have the affection of his companions. You ask me what you shall do. I will tell you. I will give you an infallible rule: Do all in your power to make others happy. Be willing to make sacrifices, that you may promote the happiness of others.

This is the way to make friends, and the only way. When you are playing with your brothers and sisters at home, be always ready to give them more than their share of privileges. Manifest an obliging

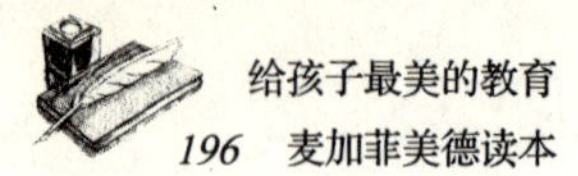

disposition, and they can not but regard you with affection. In all your intercourse with others, at home or abroad, let these feelings influence you, and you will receive a rich reward.

英美人的姓名

英美人的姓名排列次序为名在前，姓在后。如Herbert George Wells（赫伯特·乔治·威尔斯），第一、第二两个词是名，末一词是姓。

英美习俗，通常在婴儿受洗礼时，由教士或父母亲朋起名字，献为教名，排列在姓名的最前面。此外，长辈或本人也可起第二个名字，排在教名之后。这就是英美人常常有两个甚至更多名字的原因。名字可以来自许多方面。有人因其母系属于名门望族或有其他特殊荣誉，把母姓作为子女的第二个名字。也有借用名人或亲属或与家庭有密切交往者的姓为名的。有时，子孙完全袭用父辈名字，这时需在姓名后加Junior（略作Jr. 或Jun.）一词或加罗马数字，以示区别。如 John Ford Jr.（小约翰·福特），Thomas Daly Ⅲ（托马斯·戴利三世）。

英语的名字，多达几千个。有些姓也可用来作名，如Henry。为了书写或口语方便，往往将本名缩短，如Frederick缩为Fred。Margaret缩为Maggy等。亲友之间，常用昵称，以示亲切。昵称一般比本名短，但也有比本名长的，如Johnny是John的昵称。一个名字的省略形式和昵称有时不止一种，如William可以分别为Bill, Billy, Willy等。

最绅士的报复

宽容是一种美德，它可以产生爱，而爱可以泯灭仇恨，让这个世界更美好。最好的报复不是以牙还牙，而是化敌为友。当仇敌都变成了你的兄弟，还有什么是你不能做到的呢！

“我一定会报复他的，让他幡然悔悟。”菲利普对自己发誓，怒气已经让他的脸变得通红。他沉浸在自己的情绪中，没有发现正好在这个时候遇到了斯蒂芬。

“怎么了，”斯蒂芬问，“是谁让你如此急于报复？”菲利普仿佛从梦中醒来，他先冷静了一小会，才转头看向他的朋友，笑容又回到了他的脸上。“啊，”他回答说，“你还记得我父亲给我的那根很漂亮的竹手杖吗？瞧，已经碎成了几块，完全不能用了。这全要拜那个农场主罗宾逊的儿子所赐。”

斯蒂芬十分冷静地询问是什么导致小罗宾逊要折断手杖。“我一个人好好地在路上走着，”菲利普委屈地说，“边走边甩着手杖玩。一不留神，把它从我手里甩脱出去。当时，我正好走到那座木桥旁的水闸那，那个没教养的家伙把一罐水放在了地上，那是他从井里打上来准备带回家的。”

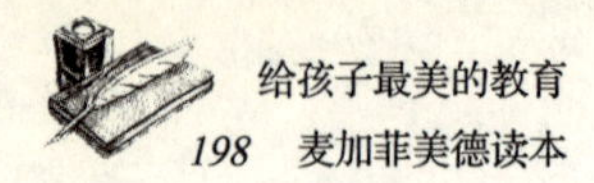

“很不凑巧的，手杖反弹回来碰倒了水罐，但并没有打碎它。他就站起身来走近我，一边喊着我的名字，而我一再向他保证这只是个意外，我对此感到很抱歉。但他根本不听我说什么，一把抓过我的手杖，就把它弄成了你看到的样子。但我一定会让他为此后悔的。”

“看起来他的行为的确十分恶劣，”斯蒂芬点头道，“而且已经为这种行为受到过惩罚了，大家不喜欢他或者和他发生什么联系。他很少能找到同伴和他一起玩，很少有娱乐的机会，这都是他应得的。我觉得，这已经为你很好的报复他了。”

“是这样的，”菲利普回答，“但他弄断了我的手杖。这可是我父亲送我的礼物，它是那么的漂亮。我只是不小心碰倒了他的水罐，我会再装满给他的。不，我一定要报复。”

“菲利普，”斯蒂芬说，“我觉得你现在最好是不要去理他，你对他的轻视就是对他最好的惩罚了。我相信，他会因为你的报复对你做更多的反击。而且，我现在想起不久之前发生在他身上的一件事。”

“那对他来说很是不幸。他碰巧看到一只蜜蜂在花上飞舞，当他抓住它打算拔掉它的翅膀以此取乐的时候，蜜蜂蛰了他一下，安全地飞回了蜂巢。疼痛让他陷入了暴怒，就如你一样，他发誓要报复。因此他找到一根棍子，将它向蜂巢扔了过去。”

“瞬时间，整群蜂飞了出来，冲向他将他浑身蛰了个遍。他尖声大叫，因为极度痛苦而满地打滚。他父亲立刻跑向他，但无法阻止蜂群，蜜蜂们狠狠教训了他一顿让他在床上躺了好多天。”

“因此，你瞧，他寻求报复却并不成功。我也建议你，不管怎样，不要追求他的无礼行为。他是个坏男孩，比你强壮的多，所以你有没有能力去报复也很值得怀疑。”斯蒂芬最后说。

“我必须承认，”菲利普说道，“你的建议听起来十分正确。和我一起来吧，我会告诉父亲整件事情的经过，我想他不会生我的气的。”他们一起走了，菲利普告诉了父亲发生了什么。菲利普的父亲很感谢斯蒂芬给他儿子的好建议，并且许诺他会再给菲利普一根和之前那根一样好的手杖。

过了没几天，菲利普看到那个坏脾气的男孩正准备把一根非常重的木头运回家，但他实在没有力气再把它扛上肩了。菲利普跑向他，帮他把木头放到了他的肩上。小罗宾逊因为这意外的善意感到十分羞愧，对他之前的行为也感到十分的后悔。菲利普十分高兴的回到家。“以善良回应邪恶，这就是我所做的最绅士的报复了。我不会对此感到丝毫的后悔。”

英美人的姓名来源（一）

英国人在历史上一个很长时期内，只有名，没有姓。大约到了十一世纪，一些贵族家庭用宅邸的名称来称呼一家之长，后又传诸子孙，世代相袭，形成了姓。姓的使用首先兴起于伦敦等城市。其形成大致有以下几种：

1. 表明血统关系：有的在父名后加s, son等词尾，以表明系某某之子，例如父名Adam，子以Adams为姓，父名Jack，子以Jackson为姓；有的在父名前冠以Fits, O'，Mac、Mc（均有“之子”、“的”等表示从属关系之意）等词头，如父名Gerald，子以Fitsgerald为姓，父名Brian，子以O'Brian为姓，MacDonald，意为Donald之子，而McMahon，则为Mahon之子。

2. 起源于出生或居住地名：有的直接以地为姓，如London（伦敦），cleveland（克利夫兰），有的以ton, ham（含有村庄、部落之意）等为词尾，如Washington, Needham等，还有些姓的词尾是brook（小溪），wood（树林）等，表示居住地的环境，如Holbrook（谷中小溪），Heywood（绿色森林）等。

3. 表明容貌、特征，如Black（黑色），Longfellow（高个子）等。

4. 来源于职业，如Smith（工匠），Tyler（看门人）等。

The Noblest Revenge

"I will have revenge on him, that I will, and make him heartily repent it," said Philip to himself, with a countenance quite red with anger. His mind was so engaged that he did not see Stephen, who happened at that instant to meet him.

"Who is that," said Stephen, "on whom you intend to be revenged?" Philip, as if awakened from a dream, stopped short, and looking at his friend, soon resumed a smile that was natural to his countenance. "Ah," said he, "you remember my bamboo, a very pretty cane which was given me by my father, do you not? Look! there it is in pieces. It was farmer Robinson's son who reduced it to this worthless state."

Stephen very coolly asked him what had induced young Robinson to break it. "I was walking peaceably along," replied he, "and was playing with my cane by twisting it round my body. By accident, one of the ends slipped out of my hand, when I was opposite the gate, just by the wooden bridge, where the ill natured fellow had put down a pitcher of water, which he was taking home from the well."

"It so happened that my cane, in springing back, upset the pitcher, but did not break it. He came up close to me, and began to call me names, when I assured him that what I had done had happened by accident, and that I was sorry for it. Without regarding what I said, he instantly seized my cane, and twisted it, as you see; but I will make him repent of it."

"To be sure," said Stephen, "he is a very wicked boy, and is already very properly punished for being such, since nobody likes him or will have anything to do with him. He can scarcely find a companion to play with him; and is often at a loss for amusement, as he deserves to be. This, properly considered, I think will appear sufficient revenge for you."

"All this is true," replied Philip, "but he has broken my cane. It was a present from my father, and a very pretty cane it was. I offered to fill his pitcher for him again, as I knocked it down by accident. I will be revenged."

"Now, Philip;" said Stephen, "I think you will act better in not minding him, as your contempt will be the best punishment you can inflict upon him. Be assured, he will always be able to do more mischief to you than you choose to do to him. And, now I think of it, I will tell you what happened to him not long since."

"Very unluckily for him, he chanced to see a bee hovering about a flower which he caught, and was going to pull off its wings out of sport, when the animal stung him, and flew away in safety to the hive. The pain put him into a furious passion, and, like you, he vowed revenge. He accordingly procured a stick, and thrust it into the beehive."

"In an instant the whole swarm flew out, and alighting upon him stung him in a hundred different places. He uttered the most piercing cries, and rolled upon the ground in the excess of his agony. His father immediately ran to him, but could not put the bees to flight until they had stung him so severely that he was confined several days to his bed."

"Thus, you see, he was not very successful in his pursuit of revenge. I would advise you, therefore, to pass over his insult. He is a wicked boy, and much stronger than you; so that your ability to obtain this revenge may be doubtful."

"I must own," replied Philip, "that your advice seems very good. So come along with me, and I will tell my father the whole matter, and I think he will not be angry with me." They went, and Philip told his father what had happened. He thanked Stephen for the good advice he had given his son, and promised Philip to give him another cane exactly like the first.

A few days afterward, Philip saw this ill-natured boy fall as he was carrying home a heavy log of wood, which he could not lift up again. Philip ran to him, and helped him to replace it on his shoulder. Young Robinson was quite ashamed at the thought of this unmerited kindness, and heartily repented of his behavior. Philip went home quite satisfied. "This," said he, "is the noblest vengeance I could take, in returning good for evil. It is impossible I should repent of it."

小证人

当潘多拉的魔盒打开，谎言飞向了人间，但它显然没有沾染这位纯洁的小姑娘——她让我们见识到了诚实的力量。当诚实变成一种信仰，它将展开灵魂的翅膀，载着你在人生中自由翱翔。

有一位九岁的小姑娘被带上法庭，作为一名证人，证明一名受审的被告在她父亲的房子里做了违法的事。

“现在，艾米莉，”被告的辩护律师说，“我希望知道你是否理解誓词的性质？”

“我不明白你的意思。”小女孩简单回答道。

“法官大人，”律师对法官说，“很显然，这位证人无效。她连誓词的性质都不明白。”

“让我们看一下，”法官说，“到这边来，我的孩子。”

小女孩被法官和蔼的声音和亲切的态度所鼓舞，慢慢地向他走去，平静、清澈的眼睛充满信任地看着法官，目光是那么的天真而坦诚，一直照进人的心灵。

“你曾经宣过誓吗？”法官问道。

小女孩惊恐地朝后退了几步，血涌上来，脸和脖子涨得通红，回答

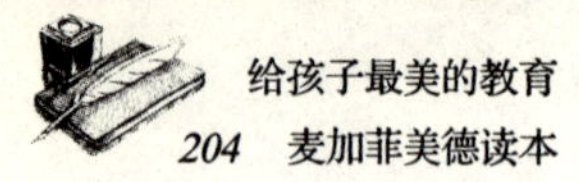

道："没有，先生。"她认为法官是想问她是否说过异教徒的语言。

"我不是那个意思，"法官看出小女孩误会了，解释道，"我的意思是你曾经做过证人吗？"

"没有，先生，我以前从来没有来过法庭。"小女孩回答道。

法官将一本翻开的《圣经》递给小女孩："你知道这本书吗？我的孩子。"

小女孩看了看，回答道："是的，先生，这是一本《圣经》。"

"你曾经读过它吗？"法官问道。

"是的，先生，每天晚上。"

"你能告诉我《圣经》是什么吗？"法官问道。

"它是全能的上帝的话。"小女孩回答道。

"很好，"法官说道，"请把你的手放在《圣经》上，仔细听我说的。"然后他慢慢地严肃地说出以下誓词："你能保证你在法庭上所说的一切都是事实吗？你能保证请求上帝来帮助你吗？"

"是的，我能。"小女孩回答道。

"现在，"法官说道，"你已经作为一名证人发过誓了。你能告诉我如果你不说真话，你会受到什么惩罚吗？"

"我将会被关进监狱。"小女孩回答道。

"还有呢？"法官问道。

"我永远也不能进入天堂。"小女孩说。

"你怎么知道这个？"法官又问道。

小女孩拿起《圣经》，迅速翻到十诫那一章，用手指着其中一诫读道："你不应该用伪证来陷害你的邻人。"然后小女孩说道："在我能读《圣经》之前我就知道这个了。"

"是否有人和你谈过你要在法庭上作为一名证人来指证这个人吗？"法官询问道。

"是的，先生，"小女孩回答道，"我的母亲听说他们想让我作证，昨天晚上她把我叫到她的房间，要我告诉她十诫。然后我们跪在一起，她祈祷，希望我能够理解用伪证陷害邻人是多么的邪恶；她祈祷，希望上帝能够帮助我——一个孩子，讲出实话，就如同在他面前一样。”

“而且当我和父亲来这里的时候，母亲吻了我，提醒我别忘了第九诫，别忘了上帝能听见我说的每一个字。”

“你相信这个吗？”法官问道，泪光在眼睛里闪动，激动得嘴唇有点颤动。

“是的，先生。”小姑娘说道，她的声音和神态都让人觉得她对她的信仰是十分坚定的。

“上帝保佑你，我的孩子，”法官说道，“你有一个好母亲。这位证人是完全合格的。”他继续说道：“假如在以后的生命中我受到审判，无辜受到控告，我将祈求上帝赐给我这样一位证人。现在，可以开始盘问证人了。”

小女孩用她那孩子般的语言简单地陈诉了证词，但她的声音和神态透露出的对真实的信仰打动了每个人的心。

律师们问了她很多相关的问题，但她从头至尾都没有改变她的陈诉。

事实是令人惊叹的，就如同这个孩子所说的一样。在她之前的证词都是谎言和伪证，但在她的证词前，所有的虚假都被击得粉碎。

这个孩子，她的母亲为她祈求如同在上帝面前一样说真话的力量，将处心积虑的邪恶和狡猾的计谋击得粉碎。她母亲为她祈求的力量已经赐予了她；那令人惊叹和可怕的简单证词——对被告和他的律师来说是可怕的——就像上帝亲自的揭露。

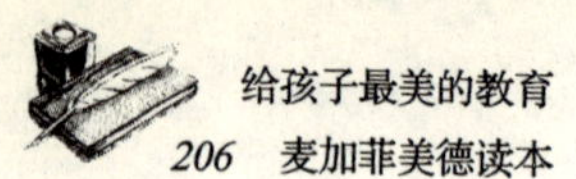

The Young Witness

A little girl nine years of age was brought into court, and offered as a witness against a prisoner who was on trial for a crime committed in her father's house.

"Now, Emily," said the counsel for the prisoner, "I wish to know if you understand the nature of an oath?"

"I don't know what you mean," was the simple answer.

"Your Honor," said the counsel, addressing the judge, "it is evident that this witness should be rejected. She does not understand the nature of an oath."

"Let us see," said the judge. "Come here, my daughter."

Assured by the kind tone and manner of the judge, the child stepped toward him, and looked confidingly in his face, with a calm, clear eye, and in a manner so artless and frank that it went straight to the heart.

"Did you ever take an oath?" inquired the judge.

The little girl stepped back with a look of horror; and the red blood rose and spread in a blush all over her face and neck, as she answered, "No, sir." She thought he intended to ask if she had ever used profane language.

"I do not mean that," said the judge, who saw her mistake; "I mean were you ever a witness?"

"No, sir; I never was in court before," was the answer.

He handed her the Bible open. "Do you know that book, my daughter?"

She looked at it and answered, "Yes, sir; it is the Bible."

"Do you ever read in it?" he asked.

"Yes, sir; every evening."

"Can you tell me what the Bible is?" inquired the judge.

"It is the word of the great God," she answered.

"Well," said the judge, "place your hand upon this Bible, and listen to what I say;" and he repeated slowly and solemnly the following oath: "Do you swear that in the evidence which you shall give in this case, you will tell the truth, and nothing but the truth; and that you will ask God to help you?"

"I do," she replied.

"Now," said the judge, "you have been sworn as a witness; will you tell me what will befall you if you do not tell the truth?"

"I shall be shut up in the state prison," answered the child.

"Anything else?" asked the judge.

"I shall never go to heaven," she replied.

"How do you know this?" asked the judge again.

The child took the Bible, turned rapidly to the chapter containing the commandments, and, pointing to the one which reads, "Thou shalt not bear false witness against thy neighbor," said, "I learned that before I could read."

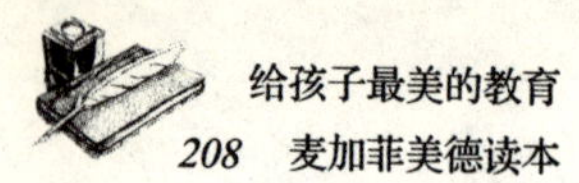

"Has anyone talked with you about being a witness in court here against this man?" inquired the judge.

"Yes, sir," she replied, "my mother heard they wanted me to be a witness; and last night she called me to her room, and asked me to tell her the Ten Commandments; and then we kneeled down together, and she prayed that I might understand how wicked it was to bear false witness against my neighbor, and that God would help me, a little child, to tell the truth as it was before him.

"And when I came up here with father, she kissed me, and told me to remember the Ninth Commandment, and that God would hear every word that I said."

"Do you believe this?" asked the judge, while a tear glistened in his eye, and his lip quivered with emotion.

"Yes, sir," said the child, with a voice and manner which showed that her conviction of the truth was perfect.

"God bless you, my child," said the judge, "you have a good mother. The witness is competent," he continued. "Were I on trial for my life, and innocent of the charge against me, I would pray God for such a witness as this. Let her be examined."

She told her story with the simplicity of a child, as she was; but her voice and manner carried conviction of her truthfulness to every heart.

The lawyers asked her many perplexing questions, but she did not vary in the least from her first statement.

The truth, as spoken by a little child, was sublime. Falsehood and perjury had preceded her testimony; but before her testimony, falsehood was scattered like chaff.

The little child, for whom a mother had prayed for strength to be given her to speak the truth as it was before God, broke the cunning device of matured villainy to pieces, like a potter's vessel. The strength that her mother prayed for was given her; and the sublime and terrible simplicity,—terrible to the prisoner and his associates,—was like a revelation from God himself.

英美人的姓名来源（二）

5. 名字缩写时，按英国习惯一般把名字全缩写，例如G. P. Thomson，或缩写第一个名字，如G.Paget Thomson；美国则习惯于缩写中间的名字，如George P. Thomson。一般没有将姓加以缩写的习惯。但一些举世知名的人物，也有全部姓名都用缩写形式的，例如G.B.S.即George Bernard Shaw（萧伯纳），F.D.R.即Franklin Delano Roosevelt（富兰克林·罗斯福）等。

6. 口语中对一个人怎样称呼才算合适、得体，则看具体场合和相互关系而定。过去晚辈对长辈，从不直呼其名；现在有少数青年人，不论对父母还是师长，均直呼其名不讳。已婚妇女一般不用原姓，用丈夫姓名冠以Mrs 一词。例如女子Mary Lakins 与男子John Cumings 结婚，女方改称Mrs. John Cumings 或Mrs. Cumings（约翰·卡明斯夫人或卡明斯夫人）。也可在夫姓前写自己本名以代替夫名，如Mary Cumings。丈夫死后的妇女，就不再用丈夫的名字，必须写成Mrs. Mary Cumings。现代提倡女权的妇女，则有破除旧俗，而使用原姓的。

7. 英国贵族姓名，常加上其封地名，如Lord Greenhill Harrow（哈罗·格林希尔勋爵），习惯上也可写为Lord of Harrow ，其中Harrow 是地名。

8. 以上各条，同样适用于加拿大、澳大利亚、新西兰的英语姓名，也适用于英联邦一部分成员国中使用英语姓名的白人移民。

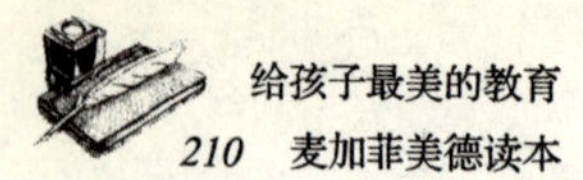

温柔之手

提莫迪·S·亚瑟（1809～1885），出生于纽约的纽堡附近，但他一生中大多数时光在巴尔的摩和费城度过。他没有受过多少良好的教育，应该说他是靠自学成才。他创作了100多部作品，其中很多都是描写家庭和道德的小说，也有很多是发表在杂志上的短小的寓言等等。《酒吧里的十个夜晚》和《陷阱中的三年》是他最知名的作品。

这件事发生在哪儿、什么时候发生的，也许并不重要。反正有一天，我路过一个人烟稀少的地方，夜幕不知不觉地降临了。由于是步行，我估计还要一个小时才能到达要去的小村庄，因此，我计划在第一个出现的房屋中歇脚过夜。

暗夜逐渐笼罩了朦胧的晚霞，这时我发现自己走到了一个小屋子旁边，窗户上没有窗帘，灯光射出来，让人感到愉快而舒适。小屋子坐落在一个院子里，与我脚下的道路距离不远。我拐到旁边，穿过歪斜的大门，向小屋走去。大门轻轻地晃动，缓慢地闭合起来，门轴发出“咔哒”的响声，不过我没有注意这些，而是向门廊走去。那里站着一个瘦弱的女孩，她听到了动静，站在那里看着我。

伴随着门闭合的声音，一串深沉、急促的狗吠声就像回声一样响起，一只大狗突然出现在门口，仿若幽灵一般。就在它要跃起的时候，一只手轻轻抚在它那毛发蓬松的脖颈上，同时一个声音轻轻说道："进去，老虎。"女孩说道，不是用命令的口气，但是她的声音非常坚定，似乎清楚它一定会服从命令。她一边说，一边用手轻轻压了压这只狗。它转过头，消失在房间里。

"你是谁？"一个沙哑的声音问道。一个结实的男子出现在门口。

"这里离G城有多远？"我问道。我想，我是要找个地方过夜，开始时还是不要说太多。

"去G城！"男子抱怨地说，但是不像开始时那么严厉，"离这儿还有整整六英里。"

"那么远！我从来没来过这里，而且我是步行来的。"我说道，"如果您能为我腾个地方让我待到早晨，我会不胜感激。"

我看到那个女孩的手快速地移向他的手臂，扶在他的肩膀上。女孩紧紧地靠在他的身上。

"进来吧，我们会尽力帮你。"男子的声音变了，这让我很奇怪。我走进一个大房间，房间里燃着一团火。火堆前坐着两个粗壮的小伙，他们睡眼惺忪地看看我，没什么欢迎的表示。桌子旁站着一位中年妇人，两个孩子在与地板上的小猫玩耍。

"一个陌生人，母亲！"刚才在门口非常无礼地迎接我的那个男子说，"他希望在这里留宿。"

妇人怀疑地看了我好一会儿，然后冷冷地回答："我们这里又不是旅店。"

"我知道，女士。"我说道，"但是我不能在外面过夜，而且这里离G城还很远。"

"他很疲惫，而且是步行，那太远了，"一家之主温和地说道，"所以让我们别再争论这件事了，母亲，我们必须给他一张床。"

女孩已经悄悄走到了她母亲身旁，我都没有注意到。她低声而快速地向她母亲说了些什么，我没有听到，只是注意到在她说话的时候，她把一只小小的、白皙的手放在她母亲的手上。这一触摸是否有什么魔力？妇人的态度从排斥变为欢迎，她说：“是呀，这里离G城真的是很远，我想我们可以为他安排个地方。”

那晚有很多次，我观察到了这只手和这个声音的魔力——虽然轻微，但对对方却非常有效。第二天早上，吃过早饭后，我打算离开，这时房子的主人告诉我，如果我再等上半个小时，就可以搭他的马车去G城，因为他恰好有事要去那里。我非常高兴地接受了这个邀请。

半个小时后，农夫驾着马车来到屋前的路上，并请我上去。我注意到拉车的马是一匹暴烈的加拿大矮种马，看上去非常耐用。农夫坐到我身边，家里人都出来和我们告别。

“迪克！”农夫专横地嚷道，同时用缰绳飞速一抽。但是迪克一动未动。“迪克！你这个无赖！走啊！”农夫的鞭子清脆地抽在马儿的耳朵上。

但还是没有动。迪克很不驯服地站着。农夫又不耐烦地给了它一鞭，但马儿只是跳了跳。农夫又着急地抽打了六七下，他的力气都用尽了，但马儿就是无动于衷。一个粗壮的小伙走到路上，抓住了迪克的缰绳，把它往前拽，同时用粗暴的声音吆喝着，但迪克这时更倔强了，它的蹄子贴住地面，一动不动，小伙子用拳头不耐烦地击打着马儿的头，粗暴地拽着它的缰绳。这样还是没有用处，这样的对抗对迪克没用。

“别这样，约翰！”听到小女孩甜美的声音，我转过头。她穿过大门，来到马路上，抓住小伙子，把他拖到一旁。她并没有用力，只是握住他的胳膊，而他自然地服从了，似乎他除了使她满意之外没有其他念头。

现在，她一边用她这只温柔的手轻轻抚摸着马的脖颈，一边对马儿轻声地说着什么。马儿绷紧的肌肉立即放松了——紧张的气氛很快消散在空气中。

“可怜的迪克！”女孩说，轻轻地抚摸着它的脖颈，就像孩子一样温柔地摩挲着它。“出发吧，你这个让人恼火的家伙！”她抓起缰绳，用一种半责备、半爱抚的声音说。

马儿向她转过头，用头在她的胳膊上轻轻蹭了一会儿，然后竖起耳朵，轻快地小跑起来，就好像它从来没有起过叛逆的念头一样。

“这只手的力量真神奇！”在路上，我对我的同伴说。

他看了我一会儿，好像我的话让他很吃惊。然后他的眼睛一亮，简短地说：“她是个好孩子，我们都很爱她。”

这真的就是她那神奇力量的秘密吗？她那纤弱的小手的动作所表现出来的精神力量，甚至能感化粗野的心灵！她父亲的解释当然是真的。但我还是曾经被女孩的神奇触摸所感动，并且直到今天仍然感动。我曾经见到过有同样力量的、充满爱意的美好的东西，但是它们都不如女孩的手那样具有魔力。我找不到什么更好的名字，只好称它为“温柔之手”。

The Gentle Hand

Timothy S. Arthur (b. 1809, d. 1885) was born near Newburgh, N.Y., but passed most of his life at Baltimore and Philadelphia. His opportunities for good schooling were quite limited, and he may be considered a self-educated man. He was the author of more than a hundred volumes, principally novels of a domestic and moral tone, and of many shorter tales—magazine articles, etc. "Ten Nights in a Barroom," and "Three Years in a Mantrap," are among his best known works.

When and where it matters not now to relate—but once upon a time, as I was passing through a thinly peopled district of country, night came down upon me almost unawares. Being on foot, I could not hope to gain the village toward which my steps were directed, until a late hour; and I therefore preferred seeking shelter and a night's lodging at the first humble dwelling that presented itself.

Dusky twilight was giving place to deeper shadows, when I found myself in the vicinity of a dwelling, from the small uncurtained windows of which the light shone with a pleasant promise of good cheer and comfort. The house stood within an inclosure, and a short distance from the road along which I was moving with wearied feet.

Turning aside, and passing through the ill–hung gate, I approached the dwelling. Slowly the gate swung on its wooden hinges, and the rattle of its latch, in closing, did not disturb the air until I had nearly reached the porch in front of the house, in which a slender girl, who had noticed my entrance, stood awaiting my arrival.

A deep, quick bark answered, almost like an echo, the sound of the shutting gate, and, sudden as an apparition, the form of an immense dog loomed in the doorway. At the instant when he was about to spring, a light hand was laid upon his shaggy neck, and a low word spoken.

"Go in, Tiger," said the girl, not in a voice of authority, yet in her gentle tones was the consciousness that she would be obeyed; and, as she spoke, she lightly bore upon the animal with her hand, and he turned away and disappeared within the dwelling.

"Who's that?" A rough voice asked the question; and now a heavy–looking man took the dog's place in the door.

"How far is it to G—?" I asked, not deeming it best to say, in the beginning, that I sought a resting place for the night.

"To G—!" growled the man, but not so harshly as at first. "It's good six miles from here."

"A long distance; and I'm a stranger and on foot," said I. "If you can make room for me until morning, I will be very thankful."

I saw the girl's hand move quickly up his arm, until it rested on his shoulder, and now she leaned to him still closer.

"Come in. We'll try what can be done for you." There was a change in the man's voice that made me wonder. I entered a large room, in which blazed a brisk fire. Before the fire sat two stout lads, who turned upon me their heavy eyes, with no very welcome greeting. A middle-aged woman was standing at a table, and two children were amusing themselves with a kitten on the floor.

"A stranger, mother," said the man who had given me so rude a greeting at the door; "and he wants us to let him stay all night."

The woman looked at me doubtingly for a few moments, and then replied coldly, "We don't keep a public house."

"I'm aware of that, ma'am," said I; "but night has overtaken me, and it's a long way yet to G—."

"Too far for a tired man to go on foot," said the master of the house, kindly, "so it's no use talking about it, mother; we must give him a bed."

So unobtrusively that I scarce noticed the movement, the girl had drawn to her mother's side. What she said to her I did not hear, for the brief words were uttered in a low voice; but I noticed, as she spoke, one small, fair hand rested on the woman's hand.

Was there magic in that touch? The woman's repulsive aspect changed into one of kindly welcome, and she said, "Yes, it's a long way to G—. I guess we can find a place for him."

Many times more during that evening, did I observe the magic power of that hand and voice—the one gentle yet potent as the other. On the next morning, breakfast being over, I was preparing to take my departure when my host informed me that if I would wait for half an hour he would give me a ride in his wagon to G—, as business required him to go there. I was very well pleased to accept of the invitation.

In due time, the farmer's wagon was driven into the road before the house, and I was invited to get in. I noticed the horse as a rough-looking

Canadian pony, with a certain air of stubborn endurance. As the farmer took his seat by my side, the family came to the door to see us off.

"Dick!" said the farmer in a peremptory voice, giving the rein a quick jerk as he spoke. But Dick moved not a step. "Dick! you vagabond! get up." And the farmer's whip cracked sharply by the pony's ear.

It availed not, however, this second appeal. Dick stood firmly disobedient. Next the whip was brought down upon him with an impatient hand; but the pony only reared up a little. Fast and sharp the strokes were next dealt to the number of half a dozen. The man might as well have beaten the wagon, for all his end was gained.

A stout lad now came out into the road, and, catching Dick by the bridle, jerked him forward, using, at the same time, the customary language on such occasions, but Dick met this new ally with increased stubbornness, planting his fore feet more firmly and at a sharper angle with the ground.

The impatient boy now struck the pony on the side of the head with his clinched hand, and jerked cruelly at his bridle. It availed nothing, however; Dick was not to be wrought upon by any such arguments.

"Don't do so, John!" I turned my head as the maiden's sweet voice reached my ear. She was passing through the gate into the road, and in the next moment had taken hold of the lad and drawn him away from the animal. No strength was exerted in this; she took hold of his arm, and he obeyed her wish as readily as if he had no thought beyond her gratification.

And now that soft hand was laid gently on the pony's neck, and a single low word spoken. How instantly were the tense muscles relaxed—

how quickly the stubborn air vanished!

"Poor Dick!" said the maiden, as she stroked his neck lightly, or softly patted it with a childlike hand. "Now, go along, you provoking fellow!" she added, in a half-chiding, yet affectionate voice, as she drew up the bridle.

The pony turned toward her, and rubbed his head against her arm for an instant or two; then, pricking up his ears, he started off at a light, cheerful trot, and went on his way as freely as if no silly crotchet had ever entered his stubborn brain.

"What a wonderful power that hand possesses!" said I, speaking to my companion, as we rode away.

He looked at me for a moment, as if my remark had occasioned surprise. Then a light came into his countenance, and he said briefly, "She's good! Everybody and everything loves her."

Was that, indeed, the secret of her power? Was the quality of her soul perceived in the impression of her hand, even by brute beasts! The father's explanation was doubtless the true one. Yet have I ever since wondered, and still do wonder, at the potency which lay in that maiden's magic touch. I have seen something of the same power, showing itself in the loving and the good, but never to the extent as instanced in her, whom, for want of a better name, I must still call "Gentle Hand."

查尔斯国王二世和威廉·佩恩

查尔斯二世，公元1660～1685年期间英格兰统治者。威廉·佩恩(1644～1718)，一位著名的教友会成员，他于1682年来到美国，建立了现在的宾夕法尼亚州。他从印第安人手中购买此州，印第安人对佩恩和他的同伴的公正和善良非常感动，在其他移民者骚扰佩恩等时，常常给他们保护。

查尔斯国王：（以下简称为“查”）嗨，威廉，我的朋友！我把美利坚北部那么富裕的地方卖给了你，但是我看好像你并不打算自己去那里。

佩恩：（以下简称“佩”）不，我打算去的，我向您保证，我的朋友查尔斯。我正是来向您告别的。

查：什么？去美利坚北部的荒蛮之地探险！怎么啦，伙计，你有足够的护卫，可以保护你上岸两个小时以内不会卷入到和野蛮人的战争中去?

佩：是呀，世界上最好的护卫。

查：我对此表示怀疑，威廉。除非你的身边有一大群佩带刺刀和毛瑟枪的勇士保护，否则你无法抵抗那些食人生番。而且别忘了，我

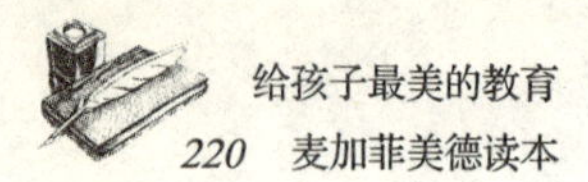

可事先告诉你，我给你和你的家人最好的祝愿，我曾受过你们的恩惠，但是我一个士兵也不会派给你。

佩：我不想要您的士兵，查尔斯，我依赖于比士兵还好的东西。

查：啊！那是什么？

佩：我依赖那些野蛮人本身，依赖他们的心灵，依赖他们的公正，依赖他们的道德观念。

查：很好，道德观念，没错。但是我恐怕美利坚北部的印第安人跟你的想法可不一样。

佩：为什么他们会和别人不一样？

查：因为如果他们有哪怕一点道德观念，就不会那么野蛮地对待我的臣民了。

佩：查尔斯，我的朋友，这并不能说明什么。你的臣民才是侵略者。他们刚到北美时，发现那里的人是世界上最友好、最和善的生灵。每天当地人看到他们上岸，就匆忙地跑去迎接他们，拿出所有最好的鱼、鹿肉和粮食招待他们。作为对这群好客的所谓“野蛮人”的报答，你所谓的“基督教徒”抢走了他们的家园和富饶的猎场，作为自己的农场。现在这些备受伤害的人当然会对这样的不公正感到绝望，为了报复做出一些极端的事来。

查：好吧，他们那样对待你的话，你可别抱怨。

佩：我倒不担心这个。

查：哈！你逃不脱的，我猜你也想得到他们的猎场，对吗？

佩：是的，但是我不会把这些可怜的人赶走。

查：真的不会吗？那你怎么得到他们的土地？

佩：我想购买他们的土地。

查：从他们的手里购买土地？可是，伙计，你不是已经从我这里买走了吗？

佩：是的，我知道，而且您的价格不菲呀。但是我这么做只是想接受您的好意，我并不认为他们的土地归您所有。

查：那怎么可能，朋友？他们的土地不归我所有？

佩：是的，查尔斯，我的朋友。不归您所有，根本不归您所有。他们的土地怎么可能归您所有呢？

查：怎么，发现权，当然啦。教皇和所有基督教国王都承认相互给予这种权利。

佩：发现权？这种权利真是奇怪。朋友，那么假设这些印第安人乘着木筏漂洋过海，发现了大不列颠岛，他们是不是也可以宣布这个岛屿是属于他们的，并卖掉它呢，您对此怎么看？

查：什么……什么……什么……我只能说，他们真是厚颜无耻。

佩：那么，您作为一名基督徒，一名基督徒国王，怎么能做你严厉谴责野蛮人做的事情呢？那么再假设一下，您拒绝放弃大不列颠岛，这些印第安人就对您发动战争，而且他们的武器比您的更有威力，杀死了您很多的臣民，其余人也都逃跑了——您是否认为这太残忍了？

查：我不得不说，威廉，我确实认为这太残忍了。我还能说其他什么吗？

佩：那么就是了，我，作为一名基督徒，怎么能做我讨厌的蛮夷人做的事呢？不，我不会这么做的。但是我会从真正的所有者那里购买，即使他们是印第安人也好。这样做，我遵照了上帝的公正和仁慈的旨意，这样他才会降福于我的领地——如果我能活着在北美建立自己的领地的话。

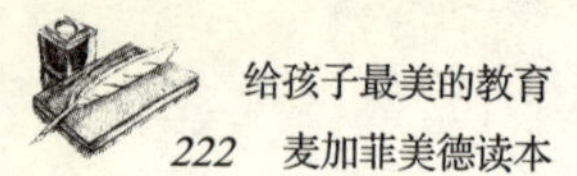

King Charles Ⅱ and William Penn

King Charles. Well, friend William! I have sold you a noble province in North America; but still, I suppose you have no thoughts of going thither yourself?

Penn: Yes, I have, I assure thee, friend Charles; and I am just come to bid thee farewell.

K.C: What! venture yourself among the savages of North America! Why, man, what security have you that you will not be in their war kettle in two hours after setting foot on their shores?

P: The best security in the world.

K.C: I doubt that, friend William; I have no idea of any security against those cannibals but in a regiment of good soldiers, with their muskets and bayonets. And mind, I tell you beforehand, that, with all my good will for you and your family, to whom I am under obligations, I will not send a single soldier with you.

P: I want none of thy soldiers, Charles: I depend on something better than thy soldiers.

K.C: Ah! what may that be?

P: Why, I depend upon themselves; on the working of their own hearts;

on their notions of justice; on their moral sense.

K.C: A fine thing, this same moral sense, no doubt; but I fear you will not find much of it among the Indians of North America.

P: And why not among them as well as others?

K.C: Because if they had possessed any, they would not have treated my subjects so barbarously as they have done.

P: That is no proof of the contrary, friend Charles. Thy subjects were the aggressors. When thy subjects first went to North America, they found these poor people the fondest and kindest creatures in the world. Every day they would watch for them to come ashore, and hasten to meet them, and feast them on the best fish, and venison, and corn, which were all they had. In return for this hospitality of the savages, as we call them, thy subjects, termed Christians, seized on their country and rich hunting grounds for farms for themselves. Now, is it to be wondered at, that these much–injured people should have been driven to desperation by such injustice; and that, burning with revenge, they should have committed some excesses?

K.C: Well, then, I hope you will not complain when they come to treat you in the same manner.

P: I am not afraid of it.

K.C: Ah! how will you avoid it? You mean to get their hunting grounds, too, I suppose?

P: Yes, but not by driving these poor people away from them.

K.C: No, indeed? How then will you get their lands?

P: I mean to buy their lands of them.

K.C: Buy their lands of them? Why, man, you have already bought them of me!

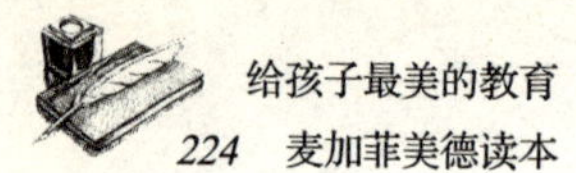

P: Yes, I know I have, and at a dear rate, too; but I did it only to get thy good will, not that I thought thou hadst any right to their lands.

K.C: How, man? no right to their lands?

P: No, friend Charles, no right; no right at all: what right hast thou to their lands?

K.C: Why, the right of discovery, to be sure; the right which the Pope and all Christian kings have agreed to give one another.

P: The right of discovery? A strange kind of right, indeed. Now suppose, friend Charles, that some canoe load of these Indians, crossing the sea, and discovering this island of Great Britain, were to claim it as their own, and set it up for sale over thy head, what wouldst thou think of it?

K.C: Why—why—why—I must confess, I should think it a piece of great impudence in them.

P: Well, then, how canst thou, a Christian, and a Christian prince, too, do that which thou so utterly condemnest in these people whom thou callest savages? And suppose, again, that these Indians, on thy refusal to give up thy island of Great Britain, were to make war on thee, and, having weapons more destructive than thine, were to destroy many of thy subjects, and drive the rest away—wouldst thou not think it horribly cruel?

K.C: I must say, friend William, that I should; how can I say otherwise?

P: Well, then, how can I, who call myself a Christian, do what I should abhor even in the heathen? No. I will not do it. But I will buy the right of the proper owners, even of the Indians themselves. By doing this, I shall imitate God himself in his justice and mercy, and thereby insure his blessing on my colony, if I should ever live to plant one in North America.

—Mason L. Weems.

CHAPTER 6

五味的人生

不管一切如何，你仍然要平静和愉快。生活就是这样，我们也就必须这样对待生活，要勇敢、无畏、含着笑容地——不管一切如何。

——[波]罗莎·卢森堡

争吵的后果

人生路上，我们总会遇到各种各样的困难。面对困难，除了争吵，有很多其他解决问题的方法。而争吵只会造成对立，甚至会将事情变得更糟。

在树林边的一个大树下，两个男孩看到了一颗又大又好的坚果，于是，他们争先恐后地冲了过去。

詹姆士首先跑到那里，把坚果紧紧地抓在手里。“这应该是我的，”约翰气愤地说，“是我先看到的。”

“不对，这是我的，我先拿到的。”詹姆士一点也不肯让步。就这样，两个男孩为了坚果争吵起来。

由于他们始终不能达成一致，最后他们叫来了一个年龄稍大一些的孩子，请他来做决定。

大孩子轻松地说：“这件事很容易解决。”他从詹姆士手中拿过坚果，敲碎硬壳，将果仁取了出来。然后，他尽可能地将果壳分成相等的两半。

“壳的这一半，给最先看到坚果的那个人。”大孩子说，“而壳的另一半，就属于最先拿到坚果的人。至于果仁嘛，就当作我为你们解决这次争吵的报酬好了。”

“就这样，”随后，他大笑着说：“哈哈，知道了吧，这就是争吵最容易出现的结局了。”

英文地址书写格式

英文地址格式和中文刚好相反，按地址单元从小到大的顺序从左到右书写，并且地址单元间以半角逗号(,)分隔，同时邮政编码可以直接写到地址中，其位置通常位于国家和省（州）之间，书写格式如下：

xx室，xx号，xx路，xx区，xx市，xx省，xx国

下面我们看一个简单的例子：

上海市延安西路1882号东华大学186信箱（邮编：200051）

Mailbox 186, 1882 West Yan'an Rd., Donghua University, Shanghai, 200051, China.

The Quarrel

Under a great tree in the woods, two boys saw a fine, large nut, and both ran to get it.

James got to it first, and picked it up.

"It is mine," said John, "for I was the first to see it."

"No, it is mine" said James, "for I was the first to pick it up."

Thus, they at once began to quarrel about the nut.

As they could not agree whose it should be, they called an older boy, and asked him.

The older boy said, "I will settle this quarrel."

He took the nut, and broke the shell. He then took out the kernel, and divided the shell into two parts, as nearly equal as he could.

"This half of the shell," said he, "belongs to the boy who first saw the nut. And this half belongs to the boy who picked it up. The kernel of the nut, I shall keep as my pay for settling the quarrel."

"This is the way," said he, laughing, "in which quarrels are very apt to end."

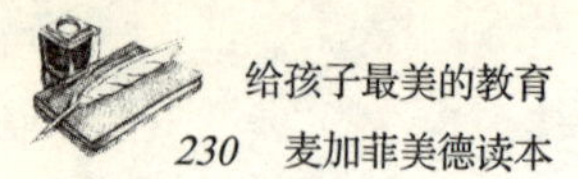

可怜的戴维

获取财富的过程，可以让孩子们懂得生活的艰辛，但也可以让他们赚取阅历和自信。人并不能选择自己的出身，但可以选择自己的人生。只要你足够坚强，那贫穷不过是一块小小的绊脚石，用你自己的双手就可以搬走它。记住，天助自助之人。

现在是乡村中学的休息时间，铃声刚响过，孩子们便跑出来，在明亮的阳光下，兴高采烈地笑着、闹着。

所有的人都很快乐，除了可怜的戴维。他最后一个慢慢地走出教室，脸上没有一丝笑容。他遇到了麻烦，金灿灿的阳光也不能让他高兴起来。

他穿过操场，坐在老枫树后的石头上。为让他笑起来，一只小鸟站在高高的枝头上大声唱着歌。

但是戴维没有注意到它，他在想着别人因为他破旧的衣着说出的刻薄话，眼泪不知不觉地从眼中淌出，顺着脸颊往下流。可怜的戴维没了父亲，他的母亲为了能让他上得起学，不得不没日没夜地干活。

那天晚上，戴维顺着那条横跨田野，穿过树林的小路往回家走。他还是沉浸在自己的悲伤中。

戴维不希望让他的妈妈烦恼，于是在林中逗留了很长时间，最后他干脆躺在树下的青苔上。恰好他的老师路过那里。老师看到了戴维，停下来蹲在他身边，温和地说："有什么麻烦吗，戴维？"

戴维没有吭声，可是眼泪却又情不自禁地落了下来。

"难道你不想把遇到的麻烦告诉老师吗？或许我能帮助你呢。"

于是戴维把自己的烦恼全都告诉了老师。听他讲完，老师却快乐地说："我想，我有一个计划，那应该可以帮到你的。"

"哦，什么计划？"戴维很感兴趣，一下子坐了起来，一滴泪水掉在了紫罗兰上。

"嗯，你愿意当一个小花商吗？"

"卖花赚钱？"戴维说，"那太好了，不过我到哪儿去弄花呢？"

"就在这儿，看这片树林，看那漂亮的田野。"他的老师说，"这儿有讨人喜爱的蓝色紫罗兰，沿着小溪走不多远，那里盛开着白色的花儿，在那些石头中间，有许多满天星和其他一些什么，正好做花束的配饰。把它们都带到我的房子去，我可以帮助你将它们扎成花束。"

从此，戴维每天都在树林里采集着最美丽的鲜花。老师会帮他把它们扎成花束，然后戴维带去最近的城镇，大声叫卖。

不久，他就挣到了足够的钱去买一套新衣服。现在，戴维也能感受到明媚的阳光和小鸟欢唱所带来的快乐了。

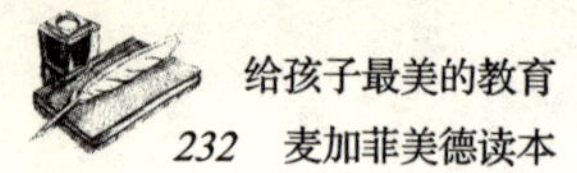

Poor Davy

It was recess time at the village school. The bell had rung, and the children had run out into the bright sunshine, wild with laughter and fun.

All but poor Davy. He came out last and very slowly, but he did not laugh. He was in trouble, and the bright, golden sunlight did not make him glad.

He walked across the yard, and sat down on a stone behind the old maple. A little bird on the highest branch sang just to make him laugh.

But Davy did not notice it. He was thinking of the cruel words that had been said about his ragged clothes. The tears stole out of his eyes, and ran down his cheeks.

Poor Davy had no father, and his mother had to work hard to keep him at school.

That night, he went home by the path that led across the fields and through the woods. He still felt sad.

Davy did not wish to trouble his mother; so he lingered a while among the trees, and at last threw himself on the green moss under them.

Just then his teacher came along. She saw who it was, and stopped, saying kindly, "What is the matter, Davy?"

He did not speak, but the tears began again to start.

"Won't you tell me? Perhaps I can help you."

Then he told her all his trouble. When he ended, she said, cheerily, "I have a plan, Davy, that I think will help you."

"Oh, what is it?" he said, sitting up with a look of hope, while a tear fell upon a blue violet.

"Well, how would you like to be a little flower merchant?"

"And earn money?" said Davy. "That would be jolly. But where shall I get my flowers?"

"Right in these woods, and in the fields," said his teacher. " Here are lovely blue violets, down by the brook are white ones, and among the rocks are ferns and mosses. Bring them all to my house, and I will help you arrange them."

So, day after day, Davy hunted the woods for the prettiest flowers, and the most dainty ferns and mosses. After his teacher had helped to arrange them, he took them to the city that was near, and sold them.

He soon earned money enough to buy new clothes. Now the sunshine and the bird's songs make him glad.

哈瑞和他的狗

很多人家中都会养有动物，它们虽然不会说话，但却用行动证明着它们的忠诚与友谊。我们时常说，动物是人类最好的朋友。然而现实中，我们人类却往往表现得非常自私，常为一己之利而去出卖、折磨，甚至牺牲自己的动物朋友。

人类最应该学习的一点就是，如何和动物们和睦相处。

“来呀，弗里斯克，上来咬。”小哈瑞喊着。他正坐在祖母家门前一个倒置的竹筐上，吃着麦片面包，喝着牛奶，他看起来满足极了。他的小妹妹，安妮早已经吃完了早餐，她坐在她哥哥的对面，把手中的花编成了一个花环，然后又把它扔开了。

“来呀，弗里斯克，上来咬！”哈瑞继续喊着，把一块小面包举到弗里斯克刚好够不到的地方。顺从的弗里斯克蹲坐在后腿上，举着前爪，等着它的主人把诱人的食物丢给它。

哈瑞和他的狗是极好的朋友。弗里斯克非常爱它的主人，远超过它爱其他的人，这或许是因为哈瑞是它在困难时期遇到的最早、最忠诚的朋友。

可怜的弗里斯克原来是一只在密尔顿的流浪狗，哈瑞就住在这里。如果弗里斯克能说话的活，它所讲述的一定是一个悲惨的故事，里面充满了棍棒、饥饿和恶劣的天气。

它第一次出现在哈瑞面前的时候，哈瑞就坐在现在他坐的地方，弗里斯克又湿又脏，还饿着肚子，它就是在如此困苦的情况下遇见了哈瑞。哈瑞很喜欢它，但哈瑞的祖母却用笤帚把它赶了出去。

哈瑞最后终于为小狗争取到了留在屋外等候救济的权利，他喂给他剩下的骨头和马铃薯，以及其他一些他能搞到的食物。他还给弗里斯克找来一个筐子，让它在里面睡觉，就是这只筐子倒过来后就成了他的板凳。

过了一阵，弗里斯克证明了自己的能力，它咬走了好多觊觎家中那棵大桃树的小偷。为此它被让进了大门，成了家中最机警的成员。它会跑过陆地或是游过水面取来东西，还会捡起小安妮掉在地上的顶针或棉球，或是去学校给哈瑞送去午餐，还绝不偷吃。

“来呀，弗里斯克，上来咬！”哈瑞说着，并最终让它吃着了一直期待着的面包片。弗里斯克感到很满意，但哈瑞却不是。这个小家伙虽然大体上是一个性情温和的孩子，但也有非常淘气的时候，而他淘起气来会淘上一天。这一天看来是他最淘气的一天。因为是假日，中午的时候，他的表姐和表弟、珍妮和威廉会来看望他和安妮。到时他们会采桃子，孩子们会有一顿大餐。

哈瑞实在等得不耐烦了，他抱怨早晨好像永远也过不完似的。他开始恶作剧——折磨完了弗里斯克，他又剪掉了安妮的布娃娃的头发，最后又打碎了祖母的眼镜。因为这样，午饭刚过，珍妮和威廉还没有来的时候，他就被遣送回了卧室，不准出来。

可怜的哈瑞！他躺在那儿不停地翻身、踢着被子，而此时威廉、安妮和珍正忙着采桃子。威廉爬到了树上，摇晃着树干，珍和安妮在下面忙着用围裙接住桃子，或是把桃子从地上捡起来，竹篮很快就装满了，他们就坐在树下品尝着最好、最甘美的桃子。弗里斯克就在他们中间高兴地叫着，好像它也在摘桃子似的！

可怜的哈瑞！他躺在床上，听得见从窗户外面传来的阵阵笑声。听着这笑声，哈瑞躺在床上伤心地哭了，从被子里不停地传出一两声他的抽泣。他想如果不是自己太过淘气的话，他也可以和他们一起欢笑，他一定会非常非常开心的。

他开始想，安妮会不会好心地给他带一个桃子来。这时，突然他听到楼梯上有轻轻的脚步声，他想一定是安妮来了。脚步声越来越近，最后有一颗小脑袋从半开的门里伸了进来，好像还有点害怕。

但那不是安妮，是弗里斯克——可怜的弗里斯克。一早上哈瑞都在逗它、折磨它，现在它跑到了哈瑞的卧室，口中叼着一个大桃子，它摇着尾巴，跳上了床，把桃子放进了哈瑞的手里。

你看，弗里斯克是一个多好的伙伴呀。他理应得到哈瑞的一部分早餐，不管它是不是追着抢到的。从这一天起，小哈瑞也明白了友善将会得到回报，即使是对于一只狗也是如此，恶意和坏脾气除了痛苦和失望什么也带不来。

英文通信地址常用翻译（一）

自治区 Autonomous Region

直辖市 Municipality

特别行政区 Special Administration Region 简称SAR

自治州 Autonomous Prefecture

盟、专区 Prefecture

县、旗、郡 County

自治县 Autonomous County

乡 Township

镇 Town

村 Village

Harry and His Dog

"Beg, Frisk, beg," said little Harry, as he sat on an inverted basket, at his grandmother's door, eating, with great satisfaction, a porringer of bread and milk. His little sister Annie, who had already dispatched her breakfast, sat on the ground opposite to him, now twisting her flowers into garlands, and now throwing them away.

"Beg, Frisk, beg!" repeated Harry, holding a bit of bread just out of the dog's reach; and the obedient Frisk squatted himself on his hind legs, and held up his fore paws, waiting for master Harry to give him the tempting morsel.

The little boy and the little dog were great friends. Frisk loved him dearly, much better than he did anyone else; perhaps, because he recollected that Harry was his earliest and firmest friend during a time of great trouble.

Poor Frisk had come as a stray dog to Milton, the place where Harry lived. If he could have told his own story, it would probably have been a very pitiful one, of kicks and cuffs, of hunger and foul weather.

Certain it is, he made his appearance at the very door where Harry was now sitting, in miserable plight, wet, dirty, and half starved; and that there he met Harry, who took a fancy to him, and Harry's grandmother, who drove him off with a broom.

Harry, at length, obtained permission for the little dog to remain as a sort of outdoor pensioner, and fed him with stray bones and cold potatoes, and such things as he could get for him. He also provided him with a little basket to sleep in, the very same which, turned up, afterward served Harry for a seat.

After a while, having proved his good qualities by barking away a set of pilferers, who were making an attack on the great pear tree, he was admitted into the house, and became one of its most vigilant and valued inmates. He could fetch or carry either by land or water; would pick up a thimble or a ball of cotton, if little Annie should happen to drop them; or take Harry's dinner to school for him with perfect honesty.

"Beg, Frisk, beg!" said Harry, and gave him, after long waiting, the expected morsel. Frisk was satisfied, but Harry was not. The little boy, though a good-humored fellow in the main, had turns of naughtiness, which were apt to last him all day, and this promised to prove one of his worst. It was a holiday, and in the afternoon his cousins, Jane and William, were to come and see him and Annie; and the pears were to be gathered, and the children were to have a treat.

Harry, in his impatience, thought the morning would never be over. He played such pranks—buffeting Frisk, cutting the curls off of Annie's doll, and finally breaking his grandmother's spectacles—that before his visitors arrived, indeed, almost immediately after dinner, he contrived to be sent to bed in disgrace.

Poor Harry! there he lay, rolling and kicking, while Jane, and William, and Annie were busy about the fine, mellow Windsor pears.

William was up in the tree, gathering and shaking; Annie and Jane catching them in their aprons, and picking them up from the ground; now piling them in baskets, and now eating the nicest and ripest; while Frisk was barking gayly among them, as if he were catching Windsor pears, too!

Poor Harry! He could hear all this glee and merriment through the open window as he lay in bed. The storm of passion having subsided, there he lay weeping and disconsolate, a grievous sob bursting forth every now and then, as he heard the loud peals of childish laughter, and as he thought how he should have laughed, and how happy he should have been, had he not forfeited all this pleasure by his own bad conduct.

He wondered if Annie would not be so good-natured as to bring him a pear. All on a sudden, he heard a little foot on the stair, pitapat, and he thought she was coming. Pitapat came the foot, nearer and nearer, and at last a small head peeped, half afraid, through the half-open door.

But it was not Annie's head; it was Frisk's—poor Frisk, whom Harry had been teasing and tormenting all the morning, and who came into the room wagging his tail, with a great pear in his mouth; and, jumping upon the bed, He laid it in the little boy's hand.

Is not Frisk a fine, grateful fellow? and does he not deserve a share of Harry's breakfast, whether he begs for it or not? And little Harry will remember from the events of this day that kindness, even though shown to a dog, will always be rewarded; and that ill nature and bad temper are connected with nothing but pain and disgrace.

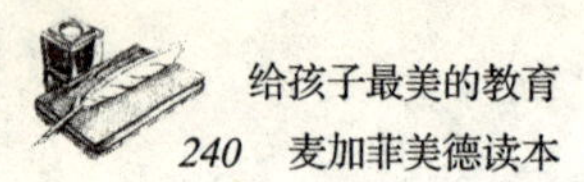

不满的钟摆

简·泰勒（1783~1824），生于伦敦。她的母亲是一位颇有名气的作家。简·泰勒和姐姐安妮一起写了几本非常优秀的青少年读物，如《婴儿的赞美诗》、《新颖的诗歌》。除此之外，她还创作了《演出，寓言》、《散文的韵律》和《QQ的贡献》。她的作品文字优美，而且富有寓意。

在一个农夫的厨房里有座古老的钟，它已经毫无怨言地走了五十年了。在一个夏天的清晨，当家人还在梦中的时候，老钟忽然停下了。这时，表盘（也许应归功于童话）换上一副惊讶的表情，指针徒劳地想继续跳动，轮轴惊讶地一动不动，钟坠沉默地吊着，每个成员都觉得自己必须把责任推卸到其他人身上。不久，表盘开展了正式调查，看看到底是谁导致了老钟的停摆。指针、轮轴、钟坠都异口同声地申明自己是无辜的。

这时，下面传来钟摆轻轻的滴答一声，它说："我坦白，是我导致了现在的停摆。我希望我的理由能让大家满意。实际上，我对每天都要滴答摇摆已经厌倦了。"听到这，老钟愤怒了，恨不得狠狠地揍它一下。"懒鬼！"表盘扬着手说。

“是呀！”钟摆回答，“表盘女士，你多轻松呀，大家都知道，你总是高高在上——你多轻松呀，我说，还指责别人懒惰！你什么都不用干，天天盯着别人，看着厨房里发生的事儿自娱自乐。求你想想看，如果你一辈子被关在一个小黑匣子里，年复一年地摆来摆去，你会乐意吗？”

“这个嘛，”表盘说，“你的房间里不是有个窗户，让你向外看吗？”“虽说如此，”钟摆继续说，“里面太暗了，虽然有个窗户，可是我从来不敢停下哪怕短短一下，探头看一眼。而且，我真的对我的生活方式感到厌倦了。我可以告诉你我对自己的职责有多厌恶。这个早上，我碰巧计算了一下下一个二十四小时中我要摇摆的次数，没准你们谁能告诉我准确的数字。”

分针计算的速度很快，它很快回答道：“86400次。”“完全正确。”钟摆回答。“那么，请你们大家都想像一下，这个数字会不会让人精疲力竭，而且，我还要把这个数字乘以数月、数年。现在你们明白了吧，我为什么会感到绝望。所以，在我推想、犹豫、思考了很久之后，我就停下来了。”

在钟摆进行这套长篇大论的时候，表盘几乎忍俊不禁。不过，她还是努力恢复严肃，这样回答道：“亲爱的钟摆先生，像您这么有用、勤奋的人，竟然会被这种突如其来的疲惫制服，真让我吃惊。的确，您已经做出了伟大的成就，但是我们也没闲着，而且也非常乐意这么做。您做的工作，想来非常让人疲惫，但问题是，如果真正做起来，它是不是真的一样让人疲惫。现在，您能不能帮我做件事，摇摆五六下，以证明我的观点？”

钟摆依言，按照通常的速度摇摆了六次。“现在，”表盘接着说，“我能不能问问，这么做让您觉得很疲惫，或很厌恶吗？”“一点也不，”钟摆回答，“我抱怨的不是六次，也不是六十次，而是千万次。”

“很好，”表盘回答，“但是回忆一下，虽然你在某一时刻可能想起一千万次摇摆，但你只需要在这一时刻里摇摆一次。而且，不论这之后你还需要摇摆多少下，那总是下一个时刻的问题。”“我承认，这种考虑让我有点犹豫。”钟摆说。“那么我希望，”表盘接着说，“我们立即回到各自的岗位上去，因为如果我们继续这么闲待着的话，女仆就会起晚了。”

听到这话：从没有被别人指责为渎职的钟坠，竭力劝说它继续工作。这时，好像心有灵犀一样，轮轴开始运转，指针开始跳动，钟摆也开始摇摆，而且它为了得到表扬，发出的滴答声比以前都要响亮。红彤彤的太阳放射出的光线，从墙上的一个小洞洒进了厨房，照在表盘上，让她亮闪闪的，好像什么都没有发生过一样。

早晨，农夫下楼来吃早饭时，看了看钟表，发现他的手表在夜里走快了半个小时。

The Discontented Pendulum

Jane Taylor (b. 1783, d. 1824) was born in London. Her mother was a writer of some note. In connection with her sister Ann, Jane Taylor wrote several juvenile works of more than ordinary excellence. Among them were "Hymns for Infant Minds" and "Original Poems." Besides these, she wrote "Display, a Tale," "Essays in Rhyme," and "Contributions of QQ." Her writings are graceful, and often contain a useful moral.

An old dock that had stood for fifty years in a farmer's kitchen, without giving its owner any cause of complaint, early one summer's morning, before the family was stirring, suddenly stopped. Upon this, the dial plate (if we may credit the fable) changed countenance with alarm; the hands made a vain effort to continue their course; the wheels remained motionless with surprise; the weights hung speechless; and each member felt disposed to lay the blame on the others. At length the dial instituted a formal inquiry as to the cause of the stagnation, when hands, wheels, weights, with one voice, protested their innocence.

But now a faint tick was heard below from the pendulum, who spoke thus: "I confess myself to be the sole cause of the present stoppage; and I am willing, for the general satisfaction, to assign my reasons. The truth is, that I am tired of ticking." Upon hearing this, the old clock became so enraged that it was upon the very point of striking. "Lazy wire!" exclaimed the dial plate, holding up its bands.

"Very good!" replied the pendulum; "it is vastly easy for you, Mistress Dial, who have always, as everybody knows, set yourself up above me,—it is vastly easy for you, I say, to accuse other people of laziness! you who have had nothing to do all your life but to stare people in the face, and to amuse yourself with watching all that goes on in the kitchen. Think, I beseech you, how you would like to be shut up for life in this dark closet, and to wag backward and forward year after year, as I do."

"As to that," said the dial, "is there not a window in your house on purpose for you to look through?" "For all that," resumed the pendulum, "it is very dark here; and, although there is a window, I dare not stop even for an instant to look out at it. Besides, I am really tired of my way of life; and, if you wish, I'll tell you how I took this disgust at my employment. I happened, this morning, to be calculating how many times I should have to tick in the course of only the next twenty-four hours; perhaps some one of you above there can give me the exact sum."

The minute hand, being quick at figures, presently replied, "Eighty-six thousand four hundred times." "Exactly so," replied the pendulum. "Well, I appeal to you all, if the very thought of this was not enough to fatigue anyone; and when I began to multiply the strokes of one day by those of months and years, really it was no wonder if I felt discouraged at the prospect. So, after a great deal of reasoning and hesitation, thinks I to myself, I'll stop."

The dial could scarcely keep its countenance during this harangue; but, resuming its gravity, thus replied: "Dear Mr. Pendulum, I am really astonished that such a useful, industrious person as yourself should have been seized by this sudden weariness. It is true, you have done a great deal of work in your time; so have we all, and are likely to do; which, although it may fatigue us to think of, the question is, whether it will fatigue us to do. Would you now do me the favor to give about half a dozen strokes to illustrate my argument?"

The pendulum complied, and ticked six times at its usual pace. "Now," resumed the dial, "may I be allowed to inquire if that exertion is at all fatiguing or disagreeable to you?" "Not in the least," replied the pendulum; "it is not of six strokes that I complain, nor of sixty, but of millions."

"Very good," replied the dial; "but recollect that, although you may think of a million of strokes in an instant, you are required to execute but one; and that, however often you may hereafter have to swing, a moment will always be given you to swing in." "That consideration staggers me, I confess," said the pendulum. "Then I hope," resumed the dial plate, "that we shall all return to our duty immediately; for the maids will be in bed if we stand idling thus."

Upon this, the weights, who had never been accused of light conduct, used all their influence in urging him to proceed; when, as if with one consent, the wheels began to turn, the hands began to move, the pendulum began to swing, and, to its credit, ticked as loud as ever; while a red beam of the rising sun, that streamed through a hole in the kitchen, shining full upon the dial plate, it brightened up as if nothing

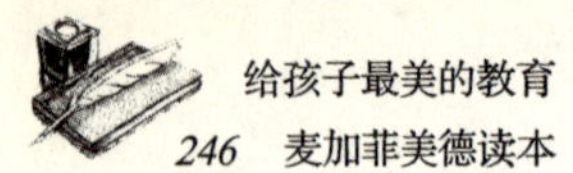

had been the matter.

When the farmer came down to breakfast that morning, upon looking at the clock, he declared that his watch had gained half an hour in the night.

英文通信地址常用翻译（二）

201室/房 Room 201
二单元 Unit 2
一号楼/栋 Building 1
2号 No. 2
宿舍 Dormitory
楼/层 Floor
住宅区/小区 Residential Quarter
巷/弄 Lane
路 Road（也简写作Rd.，注意后面的点不能省略）
一环路 1st Ring Road
花园 Garden
院 Yard
街 Street/Avenue
大学 College/University
信箱 Mailbox
区 District
A座 Suite A
广场 Square
州 State
大厦/写字楼 Tower/Center/Plaza
胡同 Alley（北京地名中的条即是胡同的意思）

哈瑞的财富

贫穷并不可怕，可怕的是你因此不自信，放弃了努力。财富是由人创造的。如果你只看见财富，而不愿意成为创造财富的人，即便拥有金山银山，也很快会坐吃山空。

生活中会存在一些不平等，但上帝对每个人是公平的。只是，你想要的生活，需要自己去争取。

一天，小哈瑞与他的小玩伴强尼·克莱恩一起玩了一个上午。强尼住在一幢漂亮的大房子里，在星期天的时候他会坐着气派的马车去教堂，全镇上的人都能看见。

哈瑞回到家后说："妈妈，强尼的两个口袋里都是钱。"

"是吗？亲爱的。"

"是的，妈妈。他还说，只要他想要的话他还可以有更多的钱。"

"噢，是吗，那他一定很开心。"我愉快地回答说，"非常好，你说呢？"

"是的，妈妈，只是——"

"只是什么，哈瑞？"

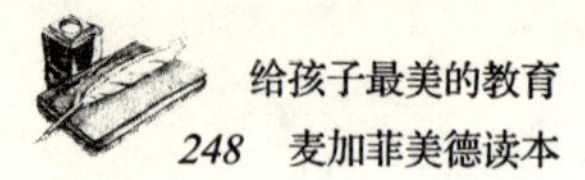

“嗯，他有一条很大的玩具枪，一块手表，一个摇动木马，还有好多好多玩具。”哈瑞抬起头闷闷不乐地看着我。

“怎么回事，我的孩子？”

“没什么，妈妈，”此时涌出眼睛的泪水暴露了秘密，“我只是想我们很穷，是吗？”

“不，不是的，哈瑞，我们离贫穷还远着呢，但我们也并不像克莱恩家那样富有，如果这就是你所说的穷的话。”

“不，妈妈，”小家伙坚持着，“我们就是非常穷，无论怎么说，我们是的！”

“哈瑞！”我带着责备的口气叫他。

“是的，妈妈，我就是太穷，”他抽泣着，“我几乎什么都没有——我指那些值钱的东西——除了吃的和穿的，那些必须拥有的东西我都没有。”

“必须拥有的东西？”我重复着他的话，把手中的针线活放到了桌上，这样，我就可以和他好好谈谈这个问题，“你不知道吗，我的孩子——”

就在这时，正在读报纸的本叔叔抬起了头，“哈瑞，”他说，“我想研究一下人的眼睛，因此如果你愿意给我你的眼睛，我会给你每只一美元。”

“要我的眼睛？”哈瑞大声喊道，他对此大吃一惊。

“是的，”本叔叔平静地说，“要你的眼睛。我可以给你麻醉，这样你就不会感到疼了，你可以戴一副漂亮的玻璃眼球。快点，一美元一只，否则要降价了。你看怎么样？我很快就可以把它们取出来。”

“把我的眼睛给你？”哈瑞像是无法相信这个离奇的想法，“我想不行。”受惊的小家伙坚决地摇着头。

“好吧，五美元，十美元，二十美元。”每一次报价哈瑞都不断地摇头。

“不，先生，您给我一千美元我也不会让你取走我的眼睛的。没有了眼睛我怎么办？我将再也看不见妈妈，看不见宝宝，看不见花，也看不见马，所有的一切一切。”哈瑞补充着，越来越激动起来。

“我给你二千美元。”本叔叔继续说着，从他的口袋里掏出一卷支票。哈瑞站得远远的，大声喊道他永远也不会做这样的事。

“那么好吧，”本叔叔说。他此时神情十分严肃，一边在本子上写着什么，一边说：“我不能给你高过二千美元的价格，所以我只能放弃你的眼睛了。但是，”他又说道，“我要告诉你我要怎么做，如果你让我把这瓶子里的东西滴几滴到你耳朵里的话，我会给你二十美元。你并不会觉得疼，但却会让你变聋。你知道我想做一个关于耳聋的实验。快，现在就做决定。这里的二十美元是给你准备的。”

“把我变聋！”哈瑞已经快气疯了，他看也不看摆在桌子上的那些金币，大声喊道，“我想你也不会那么做的，如果我聋了，我就再也听不见了，不是吗？”

“可能吧。”本叔叔说。

当然，哈瑞再次拒绝了。他不会放弃他的听力。他说：“不，三千美元也不行。”

本叔叔在本子上又记下了一条。之后又出更高的价要“哈瑞的右手”，然后是“左手”、“双手”、“双脚”、“鼻子”，最后出价一万要他的“妈妈”，五千美元要他的“宝宝”。

哈瑞拒绝了所有这些提议，他的眼睛闪着光，不停地表达着他的震惊和愤怒。最后本叔叔说他必须放弃他的实验，因为哈瑞的价格实在是太高了。

“哈！哈！”哈瑞高兴地笑了，他架起胳膊，样子似乎在说，“我倒要看看谁能买得起！”

“天哪，哈瑞，来看这儿！”本叔叔对着笔记本看着，“这有一大笔钱呢！让我来告诉你总数。”他把所有的数目加起来，一共是三万二千美元。

“现在，哈瑞，”本叔叔说，“你不觉得放弃这么多钱太蠢了吗？”

“不，先生，我不要。”哈瑞坚决地说。

“那么，”本叔叔说，“你说你很穷，但你又不肯拿你拥有的来换取三万二千美元，这是怎么回事呢？”

哈瑞并不知道该怎么回答。他涨红了脸，泪水滑下了脸颊，他用胖乎乎的胳膊搂住我的脖子。“妈妈，”他在我耳边说道，“上帝实在是太好了，他让我们每个人都那么富有。”

英语地址写法中的常用缩写词

Avenue: Ave.　Road: Rd.　Square: Sq.

Province: Prov.　Street: St.　District: Dist.

Floor: /F　Room: Rm.　Apartment: Apt.

Building: Bldg.　Mountain:Mt.

注意：简写中的点不能省略，如Rd.，Prov.；xx东路/南路/西路/北路中的东南西北可分别缩写E/S/W/N，且一定要放在路名前，如（延安西路）West Yan'an Rd. 而不是Yan'an West Rd.。

Harry's Riches

One day, our little Harry spent the morning with his young playmate, Johnny Crane, who lived in a fine house, and on Sundays rode to church in the grandest carriage to be seen in all the country round.

When Harry returned home, he said, "Mother, Johnny has money in both pockets!"

"Has he, dear?"

"Yes, ma'am; and he says he could get ever so much more if he wanted it."

"Well, now, that's very pleasant for him," I returned, cheerfully, as a reply was plainly expected. "Very pleasant; don't you think so?"

"Yes, ma'am; only—"

"Only what, Harry?"

"Why, he has a big popgun, and a watch, and a hobbyhorse, and lots of things." And Harry looked up at my face with a disconsolate stare.

"Well, my boy, what of that?"

"Nothing, mother," and the telltale tears sprang to his eyes, "only I guess we are very poor, aren't we?"

"No, indeed, Harry, we are very far from being poor. We are not so rich as Mr. Crane's family, if that is what you mean."

"O mother!" insisted the little fellow, "I do think we are very poor; anyhow, I am!"

"O Harry!" I exclaimed, reproachfully.

"Yes, ma'am I am," he sobbed; "I have scarcely any thing—I mean anything that's worth money—except things to eat and wear, and I'd have to have them anyway."

"Have to have them?" I echoed, at the same time laying my sewing upon the table, so that I might reason with him on that point; "do you not know, my son—"

Just then Uncle Ben looked up from the paper he had been reading: "Harry," said he, "I want to find out something about eyes; so, if you will let me have yours, I will give you a dollar apiece for them."

"For my eyes!" exclaimed Harry, very much astonished.

"Yes," resumed Uncle Ben, quietly, "for your eyes. I will give you chloroform, so it will not hurt you in the least, and you shall have a beautiful glass pair for nothing, to wear in their place. Come, a dollar apiece, cash down! What do you say? I will take them out as quick as a wink."

"Give you my eyes, uncle!" cried Harry, looking wild at the very thought, "I think not." And the startled little fellow shook his head defiantly.

"Well, five, ten, twenty dollars, then." Harry shook his head at every offer.

"No, sir! I wouldn't let you have them for a thousand dollars! What could I do without my eyes? I couldn't see mother, nor the baby, nor the flowers, nor the horses, nor anything," added Harry, growing warmer and warmer.

"I will give you two thousand," urged Uncle Ben, taking a roll of bank notes out of his pocket. Harry, standing at a respectful distance, shouted that he never would do any such thing.

"Very well," continued the uncle, with a serious air, at the same time writing something in his notebook, "I can't afford to give you more than two thousand dollars, so I shall have to do without your eyes; but," he added, "I will tell you what I will do, I will give you twenty dollars if you will let me put a few drops from this bottle in your ears. It will not hurt, but it will make you deaf. I want to try some experiments with deafness, you see. Come quickly, now! Here are the twenty dollars all ready for you."

"Make me deaf!" shouted Harry, without even looking at the gold pieces temptingly displayed upon the table. "I guess you will not do that, either. Why, I couldn't hear a single word if I were deaf, could I?"

"Probably not," replied Uncle Ben. So, of course, Harry refused again. He would never give up his hearing, he said, "no, not for three thousand dollars."

Uncle Ben made another note in his book, and then came out with large bids for "a right arm," then "left arm," "hands," "feet," "nose," finally ending with an offer of ten thousand dollars for "mother," and five thousand for "the baby."

To all of these offers Harry shook his head, his eyes flashing, and exclamations of surprise and indignation bursting from his lips. At last, Uncle Ben said he must give up his experiments, for Harry's prices were entirely too high.

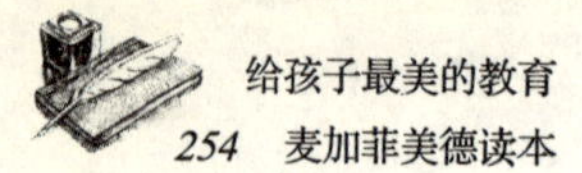

"Ha! ha!" laughed the boy, exultingly, and he folded his dimpled arms and looked as if to say, "I'd like to see the man who could pay them!"

"Why, Harry, look here!" exclaimed Uncle Ben, peeping into his notebook, "here is a big addition sum, I tell you!" He added the numbers, and they amounted to thirty-two thousand dollars.

"There, Harry," said Uncle Ben, "don't you think you are foolish not to accept some of my offers?" "No, sir, I don't," answered Harry, resolutely. "Then," said Uncle Ben, "you talk of being poor, and by your own showing you have treasures for which you will not take thirty-two thousand dollars. What do you say to that?"

Harry didn't know exactly what to say. So he blushed for a second, and just then tears came rolling down his cheeks, and he threw his chubby arms around my neck. "Mother," he whispered, "isn't God good to make everybody so rich?"

勇敢去做自己认为是对的事情

托马斯·休斯（1823～1896），英国作家。本文摘自其《在拉格比学校的日子》。他因此书及其续篇《汤姆·布朗在牛津》而闻名。

低年级的学生静静地走向自己的床铺，一边脱衣服，一边相互小声地交谈着；而高年级的学生脱下了夹克衫和马甲，坐在彼此的床上聊天，汤姆也在其中。

可怜的小阿瑟，刚来到一个新地方，脑袋里充满了新奇。与陌生的孩子们睡在同一个房间，他从前可是连想都没想过，感觉真别扭。得脱下夹克衫来，这使他几乎不能忍受，但一横心，最终还是脱了下来。然后，他踌躇地看了汤姆一眼，后者正坐在床的一角，谈笑风生。

“布朗，”他嗫嚅着，“我可以洗脸洗手吗？”

“当然可以了，你愿意洗就洗吧，”汤姆看着他说，“那是你的洗手架，在窗户下面，从你的床数第二个，如果你晚上把水都用完了，早晨还得下去打。”

说完，汤姆接着聊天去了，阿瑟胆怯地从床铺间溜到洗手架，开始洗漱，这吸引了房间里人的注意，但也只是一会儿而已。

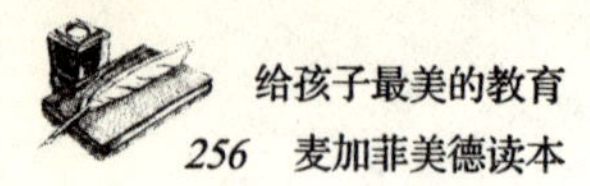

说笑仍在继续着。阿瑟洗漱完毕，换上了长睡衣。他更为不安地环视了一下房间，两三个低年级的孩子已经坐在床上了，下巴支在双膝上。灯光仍然很亮，房间里仍然很吵。

可怜、孤独的小阿瑟在试探着，但这次，他没有问汤姆可以做什么，不可以做什么，而是双膝跪倒在床边的地上，开始祈祷，就如他从小每天做的一样。因为他相信上帝能够听到哭喊，能够忍受悲伤，无论是脆弱的小孩，还是强壮却痛苦的成人的。

当时汤姆背对着阿瑟，正坐在床的一头解鞋带，没有看到正在发生的事情，这时，房间突然安静了下来，他惊奇地转过了头。接着，两三个孩子发出了嘲笑声，站在房间中央的一个高个头的粗鲁家伙捡起一只拖鞋，朝阿瑟扔过去，称阿瑟是小屁孩。

汤姆明白了一切。于是，他把刚刚脱掉的靴子向那个野蛮人的头上直直地砸过去，小阿瑟也及时抬起手臂抓住了汤姆的胳臂肘。

“去你的布朗！你什么意思？”野蛮人愤怒地吼着，脚都跺疼了。“我什么意思？不用你管，”汤姆跺着地板喊着，热血沸腾：“如果谁还想挨另一只靴子，那就来吧。”

正在这时，一个六年级的男孩进来了，屋里立即鸦雀无声，如果不是这样，事情还不知会变成什么样子呢？汤姆跟其他孩子冲到床上，脱下衣服。一会儿，管理员熄灭了蜡烛，跟往常一样道了声“晚安，先生们。”带上门，溜达着向另一个房间走去了。

许多孩子在入睡之前已将刚才那一幕深深印在了脑海里。很长一段时间，兴奋和如潮水般的记忆交替在脑海中奔突，汤姆无法思想，也无法入睡。他的头阵阵作痛，心突突地跳着，几乎控制不住自己想跳起来在房间里奔跑的冲动。

他想起了妈妈，想起了几年以前在她膝下许过的誓言，发誓在睡觉之前，决不会忘记跪在床边向上帝忏悔。他静静地躺着，哭了起来，心好像要碎了。他毕竟只是一个十四岁的孩子。

那时，一个孩子要当众祈祷，并不仅仅需要勇气，即使在开明的拉格比学校也不例外。几年之后，托马斯·阿诺德博士出任校长，他男子气概的虔诚感化了整个学校，情况才得以改观。在他去世之前，至少在校舍里，已是另一番情形。我想，在学校的其他场所也是这样的。

可惜，汤姆上学时并没有赶上那段时期。他来到学校的前几天晚上，因为吵闹他没有跪下来祈祷，而是坐在床上直到蜡烛熄灭，然后，偷偷地溜出去做祈祷，胆战心惊，惟恐别人发现他在外面。其他可怜的小家伙们也有这么做的。

后来他想为什么不在床上祈祷呢，跪着祈祷，坐着祈祷还是躺在床上祈祷并没有什么区别。这样想这样做的人不只汤姆一个，凡是不愿当众祈祷的人都采取了这种做法。去年，汤姆认真祈祷恐怕不超过十二次。

可怜的汤姆！最痛苦的莫过于感到自己的懦弱了，这种感觉刺伤了他的心。人们的堕落是他所憎恨的，如今也降临到他的身上，这灼烧着他幼小的灵魂。他不仅欺骗了母亲，欺骗了良心，也欺骗了上帝。他怎么能承受得了这种折磨呢？如今，这个他既同情又瞧不起的小男孩，那么可怜，那么软弱，竟然做了他不敢做的事情，而他只是吹吹牛而已。

他发誓将不顾一切地继续支持他，鼓励他，帮助他，与晚上的义举相呼应，这样想着，心里就舒服多了。对，第二天给家里写封信，告诉母亲一切，告诉她，儿子曾经是个懦夫。他决心明天早晨就行动起来，这样想着，他渐渐平静了下来。

真是想起来容易做起来难，但他觉得再也不能让机会白白溜走了。他几次要打退堂鼓，因为一想到他的老朋友可能因此给他冠以“假正经”、“古板”等等许多难听的名字并嘲笑他，一想到他的动机会被误解，他与那个刚来的男孩会被孤立起来，他便不寒而栗。但

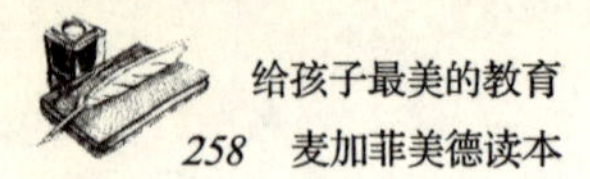

转念一想，他这样做可能对大多数的人有好处。

后来，他又想到一个折中的办法，“我这样做是不是在炫耀比别人勇敢呢？我有权利这样做吗？我是不是可以只在书房当着其他男孩的面做祈祷，然后引导他们也这样做，而在公开场合下，我仍然同之前一样呢？”最终，正义的天使占了绝对上风，他侧着身睡着了，他决心不管后果如何，要把这种强烈的冲动变成行动，而且这想法使他感到安宁。

第二天起来，他洗漱完毕，夹克衫和马甲还没有穿上，这时还差十分钟上课的铃声响了起来，在众目睽睽之下，他跪下来祈祷。他五个词还未说完，铃声又响了，好像在嘲笑他。他留神听着屋里的动静，别人会怎么想他呢？

他羞于再继续跪下去，也羞于站起来。最后，从内心深处，一个沉静、细小的声音说道：“愿上帝怜悯我这个罪人！”他一遍又一遍地重复着，最后，他惬意地、谦恭地站了起来，已经做好面对整个世界的准备。

其实，他多虑了，因为他发现除了阿瑟之外另外两个男孩也在效仿他的做法。当他走向学校的时候，有一句话在他心中闪烁：只有战胜自己内心懦弱的人才能征服整个外部世界。这使他想到了希伯来的预言者以利亚，他在何烈山的山洞里学到了同样一课。当时，他捂着脸，那个沉静、细小的声音问道，“你在这儿干什么呀，以利亚？”这使他懂得了一个道理：无论我们站在真理的一边是多么孤独，但上帝无处不在地看着你，因为在每一个社会，无论它看上去是多么腐败，多么邪恶，都有敢于不向恶势力屈服的人。

他还发现，当初将自己行为的后果想像得太严重了。当他跪下来祈祷时，尽管仍能听到嗤笑声，但只是持续了几个晚上。很快地，除了三四个男孩外，其余的人都一个接一个地效仿他的做法了。

Dare to Do Right

Adapted from "School Days at Rugby," by Thomas Hughes, an English writer well known through this book, and its sequel, "Tom Brown at Oxford." The author was born in 1823, and died in 1896.

The little schoolboys went quietly to their own beds, and began undressing and talking to one another in whispers: while the elder, amongst whom was Tom, sat chatting about on one another's beds, with their jackets and waistcoats off.

Poor little Arthur was overwhelmed with the novelty of his position. The idea of sleeping in the room with strange boys had clearly never crossed his mind before, and was as painful as it was strange to him. He could hardly bear to take his jacket off; however, presently, with an effort, off it came, and then he paused and looked at Tom, who was sitting at the bottom of his bed, talking and laughing.

"Please, Brown," he whispered, "may I wash my face and hands?" "Of course, if you like," said Tom, staring: "that's your wash–hand stand under the window, second from your bed. You'll have to go down for

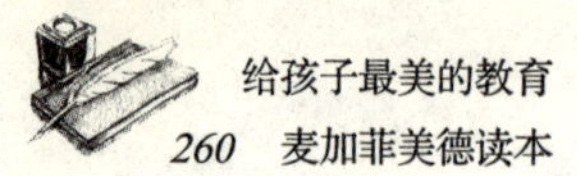

more water in the morning if you use it all."

And on he went with his talk, while Arthur stole timidly from between the beds out to his wash–hand stand, and began his ablutions, thereby drawing for a moment on himself the attention of the room.

On went the talk and laughter. Arthur finished his washing and undressing, and put on his nightgown. He then looked round more nervously than ever. Two or three of the little boys were already in bed, sitting up with their chins on their knees. The light burned clear, the noise went on.

It was a trying moment for the poor, little, lonely boy; however, this time he did not ask Tom what he might or might not do, but dropped all his knees by his bedside, as he had done every day from his childhood, to open his heart to Him who heareth the cry and beareth the sorrows of the tender child, and the strong man in agony.

Tom was sitting at the bottom of his bed unlacing his boots, so that his back was towards Arthur, and he did not see what had happened, and looked up in wonder at the sudden silence. Then two or three boys laughed and sneered, and a big, brutal fellow, who was standing in the middle of the room, picked up a slipper and shied it at the kneeling boy, calling him a sniveling young shaver.

Then Tom saw the whole, and the next moment the boot he had just pulled off flew straight at the head of the bully, who had just time to throw up his arm and catch it on his elbow. "Confound you, Brown; what's that for?" roared he, stamping with pain. "Never mind what I mean," said Tom, stepping on to the floor, every drop of blood in his body tingling: "if any fellow wants the other boot, he knows how to get it."

What would have been the result is doubtful, for at this moment the sixth–form boy came in, and not another word could be said. Tom and the rest rushed into bed and finished their unrobing there, and the old janitor had put out the candle in another minute, and toddled on to the next room, shutting the door with his usual, "Good night, gentlemen."

There were many boys in the room by whom that little scene was taken to heart before they slept. But sleep seemed to have deserted the pillow of poor Tom. For some time his excitement and the flood of memories which chased one another through his brain, kept him from thinking or resolving. His head throbbed, his heart leapt, and he could hardly keep himself from springing out of bed and rushing about the room.

Then the thought of his own mother came across him, and the promise he had made at her knee, years ago, never to forget to kneel by his bedside and give himself up to his Father before he laid his head on the pillow, from which it might never rise; and he lay down gently, and cried as if his heart would break. He was only fourteen years old.

It was no light act of courage in those days for a little fellow to say his prayers publicly, even at Rugby. A few years later, when Arnold's manly piety had begun to leaven the school, the tables turned: before he died, in the Schoolhouse at least, and I believe in the other houses, the rule was the other way.

But poor Tom had come to school in other times. The first few nights after he came he did not kneel down because of the noise, but sat up in bed till the candle was out, and then stole out and said his prayers, in fear lest some one should find him out. So did many another poor little fellow.

Then he began to think that he might just as well say his prayers in bed, and then that it did not matter whether he was kneeling, or sitting, or lying down. And so it had come to pass with Tom, as with all who will not confess their Lord before men; and for the last year he had probably

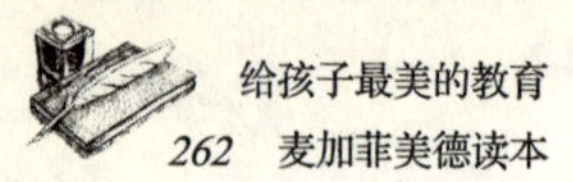

not said his prayers in earnest a dozen times.

Poor Tom! the first and bitterest feeling, which was like to break his heart, was the sense of his own cowardice. The vice of all others which he loathed was brought in and burned in on his own soul. He had lied to his mother, to his conscience, to his God. How could he bear it? And then the poor, little, weak boy, whom he had pitied and almost scorned for his weakness, had done that which he, braggart as he was, dared not do.

The first dawn of comfort came to him in vowing to himself that he would stand by that boy through thick and thin, and cheer him, and help him, and bear his burdens, for the good deed done that night. Then he resolved to write home next day and tell his mother all, and what a coward her son had been. And then peace came to him as he resolved, lastly, to bear his testimony next morning.

The morning would be harder than the night to begin with, but he felt that he could not afford to let one chance slip. Several times he faltered, for the Devil showed him, first, all his old friends calling him "Saint," and "Squaretoes" and a dozen hard names, and whispered to him that his motives would be misunderstood, and he would be left alone with the new boy; whereas, it was his duty to keep all means of influence, that he might do good to the largest number.

And then came the more subtle temptation, "shall I not be showing myself braver than others by doing this? Have I any right to begin it now? Ought I not rather to pray in my own study, letting other boys know that I do so, and trying to lead them to it, while in public, at least, I should go on as I have done?" However, his good angel was too strong that night, and he turned on his side and slept, tired of trying to reason, but resolved to follow the impulse which had been so strong, and in which he had found peace.

Next morning he was up and washed and dressed, all but his jacket and waistcoat, just as the ten minutes' bell began to ring, and then in the face of the whole room he knelt down to pray. Not five words could he say,—the bell mocked him; he was listening for every whisper in the room,—what were they all thinking of him?

He was ashamed to go on kneeling, ashamed to rise from his knees. At last, as it were from his inmost heart, a still, small voice seemed to breathe forth the words of the publican, "God be merciful to me a sinner!" He repeated them over and over, clinging to them as for his life, and rose from his knees comforted and humbled, and ready to face the whole world.

It was not needed: two other boys besides Arthur had already followed his example, and he went down to the great school with a glimmering of another lesson in his heart,—the lesson that he who has conquered his own coward spirit has conquered the whole outward world; and that other one which the old prophet learned in the cave at Mount Horeb, when he hid his face, and the still, small voice asked, "What doest thou here, Elijah?"—that however we may fancy ourselves alone on the side of good, the King and Lord of men is nowhere without his witnesses; for in every society, however seemingly corrupt and godless, there are those who have not bowed the knee to Baal.

He found, too, how greatly he had exaggerated the effect to be produced by his act. For a few nights there was a sneer or a laugh when he knelt down, but this passed off soon, and one by one all the other boys but three or four followed the lead.

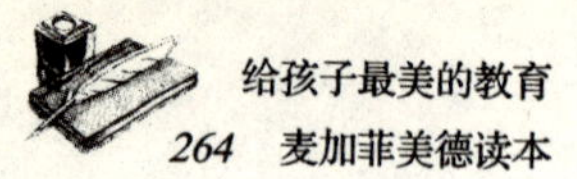

小耐丽之死

查尔斯·狄更斯（1812~1870），近代最优秀的小说家之一，出生于英国朴茨茅斯，一生中大部分时间居住于伦敦。他的父亲是个正直的人，但是缺乏谋生手段。结果，狄更斯少时只得在困窘的环境中度过。曾有人猜测他是以他父亲为原型创作了“米考伯”。作为一名法律实习生，狄更斯开始了他的职业生涯，但很快改行去做了记者。从1831年到1836年，狄更斯一直从事记者职业。狄更斯的第一本著作名叫《博兹札记》。1837年，《匹克威克外传》使他一举成名。狄更斯一生出版了大量的经典作品，但最后一部作品并没有完成他就与世长辞了。他去世后被安葬于西敏寺的诗人角。狄更斯曾于1842年和1867年两次到访美国。在1867年的那次造访中，狄更斯在许多美国主要的城市中进行了演讲，并当众朗读了他的作品。

狄更斯仿佛拥有无穷无尽的才华，他没有去复制或者模仿任何人，所有的一切完全依靠他自己的才能。他笔触幽默，充满同情，他通过仔细和准确的观察收集了大量写作素材，其笔下的人物每一个都有着独特的个性而显得栩栩如生，但有时他也会以历史影射现实，用有趣的语言进行无情的讽刺。他尤其善于描写欢乐或者悲伤的童年，小耐丽和小保罗·董贝是他笔下的著名人物，几乎每一个英语家庭都曾读过他们的故事，并为之欢乐或悲伤。狄更斯的作品生动地展现了下层人民的苦痛与要求，并且努力提倡仁慈与关爱。不过，他的作品也没有逃脱被批判的命运。有人说“他的美好品质源于一时冲动，而不是某种信条。”也有人说他展现出“一颗充满异想天开的夸大的狡猾的心灵”，更有人说他的小说有时候缺乏技巧性的情节，而且他看上去很赞成交际宴请和浪费。《老古玩店》出版于1840年，下面的片段就节选于其中。

耐丽死了，她躺在床上安静地长眠了。没有比这更美丽、更平静的了，看不出痛苦，只是分外的美丽和漂亮。她让人产生一种幻觉，好像她不是一个刚死去的人，而是一个等待上帝赋予新生命的形体。她的床上堆满了绿色的树叶、红色的浆果，这些都是她生前所喜欢的。她曾经说过：“在我死后，把一些沐浴着光明、新鲜清新的东西放在我的身边伴随着我。”

她死去了。可爱、善良、高贵、品质优秀的耐丽死去了。她那只可怜而脆弱的小鸟在笼子里跳来跳去的，她的小主人的心脏却永远地静止了，不跳动了。她的苦痛、疲劳、忧愁哪里去了呢？这些都完全消失了，随同她的悲哀·起死去了。留下来的却是幸福、安宁、平静，这些都静静地呈现在她淡淡的长眠中、安详的美丽里。

她静静地躺在那里，仿佛没有丝毫改变。老屋仍然记得那甜蜜的笑容，在夏日黄昏时分的校长室门前，在潮湿、冰冷之夜眠于温暖的火炉旁边之时，当站在垂死的小男孩的病榻前时，在那张同样温柔的面庞上所泛起的微笑。它被忧愁与灾难侵扰之后，像幻梦一般消失得无影无踪了。也就是这张可爱的容颜，让人感觉到了人死后天使卫护般的尊严与威仪。

老人跪了下来，紧握住她一只瘦小的手臂，贴在自己的心头。就是这只手，引导着他四处漂泊；就是这只手，带着最后的微笑伸向他。他深情地吻着它，然后又把它贴在心口，口中喃喃不已，仿佛耐丽的手又恢复了温暖。他用悲恸、凄惨的目光向四周伫立的人看了看，似乎恳求他们，让他们把她唤醒。

可是，她已经死去了，谁也无能为力了，救不活她的。生命迅速凋零，回忆却久久不能消失。那些古老的因为她的存在而充满了生命的房屋，她照料、伺弄过的花园，她快乐的眼睛，她漫步的小径，所有的这一切都如同昨天一般，这一切都不再了，它们再也听不到她欢快的笑声，得不到她的照料了。

“不会的，”校长说着，眼泪像断了线的珠子一样一串串地向下落。他弯下腰去再一次吻了吻她，“天国的裁决绝对不会在人世间结束的。假如把尘世与她将飞升的天国相比，尘世又算得了什么呢？即使我们当中有谁能够使她从长眠中醒来，谁又愿意这样讲出来呢？”

这是她死去的第二天。在她死去的时候，他们都在场，因为他们都知道她即将离开人世。天一亮，她就停止了呼吸。在夜晚的早些时候，他们给她读书让她听，同她聊天。渐渐地，她便沉入到了昏迷之中，说一些神志不清的话语。刚开始的时候，人们能够听得出来，她在讲她同老人一起长途跋涉的事情，但并没有什么痛苦的感觉，一路上都有人在帮助他们，因为她总是说：“愿上帝保佑你们！”醒来之后，她并没有立刻清醒起来。有时，她会说她能够听到天空中传来美妙的音乐，非常动听。苍天在上，又有谁能够知道这是不是真的？最后一次，她睁开眼，让人们亲吻她、祝福她。然后，她就冲着老人笑，大家从来没有见过这么清新、动人的笑容。她双手搂着他的脖子——他们一开始都不知道这时候她已经死去了。她就这样平静而安详地离去了，像夏天的傍晚，天边缓缓下沉的夕阳一样。

天刚亮，她的那个小男朋友带来了一束干花跑了过来，作为献给她的祭祀，安放在她的胸前。他讲了他做的梦。他梦见他的小女孩儿又回来了。他恳求让他见见她，并保证不会恐惧害怕。他还说，当他哥哥去世的时候，他就在身旁，也没有感到过害怕。看着男孩那恳切的样子，大家满足了他的愿望。他也正如所说的那样，十分沉静、镇定。而他的那种略显天真的样子，让大家十分感动。

老头在床边一直没有挪动，除了对死去的耐丽外，也一直没有和别人说过话。他在众人之前发现了男孩的到来，并让男孩靠得更近些。手指向床上，老人的泪水第一次流了出来。看到这些，大家都退了下去，只留下他们两个人在那里。

男孩用他那幼稚的童音毫无技巧的安慰着老人，劝他到外边走一走。再过一段时间，小女孩就要被埋葬，入土为安了。男孩不希望老人面临着再也不能见到小女孩的打击，也许那将使老人承受不了的。于是，他领着老人离开，采摘一些浆果、绿树叶子用来装饰她的灵床。

钟声一下、两下、三下……，无情地响着。这钟声，她白天和夜晚都听过，听的时候，她总是一脸沉静、庄重的样子，而现在，丧钟却在为她而鸣——她是多么年轻，多么美丽，多么美好！这时候，无论是老人、孩子、成年人还是年轻人，他们齐集在她的墓前。老人们站在那儿，耳聋眼花，知觉衰退。那些老祖母，她们十年前就到了离开人世的年龄，然而，她们仍然活着；还有聋子、瞎子、驼子、瘸子，各种各样的活着的死人，如今，他们都在这个夭折的女孩的墓前静立凭吊。

当她被抬着走在大街上的时候，她全身一片洁白，如同刚刚下的白雪一样纯洁、晶莹。她在人世的日子过得太快了！在门廊下，她曾静静地坐在那里。如今，仁慈的上帝又让她经过这里，灰老的教堂将身影遮在她的身上。

Death of Little Nell

Charles Dickens. 1812–1870, one of the greatest novelists of modern times, was born in Portsmouth, but spent nearly all his life in London. His father was a conscientious man, but lacked capacity for getting a livelihood. In consequence, the boy's youth was much darkened by poverty. It has been supposed that he pictured his father in the character of "Micawber." He began his active life as a lawyer's apprentice; but soon left this employment to become a reporter. This occupation he followed from 1831 to 1836. His first book was entitled "Sketches of London Society, by Boz." This was followed, in 1837, by the "Pickwick Papers," a work which suddenly brought much fame to the author. His other works followed with great rapidity, and his last was unfinished at the time of his death. He was buried in Westminster Abbey. Mr. Dickens visited America in 1842, and again in 1867. During his last visit, he read his works in public, in the principal cities of the United States.

The resources of Dickens's genius seemed exhaustless. He copied no author, imitated none, but relied entirely on his own powers. He excelled especially in humor and pathos. He gathered materials for his works by the most careful and faithful observation. And he painted his characters with a fidelity so true to their different individualities that, although they sometimes have a quaint grotesqueness bordering on caricature, they stand before the memory as living realities. He was particularly successful in the delineation of the joys and griefs of childhood. "Little Nell" and little "Paul Dombey" are known, and have been loved and wept over, in almost every household where the English language is read. His writings present very vividly the wants and sufferings of the poor, and have a tendency to prompt to kindness and benevolence. His works have not escaped criticism. It has been said that "his good characters act from impulse, not from principle," and that he shows "a tricksy spirit of fantastic exaggeration." It has also been said that his novels sometimes lack skillful plot, and that he seems to speak approvingly of conviviality and dissipation. "The Old Curiosity Shop," from which the following extract is taken, was published in 1840.

She was dead. No sleep so beautiful and calm, so free from trace of pain, so fair to look upon. She seemed a creature fresh from the hand of God, and waiting for the breath of life; not one who had lived, and suffered death. Her couch was dressed with here and there some winter berries and green leaves, gathered in a spot she had been used to favor. "When I die, put near me something that has loved the light, and had the sky above it always." These were her words.

She was dead. Dear, gentle, patient, noble Nell was dead. Her little bird, a poor, slight thing the pressure of a finger would have crushed, was stirring nimbly in its cage, and the strong heart of its child mistress was mute and motionless forever! Where were the traces of her early cares, her sufferings, and fatigues? All gone. Sorrow was dead, indeed, in her; but peace and perfect happiness were born, imaged in her tranquil beauty and profound repose.

And still her former self lay there, unaltered in this change. Yes! the old fireside had smiled upon that same sweet face; it had passed, like a dream, through haunts of misery and care; at the door of the poor schoolmaster on the summer evening, before the furnace fire upon the cold wet night, at the still bedside of the dying boy, there had been the same mild and lovely look. So shall we know the angels, in their majesty, after death.

The old man held one languid arm in his, and had the small hand tight folded to his breast for warmth. It was the hand she had stretched out to him with her last smile; the hand that had led him on through all their wanderings. Ever and anon he pressed it to his lips; then hugged it to his breast again, murmuring that it was warmer now, and, as he said it, he looked in agony to those who stood around, as if imploring them to help her.

She was dead, and past all help, or need of help. The ancient rooms she had seemed to fill with life, even while her own was waning fast, the garden she had tended, the eyes she had gladdened, the noiseless haunts of many a thoughtful hour, the paths she had trodden, as it were, but yesterday, could know her no more.

"It is not," said the schoolmaster, as he bent down to kiss her on the cheek, and gave his tears free vent, "it is not in this world that heaven's justice ends. Think what earth is, compared with the world to which her young spirit has winged its early flight, and say, if one deliberate wish, expressed in solemn tones above this bed, could call her back to life, which of us would utter it?"

She had been dead two days. They were all about her at the time, knowing that the end was drawing on. She died soon after daybreak. They had read and talked to her in the earlier portion of the night; but, as the hours crept on, she sank to sleep. They could tell by what she faintly uttered in her dreams, that they were of her journeyings with the old man; they were of no painful scenes, but of people who had helped them, and used them kindly; for she often said "God bless you!" with great fervor.

Waking, she never wandered in her mind but once, and that was at beautiful music, which, she said, was in the air. God knows. It may have been. Opening her eyes, at last, from a very quiet sleep, she begged that they would kiss her once again. That done, she turned to the old man, with a lovely smile upon her face, such, they said, as they had never seen, and could never forget, and clung, with both her arms, about his neck. She had never murmured or complained; but, with a quiet mind, and manner quite unaltered, save that she every day became more earnest and more grateful to them, faded like the light upon the summer's evening.

The child who had been her little friend, came there, almost as soon as it was day, with an offering of dried flowers, which he begged them to lay upon her breast. He told them of his dream again, and that it was of her being restored to them, just as she used to be. He begged hard to see her: saying, that he would be very quiet, and that they need not fear his being alarmed, for he had sat alone by his young brother all day long, when he was dead, and had felt glad to be so near him. They let him have his wish; and, indeed, he kept his word, and was, in his childish way, a lesson to them all.

Up to that time, the old man had not spoken once, except to her, or stirred from the bedside. But, when he saw her little favorite, he was moved as they had not seen him yet, and made as though he would have him come nearer. Then, pointing to the bed, he burst into tears for the first time, and they who stood by, knowing that the sight of this child had done him good, left them alone together.

Soothing him with his artless talk of her, the child persuaded him to take some rest, to walk abroad, to do almost as he desired him. And, when the day came, on which they must remove her, in her earthly shape, from earthly eyes forever, he led him away, that he might not know when she was taken from him. They were to gather fresh leaves and berries for her bed.

And now the bell, the bell she had so often heard by night and day, and listened to with solemn pleasure, almost as a living voice, rung its remorseless toll for her, so young, so beautiful, so good. Decrepit age, and vigorous life, and blooming youth, and helpless infancy,—on crutches, in the pride of health and strength, in the full blush of promise, in the mere dawn of life, gathered round her. Old men were there, whose eyes were dim and senses failing, grandmothers, who might have died ten years ago, and still been old, the deaf, the blind, the lame, the palsied, the living dead, in many shapes and forms, to see the closing of that early grave.

Along the crowded path they bore her now, pure as the newly fallen snow that covered it, whose day on earth had been as fleeting. Under that porch, where she had sat when heaven, in its mercy, brought her to that peaceful spot, she passed again, and the old church received her in its quiet shade.

约翰·亚当斯的假想演讲

丹尼尔·韦伯斯特（1782～1852），出生于美国新罕布什尔州的索尔兹伯里。他曾经在菲利普–埃克塞特学院待了几个月，但很快转入达特茅斯学院就读，并于1801年以优异的成绩毕业。毕业之后，他先在小学和中学里任教了几个学期。1805年，韦伯斯特通过律师执照考试后，在接下来的十一年中进行了无数次的法庭辩论，成为美国历史上最有名的辩护律师。1812年，他被选为联邦众议员。1816年，他移居波士顿，并在1827年当选为联邦参议员，并在这个位置上待了十二年。1841年，他被任命为美国国务卿。1850年，他重新出任美国国务卿直到他去世。1852年，韦伯斯特在马萨诸塞州的马什菲尔德去世。他的声望主要来自于他的演讲和国家报告。作为一名演讲家，他用清楚、纯正的英语，彰显其高贵与庄重。在其一生中，韦伯斯特对农业有很大兴趣，他也十分喜欢户外运动。

沉沦或挣扎，生活或死亡，生存或毁灭，我对我的投票完全虔诚。的确，开始时我们的目的不是独立，但是

“神明决定我们的命运。”

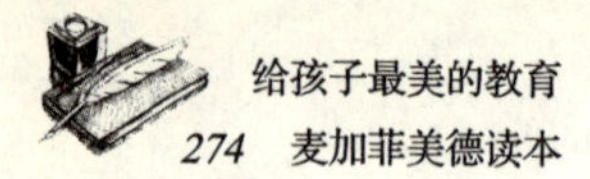

是英格兰的侵犯迫使我们举起武器。而且她被自己的利益蒙蔽了双眼，她负隅顽抗，直到独立就在我们的掌握之中。现在，我们只需倾身向前，它就是我们的了。那么，我们为什么要推迟宣言？哪个男人如此孱弱，仍在希望与英格兰和解？这样做，既不会为国家和它的解放者带来安全，也不会为他自己的生命和荣誉带来任何保障！是不是你，先生，坐在那把椅子里的那位先生（指约翰·汉考克，大陆会议主席），是不是他，坐在你旁边的、我们受人爱戴的同僚（指塞缪尔·亚当斯。在康科德和莱克星顿战役之后，盖奇总督宣布只要起义的人放下武器，就原谅他们，除了约翰·汉考克和塞缪尔·亚当斯之外），你们两个是不是已经注定是惩罚和报复的目标？不要再对皇家的仁爱抱有任何幻想，即使英格兰人仍然当政，他们也是非法的，那时你们是什么？你们能成为什么？

如果我们推迟独立，我们是要继续战争，还是放弃？我们是不是要投降，承认我们应该被碾为粉末，我们的国家和国家的权利应该被踩进泥里？我知道，我们不是要投降，**我们决不应该投降！**难道我们要违背人类最庄严的、我们在上帝面前对华盛顿的诺言？我们曾经许诺说，不论是在危险的战争中，还是在政治灾难中，我们都要将自己的命运和生命交付于他。我知道，这里的每一个人，都宁愿一场大火或地震把我们埋葬，也不愿看到诺言的任何一部分被违背。正是我自己，十二个月前，在这里，说服你们为了美国的解放选举乔治·华盛顿为军队总司令。如果我对给予他的支持稍有犹豫，就让我的手断掉、舌碎掉！

战争必须继续。我们必须坚持战斗。如果战争必须继续，为什么要推迟独立宣言的发表？这样做，会使我们更加团结有力。它会让我们的名声传遍世界。之后，国家会与我们交往，而如果我们承认自己只是拿着武器反对自己君主的臣民，其他国家永远不会这样做。不，如果我们独立，我相信英格兰自己也很快会与我们谋求和平，而不是否定她之前的行为，承认她曾经压迫并虐待过我们。这样，与向她的反叛的臣民屈服相比，她的骄傲也会受到较小伤害。如果能与我们谋求和平解决，她会认为这是命运，而如果她是在与自己叛变的臣民对话，她会感到深深的屈辱。那么，为什么我们不把这场内战变为一场国家战争？而且，既然我们必须坚持战斗，我们为什么不使自己能够享受到所有这些胜利的好处呢？

如果我们失败的话，也不会更糟。但是，我们不会失败。这一事业会带来陆战队，这一事业会带来海军。而人民——如果我们对人民真心相待的话，人民会帮助我们，帮助他们自己完成这场光辉的战斗。我不在乎其他民族是多么无情。我了解这些殖民地上的人民，我了解，对不列颠侵犯的仇视，深植于他们的心中，无法抹去。先生，独立宣言会鼓舞这些人民，使他们的气势更加高涨。持续、血腥的战争，使他们重新获得平等的权利，使正义得到伸张，使豁免权得到承认，从英王的手下，为他们获取完全的独立，这将重新赋予他们生活的意义。

在军队面前宣读这份宣言，士兵们会高擎着剑，庄严发誓誓死捍卫。在教堂的讲台前宣读，信徒们会支持它，人们对宗教自由的热爱会使他们拥护它，决心保卫它。将它张贴在公共礼堂，在那里宣读，他们的儿子和兄弟战死于庞克山的田野里，或莱克星顿和康科德的街道上，现在他们的亲人看到我们的宣言，他们一定会给我们支持。

先生，通过这些天发生的事，我发现事情是多么变幻无常，但是，你和我有朝一日真的可能会对此后悔不已。我们可能等不到独立宣言发表的那一天。我们会死亡，作为殖民地居民死亡，作为奴隶死亡，或者也可能不光彩地死于绞刑架。那么就这样吧，就这样吧。不论何时，如果上天希望我为我的国家献上我卑微的生命，我绝不会犹豫。但在我还活着的时候，让我拥有一个国家吧，或至少让我能盼望一个国家吧，一个**自由**的国家。

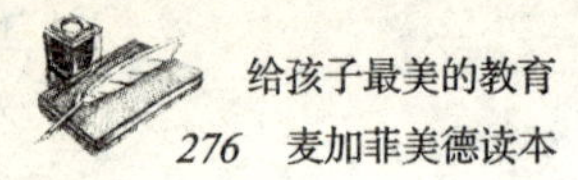

不论我们的命运怎样，请确保宣言矗立不倒。那需要财富，那需要鲜血，但是只要它矗立不倒，无论是财富还是鲜血，都是值得的。透过现实的迷雾，我看到未来的希望，它的光芒像天堂中的太阳。我们能够让它成为辉煌、不朽的一天。当我们已长眠于坟墓，我们的后代会记得。他们会充满感激地用欢宴、篝火和灯彩庆祝。每年的这一天，他们会流下热泪——簌簌而出的热泪，不是因为他们的臣民或奴隶身份，不是因为痛苦或穷困，而是因为喜悦，因为感激，因为欢乐。

先生，在上帝面前，我确信，这一时刻正在到来。我的判断证实了这点，我将所有精力投入其中。我将我所拥有的一切，将我的人格、我的希望都作为赌注。在我开始的那一刻，已经将生死置之度外，现在，我的一切努力都是为了独立宣言。它是我活着的信念，而且，但愿上帝保佑，在我离开尘世时，它仍是我的信念。现在独立，**永远独立**。

Supposed Speech of John Adams

Daniel Webster (b. 1782, d. 1852) was born in Salisbury, N.H. He spent a few months of his boyhood at Phillips Academy, Exeter, but graduated from Dartmouth College in 1801. He taught school several terms, during and after his college course. In 1805, he was admitted to the bar in Boston, and practiced law for the succeeding eleven years. In 1812, he was elected to the United States House of Representatives. In 1816, he removed to Boston, and in 1827 was elected to the United States Senate, which position he held for twelve years. In 1841, he was appointed Secretary of State. In 1850, he was reappointed Secretary of State and continued in office until his death. He died at his residence, in Marshfield, Mass. Mr. Webster's fame rests chiefly on his state papers and speeches. As a speaker he was dignified and stately, using clear, pure English. During all his life he took great interest in agriculture, and was very fond of outdoor sports.

Sink or swim, live or die, survive or perish, I give my hand and my heart to this vote. It is true, indeed, that, in the beginning, we aimed not at independence. But

"There's a divinity that shapes our ends."

The injustice of England has driven us to arms; and blinded to her own interest, she has obstinately persisted, till independence is now within our grasp. We have but to reach forth to it, and it is ours. Why then should we defer the declaration? Is any man so weak as now to hope for a reconciliation with England, which shall leave either safety to the country and its liberties, or security to his own life and his own honor! Are not you, sir, who sit in that chair, is not he, our venerable colleague, near you, are you not both already the proscribed and predestined objects of punishment and of vengeance? Cut off from all hope of royal clemency, what are you, what can you be, while the power of England remains, but outlaws?

If we postpone independence, do we mean to carry on, or to give up, the war? Do we mean to submit, and consent that we shall be ground to powder, and our country and its rights trodden down in the dust? I know we do not mean to submit. We NEVER shall submit! Do we intend to violate that most solemn obligation ever entered into by men, that plighting, before God, of our sacred honor to Washington, when, putting him forth to incur the dangers of war, as well as the political hazards of the times, we promised to adhere to him in every extremity with our fortunes and our lives? I know there is not a man here, who would not rather see a general conflagration sweep over the land, or an earthquake sink it, than one jot or tittle of that plighted faith fall to the ground. For myself, having twelve months ago, in this place, moved you that George Washington be appointed commander of the forces raised, or to be raised, for the defense of American liberty; may my right hand forget her cunning, and my tongue cleave to the roof of my mouth, if I hesitate or waver in the support I give him.

The war, then, must go on. We must fight it through. And if the war must go on, why put off the Declaration of Independence? That measure will strengthen us. It will give us character abroad. Nations will then treat with us, which they never can do while we acknowledge ourselves subjects in arms against our sovereign. Nay, I maintain that England herself will sooner treat for peace with us on the footing of independence, than consent, by repealing her acts, to acknowledge that her whole conduct toward us has been a course of injustice and oppression. Her pride will be less wounded by submitting to that course of things, which now predestinates our independence, than by yielding the points in controversy to her rebellious subjects. The former, she would regard as the result of fortune; the latter, she would feel as her own deep disgrace. Why, then, do we not change this from a civil to a national war? And since we must fight it through, why not put ourselves in a state to enjoy all the benefits of victory, if we gain the victory.

If we fail, it can be no worse for us. But we shall not fail. The cause will raise up armies; the cause will create navies. The people —the people, if we are true to them, will carry us, and will carry themselves, gloriously through this struggle. I care not how fickle other people have been found. I know the people of these colonies; and I know that resistance to British aggression is deep and settled in their hearts, and can not be eradicated. Sir, the Declaration of Independence will inspire the people with increased courage. Instead of a long and bloody war for the restoration of privileges, for redress of grievances, for chartered immunities, held under a British king, set before them the glorious object of entire independence, and it will breathe into

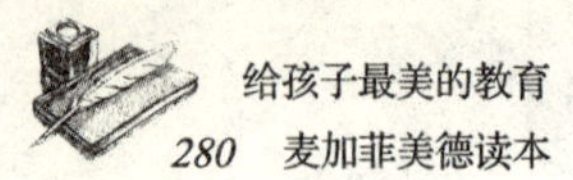

them anew the spirit of life.

Read this declaration at the head of the army; every sword will be drawn, and the solemn vow uttered to maintain it, or perish on the bed of honor. Publish it from the pulpit; religion will approve it, and the love of religious liberty will cling around it, resolved to stand with it or fall with it. Send it to the public halls; proclaim it there; let them see it who saw their brothers and their sons fall on the field of Bunker Hill and in the streets of Lexington and Concord, and the very walls will cry out in its support.

Sir, I know the uncertainty of human affairs, but I see—I see clearly through this day's business. You and I, indeed, may rue it. We may not live to see the time this declaration shall be made good. We may die; die colonists; die slaves; die, it may be, ignominiously and on the scaffold. Be it so: be it so. If it be the pleasure of Heaven that my country shall require the poor offering of my life, the victim shall be ready at the appointed hour of sacrifice, come when that hour may. But while I do live, let me have a country, or at least the hope of a country, and that a FREE country.

But whatever may be our fate, be assured—be assured that this Declaration will stand. It may cost treasure, and it may cost blood; but it will stand, and it will richly compensate for both. Through the thick gloom of the present I see the brightness of the future as the sun in heaven. We shall make this a glorious, an immortal day. When we are in our graves, our children will honor it. They will celebrate it with thanksgiving, with festivity, with bonfires, and illuminations. On its annual return they will shed tears,—copious, gushing tears; not of subjection and slavery, not of agony and distress, but of exultation, of gratitude, and of joy.

Sir, before God I believe the hour is come. My judgment approves the measure, and my whole heart is in it. All that I have, and all that I am, and all that I hope in this life, I am now ready here to stake upon it; and I leave off as I began, that, live or die, survive or perish, I am for the Declaration. It is my living sentiment, and, by the blessing of God, it shall by my dying sentiment; independence now, and INDEPENDENCE FOREVER.

美国独立日

7月4日独立日是美国主要法定节日之一。1776年7月4日，由杰斐逊起草的《独立宣言》在费城大陆会议上正式通过，庄严地宣布美利坚合众国脱离英国而独立。《独立宣言》是具有世界历史意义的伟大文献，通过《独立宣言》的这一天也成为美国人民永远纪念的节日，定为美国独立日。这一天，也是美国的国庆日。每年的独立日这一天，全美大小教堂钟声齐鸣，而头一个敲响的是费城的自由钟。

CHAPTER 7

培养良好的习惯

思想决定行动，行动养成习惯，习惯形成品质，品质决定命运。

——陶行知

一分钟的自白

时间是最公正的裁判。它不会多给一分，也不会少给一秒。它不会给你后悔的机会，因为逝去的永远不会回来。谁能牢牢地抓住它，谁就将自己的命运握在了手里。

我们是微不足道的一分钟，
每个人都有六十只翅膀，
我们用它们在看不见的轨迹上飞翔，
而且一去不返。

我们只是一分钟，但请好好珍惜我们，
关于如何对待我们，我不吐不快，
谁利用了我们，谁就可能多拥有一小时，
谁浪费了我们，就有可能失去一整年。

What the Minutes Say

We are but minutes—little things!
Each one furnished with sixty wings,
With which we fly on our unseen track,
And not a minute ever comes back.

We are but minutes; use us well,
For how we are used we must one day tell.
Who uses minutes, has hours to use;
Who loses minutes, whole years must lose.

弗兰克和沙漏

有些目标你觉得永远也达不到，因为你害怕一步一步地去走。但不积跬步，无以千里。有时候，我们应该学学那小小的水滴，只要坚持认真地做下去，总有水滴石穿的那一天。

弗兰克是一个非常喜欢问问题的小男孩，每当他看到一件新东西，总要围绕它提出一大堆的问题。他妈妈对他总是非常的耐心、和蔼，只要是她认为是弗兰克应该知道的事情，她都会告诉他答案。不过，有时她也会说："孩子，你现在还小，你提出的问题我给你说了你也不理解。等你十岁的时候，你可以再问我这些，我会告诉你的答案的。"当妈妈这样说时，弗兰克就不再追问什么了。他明白，当他提出的问题比较适合时，妈妈总会认真地予以回答的。

弗兰克第一次看到沙漏（古代的一种计时器）时，对它大感兴趣，但他并不知道这是什么。自然，他会跑去问妈妈。

妈妈说："弗兰克，那是沙漏，一般它都是8字形的。人们把沙从一端倒入，让它流过中间的小孔。一个小时能有多少沙子从小孔中漏过，人们就往里面装多少沙子。"

弗兰克看着这细细的沙流，感到很不耐烦，因为里面的沙流得实在是太慢了。“让我来帮它一下，妈妈。”他说，“沙流得太慢了，照这样永远也流不完的。”

“哦，我的儿子，它会流完的，”妈妈微笑着说：“沙子尽管流动得不快，但它却一直在流动。”

“当你观察钟表上的指针时，你会发觉它们走得非常慢。它们的确如此，但你别忘了，它们一直都没停下来过。”

“当你去玩耍时，这些沙子仍在一粒粒地流动，就如钟表指针也在一秒接一秒地走动一样。”

“整整一个晚上，沙漏里的沙子要流经小孔十二次。时钟上的时针会绕表盘转一个整圈。”

“这是因为它们每时每刻都在工作着，它们不会停下来想一想它们必须做多少，做那些工作又将花费多少时间。”

接着，弗兰克的妈妈想让他学一首很短的赞美诗，但他却说：“妈妈，我可学不会那个。”

“如果你一直坚持学习，不要停下来问学会它需要多长时间。你过不了多久便能学会的。”妈妈微笑着鼓励说。

弗兰克听从了母亲的教诲，他一行一行的学习着，学得非常刻苦。一个半小时后，他便完全学会了那首赞美诗。

Frank and the Hourglass

Frank was a very talkative little boy. He never saw a new thing without asking a great many questions about it.

His mother was very patient and kind. When it was proper to answer his questions, she would do so.

Sometimes she would say, "You are not old enough to understand that, my son. When you are ten years old, you may ask me about it, and I will tell you."

When his mother said this, he never teased any more. He knew she always liked to answer him when he asked proper questions.

The first time Frank saw an hourglass, he was very much amused; but he did not know what it was.

His mother said, "An hourglass is made in the shape of the figure 8. The sand is put in at one end, and runs through a small hole in the middle. As much sand is put into the glass as will run through in an hour."

Frank watched the little stream of sand. He was impatient, because it would not run faster. "Let me shake it, mother," said he; "it is lazy, and will never get through."

"Oh yes, it will, my son," said his mother, "The sand moves by little and little, but it moves all the time.

"When you look at the hands of the clock, you think they go very slowly, and so they do; but they never stop.

"While you are at play the sand is running, grain by grain, The hands of the clock are moving, second by second.

"At night, the sand in the hourglass has run through twelve times. The hour hand of the clock has moved all around its great face.

"This because they keep work every minute. They do not stop to think how much they have to do, and how long it will take them to do it."

Now, Frank's mother wanted him to learn a little hymn; but he said "Mother, I can never learn it."

His mother said, "Study all the time. Never stop to ask how long it will take to learn it. You will be able to say it very soon."

Frank followed his mother's advice. He studied line after line, very busily; and in one hour and a half he knew the hymn perfectly.

人生格言

当许多人在一条路上徘徊不前时，他们不得不让开一条大路，让那珍惜时间的人赶到他们的前面去。

——[古希腊]苏格拉底

不管饕餮的时间怎样吞噬着一切，我们要在这一息尚存的时候，努力博取我们的声誉，使时间的镰刀不能伤害我们。

——[英]莎士比亚

敢于浪费哪怕一个钟头时间的人，说明他还不懂得珍惜生命的全部价值。

——[英]达尔文

和蔼地说话

语言是我们与人沟通的重要工具。同样的话用不同的语气说出来，会对人产生不同的效果。语气轻柔不仅是良好修养的表现，也会使沟通变得更加容易。

和蔼地说话，让人感到爱比让人感到恐惧要好的多，不要让尖利的话语淹没我们原来的好意。

对孩子要轻声地说话，给他播下爱的种子，你会得到他的爱。如果大声地叱责，教育的效果不会长久。

对老人要轻声地说话，不要让这颗饱经风霜的心再感到悲伤，而使他丧失生活的勇气。生命之沙就要流尽，让老人们过一个平和的晚年吧。

对穷人要友善地讲话，不要用粗鲁的话语。他们已经承受了太多的不幸，不需要刻薄的语言。

对犯了错的人要和蔼地说话，他们一定有些愚蠢的举动，但也许那正是我们不友善的态度使他们这样做的。哦，让我们帮助他们吧，使他们重返我们的身边。

和蔼地讲话，它是我们心灵深处的一件小事，但它会给我们带来欢乐和益处，这是一条永恒不变的真理。

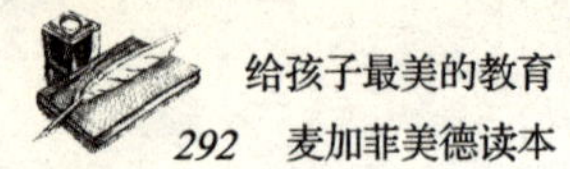

Speak Gently

Speak gently; it is better far
To rule by love than fear:
Speak gently; let no harsh words mar
The good we might do here.

Speak gently to the little child;
Its love be sure to gain;
Teach it in accents soft and mild;
It may not long remain.

Speak gently to the aged one;
Grieve not the careworn heart:
The sands of life are nearly run;
Let such in peace depart.

Speak gently, kindly, to the poor;
Let no harsh tone be heard;

They have enough they must endure,
Without an unkind word.

Speak gently to the erring; know
They must have toiled in vain;
Perhaps unkindness made them so;
Oh, win them back again.

Speak gently: 'tis a little thing
Dropped in the heart's deep well;
The good, the joy, which it may bring,
Eternity shall tell.

领子的奥妙

蓝领（Blue collar），指产业工人或服务行业的工人等体力劳动者，源于他们常着蓝色工装；

白领（White collar），指以从事脑力劳动为主的办公室工作人员，他们经常穿着白衬衣；

灰领（Gray collar），指服务性行业职工或技术维修人员，他们的工装多为灰色；

金领（Gold collar），指新型知识工人，如高级工程师、软件开发者、律师等；

粉领（Pink collar），指职业妇女或女性工人；

钢领（Steel collar），特指机器人。

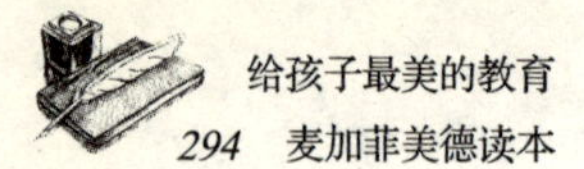

学会思考

任何知识都需要经过自己的思考才能成为自己的财富。否则，它们就会像刮过的风儿一样，你曾经感受到它，但却不曾留住它。

思考是一个学习的过程，也是一个探索的过程，正是因为人类不断地在进行思考，才促成了世界的进步。你不想把握住自己人生的发动机吗？

“学会思考”，这说起来很容易，但你知道那些源于思考的重要发现吗？我们的思维看不见，听不着，任何人都无法感知到它，但它们却有着意想不到的力量。

在一个夏日的黄昏，艾萨克·牛顿先生坐花园里，突然他看见一只苹果从树上掉了下来。他开始思考，苹果为什么会从树上掉下来。最终他发现了为什么地球、太阳、月亮和星星可以保持相对位置的规律。

一个名叫詹姆斯·瓦特的小男孩静静地坐在火炉边，观察着上下跳动的茶壶盖。他开始思考，他想知道为什么水蒸气可以使沉重的壶盖移动。他从那时起就一直思考着这个问题。长大之后，他改进了蒸汽式发动机，使它很容易就可以做需要许多匹马才能够完成的工作。

当你看到一艘汽船、一间蒸汽磨房、一辆蒸汽机头时，记住，如果没有人冥思苦想，它们是绝对不会被制造出来的。

曾经有一个叫伽利略的人站在比萨的大教堂内，对往复摆动的吊灯产生了浓厚的兴趣。这启发他思考，终于发明了摆钟。

詹姆斯·弗格森是苏格兰一名穷困的牧羊人。一次，他看过手表的内部构造后，对此产生了浓厚的兴趣。“我为什么不能做手表呢？”他想。但是上哪儿去弄那些制造齿轮和发条的材料呢？不久，他就发现了如何能得到它们。他用一根鲸须做成发条，最终他制成了一块走得很准的木制手表。与此同时，他还用钢笔为人作画，用油彩给人画像。几年后，还是个孩子的他就已经能够养活自己的父亲了。

长大后，他去了伦敦。英国一些博学人士包括国王本人都经常去聆听他的讲学。他的座右铭就是：“学会思考”。他用勤奋的思考为自己和这个世界做了许多有益的事情。

朋友，当你学习一门很难懂的课程时，千万别灰心。在请教别人之前，应该先自己帮助自己，思考，只有思考能帮助你学会如何去解决问题。

I Will Think of It

"I will think of it." It is easy to say this; but do you know what great things have come from thinking?

We can not see our thoughts, or hear, or taste, or feel them; and yet what mighty power they have!

Sir Isaac Newton was seated in his garden on a summer's evening, when he saw an apple fall from a tree. He began to think, and, in trying to find out why the apple fell, discovered how the earth, sun, moon, and stars are kept in their places.

A boy named James Watt sat quietly by the fireside, watching the lid of the tea kettle as it moved up and down. He began to think; he wanted to find out why the steam in the kettle moved the heavy lid.

From that time he went on thinking and thinking; and when he became a man, he improved the steam engine so much that it could, with the greatest ease, do the work of many horses.

When you see a steamboat, a steam mill, or a locomotive, remember that it would never have been built if it had not been for the hard thinking of some one.

A man named Galileo was once standing in the cathedral of Pisa, when he saw a chandelier swaying to and fro. This set him thinking, and it led to the invention of the pendulum.

James Ferguson was a poor Scotch shepherd boy. Once, seeing the inside of a watch, he was filled with wonder. "Why should I not make a watch?" thought he.

But how was he to get the materials out of which to make the wheels and the mainspring? He soon found how to get them: he made the mainspring out of a piece of whalebone. He then made a wooden clock which kept good time.

He began, also, to copy pictures with a pen, and portraits with oil colors. In a few years, while still a small boy, he earned money enough to support his father.

When he became a man, he went to London to live. Some of the wisest men in England, and the king himself, used to attend his lectures. His motto was, "I will think of it;" and he made his thoughts useful to himself and the world.

Boys, when you have a difficult lesson to learn, don't feel discouraged, and ask some one to help you before helping yourselves. Think, and by thinking you will learn how to think to some purpose.

玛丽的坏习惯

要改变世界，首先就得先改变自己。一些坏习惯，虽说很微小，但很可能给自己带来意想不到的伤害。好的习惯会慢慢变成美德，而坏的习惯就如同蚁穴，时刻威胁着人生的堤岸。

玛丽·阿姆斯特朗是一个可爱的小姑娘，但是她有一些坏习惯。她总是把她的书和玩具随处乱丢，妈妈总要花费很多的时间和精力，跟在她屁股后面收拾东西，将它们放回原来的地方。

妈妈经常告诉玛丽这样做不好，但妈妈的话，玛丽总是听不进去。所以，玛丽的书总是缺张少页的，玩具也经常被弄坏。更糟的是，她变得越来越粗心大意了。这给她和她的生活带来了很大的麻烦。不但会让她自己不开心，还会惹恼她的朋友们。

直到有一天，事情才发生了变化。

那天，玛丽和妈妈来到院子里。妈妈晒着太阳，忙着手里的活，玛丽则跑来跑去，兴高采烈地和她的宠物狗德西一起玩耍。玛丽觉得痛快极了。

突然，玛丽在院子的一个角落里发现一个破烂的洋娃娃，那是自己最心爱的那个。可是现在，娃娃的衣服被扯得七零八落，上面沾满了泥土。

“德西，这一定是你干的好事！”玛丽太气愤了，真想好好地教训德西一顿。

玛丽哭着把扯破的洋娃娃拿给妈妈看，她是如此悲伤，大滴大滴的眼泪像豆子一样落了下来。

妈妈说：“你一定是把洋娃娃丢在德西容易够到的地方了，对吗？”

“我想是的，妈妈。”玛丽不好意思地回答。

“那你怎么能责怪德西呢？它只是一条小狗，它并不知道洋娃娃不能这样玩。这是个教训！如果你不希望再发生这样的事情，那么你的玩具玩完后，都应该放到它们应该在的地方。”

“我会这样做的，”玛丽说，“我发誓。”

就这样，玛丽改正了她的坏习惯。而洋娃娃，经过妈妈精心地修补，也几乎和以前一样漂亮了。

女童子军誓言

以我的名义宣誓，我将努力：
恪尽职守，报效国家，
时时处处助人为乐，
遵守女童子军法令。

The Torn Doll

Mary Armstrong was a pretty little girl, but she was heedless about some things.

Her way of leaving her books and playthings just where she had used them last, gave her mother much trouble in picking them up and putting them in their proper places.

She had often told Mary the evil effects of being so careless. Her books became spoiled, and her toys broken.

But worse than this was the growing habit of carelessness, which would be of great harm to her all her life. It would make her unhappy, and would annoy her friends.

One day Mary and her mother went out into their pleasant yard, to spend an hour in the open air. Mrs. Armstrong took her work with her.

Mary ran about and played with Dash, her pet dog, and was having a happy time.

But in a corner of the yard she found her nicest doll all torn and broken, and its dress covered with mud.

She knew, at once, that Dash had done this, and she scolded him harshly.

Carrying the broken doll to her mamma. she showed it to her, and could hardly keep from crying.

Mrs. Armstrong asked Mary if she had not left the doll on the porch where Dash could easily get it; and Mary had to answer, "Yes, ma'am."

"Then you must not blame the dog, Mary, for he does not know it is wrong for him to play with your doll. I hope this will be a lesson to you hereafter, to put your things away when you are through playing."

"I will try," said Mary. And her mother promised to mend the doll as well as she could.

女童子军军法

我将努力做到：

诚实

公正

乐于助人

精神振奋

友善体贴

与其他女童子军亲如姐妹

尊重权威

善用智谋

保护和改善周围环境

言谈举止尊重他人和自己

小木匠约翰

美好的生活不是靠别人给予的，而是靠自己去争取。在奋斗的过程中，所有的伤心与喜悦，都会变成人生中的财富，这些财富，是无法用金钱衡量的。

约翰不喜欢买别人做好的玩具，他喜欢自己动手做，这是因为他从中获得了许多乐趣。

汤姆·奥斯丁是他的一个玩伴，他认为，除非是用很多钱买来的玩具，其他的都不值一提。他也从来不尝试做任何玩具，他的玩具全是买来的。

“快来看看我的木马，”一天汤姆说，“它花了我一美元，多漂亮啊，快来看啊。”

约翰非常羡慕自己的好朋友汤姆能买这样漂亮的木马。他仔细观察着这匹木马，想看看它是如何做成的，当天晚上他就开始为自己做一匹木马。

他来到他的木棚里，取出两块木料，一块用来做马头，另一块用来做马身，他花了两三天时间，便把它们变成了自己满意的形状。

他父亲送给他一块红色的皮革来做马的缰绳，还有一些铜片来做马蹄。母亲给他找出一些旧毛线用来做马鬃和马尾。

但是拿什么来做轮子呢，这可把他难住了。最终他想，应该到加工厂去一下，看看那里是否有一些可以用来做轮子的圆形木头。

他在地板上找到了许多他想要的木头。车工问他拿去做什么，约翰告诉他自己正在做木马的事。

“哦，”那人笑着说，“如果是这样，我乐意为你的马做几个轮子，但是记住，做好后要让我看看它。”约翰点头答应了他，然后将轮子装入口袋里，便跑回家了。第二天晚上，他便带着他做好的木马去了加工厂那里，车工夸他是一个天才的小家伙。

这样的赞扬使他感到很骄傲，他跑到朋友汤姆那里喊着说：“现在你看，这是我的木马。”

“哦，这匹马真漂亮，你在哪儿买的？”汤姆问。

“我不是买的，是我自己做的！”约翰答道。

“你自己做的？的确是一匹漂亮的马，不过还是没有我的好，我的那匹值一美元，而你的却一文不值。”

“但我在做这匹木马的过程中很开心呀。”说完，约翰带着自己的木马离开了汤姆。

你想知道约翰后来的情况吗？好吧，我告诉你。他在学校里学习非常刻苦，并称为班里最有学问的人。他离开学校后，到了一家机械厂工作。尽管他现在只是一名雇工，但不久的将来他一定会有一家自己的工厂。

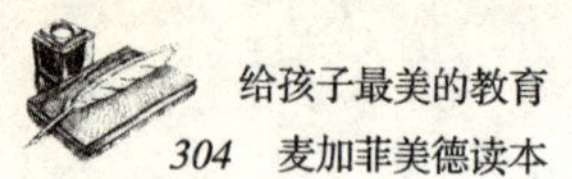

John Carpenter

John Carpenter did not like to buy toys that somebody else had made. He liked the fun of making them himself. The thought that they were his own work delighted him.

Tom Austin, one of his playmates, thought a toy was worth nothing unless it cost a great deal of money. He never tried to make anything, but bought all his toys.

"Come and look at my horse," said he, one day. "It cost a dollar, and it is such a beauty! Come and see it."

John was soon admiring his friend's horse; and he was examining it carefully, to see how it was made. The same evening he began to make one for himself.

He went into the wood shed, and picked out two pieces of wood—one for the head of his horse, the other for the body. It took him two or three days to shape them to his satisfaction.

His father gave him a bit of red leather for a bridle, and a few brass nails, and his mother found a bit of old fur with which he made a mane and tail for his horse.

But what about the wheels? This puzzled him. At last he thought he would go to a turner's shop, and see if he could not get some round pieces of wood which might suit his purpose.

He found a large number of such pieces among the shavings on the floor, and asked permission to take a few of them. The turner asked him what he wanted them for, and he told him about his horse.

"Oh," said the man, laughing, "if you wish it, I will make some wheels for your horse. But mind, when it is finished, you must let me see it."

John promised to do so, and he soon ran home with the wheels in his pocket. The next evening, he went to the turner's shop with his horse all complete, and was told that he was an ingenious little fellow.

Proud of this compliment, he ran to his friend Tom, crying, "Now then, Tom, here is my horse,—look!"

"Well, that is a funny horse," said Tom; "where did you buy it?" "I did n't buy it," replied John; I made it."

"You made it yourself! Oh, well, it's a good horse for you to make. But it is not so good as mine. Mine cost a dollar, and yours did n't cost anything."

"It was real fun to make it, though," said John, and away he ran with his horse rolling after him.

Do you want to know what became of John? Well, I will tell you. He studied hard in school, and was called the best scholar in his class. When he left school, he went to work in a machine shop. He is now a master workman, and will soon have a shop of his own.

艾米没有赚到的钱

如果只是空想，那么再美好的梦也只能是一个梦。机会只会垂青那些目标明确，行动迅速的人，生活并不会按照你计划的那样展开，除非你依照计划迅速采取行动。

艾米是一个可爱的姑娘，却有一个坏习惯，在做一件事时，不是立刻行动，而是把时间浪费在了准备工作上。

在她住的村子里，索顿先生开了一个水果店，里面卖一些本地产的莓子等各种水果。一天，索顿先生对家境贫苦的艾米说："你想挣点钱吗？"

"哦，当然，"她回答，"我想买双新鞋，可是家里没有钱。"

"好的，艾米。"索顿先生说，"我今天在格林家的牧场里看到有许多很好的成熟的黑莓，他们允许任何人去采摘。我会为你摘到的每一夸脱黑莓付你十三美分。"

艾米想到能挣到钱，高兴极了。于是她飞快地跑回家，拿了一个篮子，打算立刻去摘莓子。

这时，她想最好先算一下采五夸脱黑莓能挣多少钱。于是她拿出石板和铅笔，算出来是六十五美分。

“如果我能采十二夸脱呢？”她盘算着，“那我能赚多少钱？”

“天哪，”她算了一下，“我可以挣一美元五十六美分呢。”

艾米又算了下去，如果她采摘五十、一百、两百夸脱时，索顿先生会付给她多少钱。就为算这些花费了她不少时间，很快就到了中午吃饭的时候，她不得不下午再去了。

吃过饭，她就匆忙地拿起篮子赶往牧场。许多男孩子在午饭前就已经在那里了，好的莓子几乎被摘光了。可怜的小艾米最后连一夸脱都没有摘到。

在回家的路上，艾米想起了老师常对她讲的话：“做事情要趁早着手，做完了再去想。因为一个实干者顶得上一百个幻想家”。

男童子军誓言

以我的名誉宣誓，我将竭尽全力：
恪尽职守，报效国家，
遵守童子军法令，
时时处处助人为乐，
体魄强壮，
头脑清醒，
品行端正。

The Money Amy Didn't Earn

Amy was a dear little girl, but she was too apt to waste time in getting ready to do her tasks, instead of doing them at once as she ought.

In the village in which she lived, Mr. Thornton kept a store where he sold fruit of all kinds, including berries in their season. One day he said to Amy, whose parents were quite poor, "Would you like to earn some money? "

"Oh, yes," replied she, "for I want some new shoes, and papa has no money to buy them with."

"Well, Amy," said Mr. Thorhton, "I noticed some fine, ripe blackberries in Mr. Green's pasture to–day, and he said that anybody was welcome to them. I will pay you thirteen cents a quart for all you will pick for me."

Amy was delighted at the thought of earning some money; so she ran home to get a basket, intending to go immediately to pick the berries.

Then she thought she would like to know how much money she would get if she picked five quarts. With the help of her slate and pencil, she found out that she would get sixty–five cents.

"But supposing I should pick a dozen quarts," thought she, "how much should I earn then?" "Dear me," she said, after figuring a while, "I should earn a dollar and fifty-six cents."

Amy then found out what Mr. Thornton would pay her for fifty, a hundred, and two hundred quarts. It took her some time to do this, and then it was so near dinner time that she had to stay at home until afternoon.

As soon as dinner was over, she took her basket and hurried to the pasture. Some boys had been there before dinner, and all the ripe berries were picked. She could not find enough to fill a quart measure.

As Amy went home, she thought of what her teacher had often told her—"Do your task at once; then think about it," for "one doer is worth a hundred dreamers."

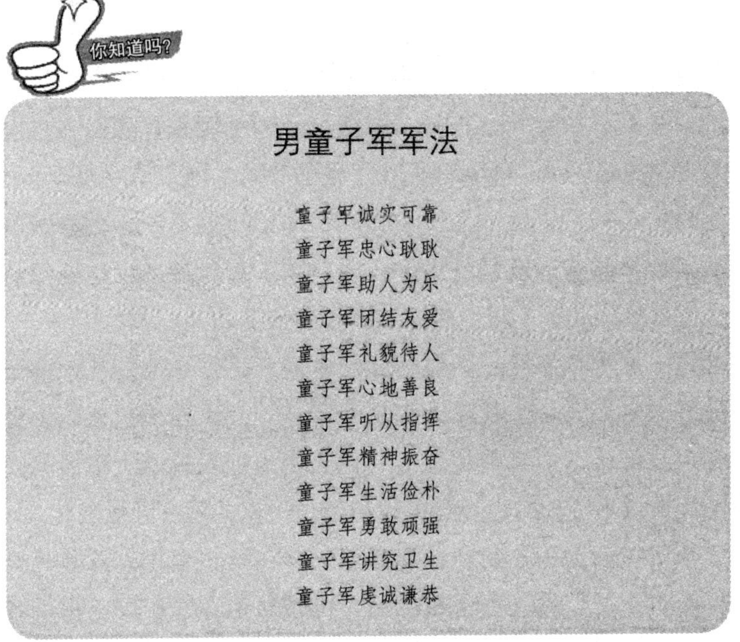

男童子军军法

童子军诚实可靠
童子军忠心耿耿
童子军助人为乐
童子军团结友爱
童子军礼貌待人
童子军心地善良
童子军听从指挥
童子军精神振奋
童子军生活俭朴
童子军勇敢顽强
童子军讲究卫生
童子军虔诚谦恭

优秀的朗诵者

说话是一门艺术，是展示自己的最好舞台，再好的想法与激情都需要语言将其展现出来，而语言的魔力也会感染他人。

在人生的战场上，语言就是始终陪伴在我们身边的士兵。人生的战役如何打响，就看你怎么操控这些忠诚的小家伙们了。

传说有一天，普鲁士国王弗雷德里克正坐在他的私人房间里。这时，士兵呈上一份诉状，等候国王御批。国王刚刚打猎回来，也许是强烈的阳光或是其他什么东西弄花了他的眼睛，他一个字也看不清。

他的私人秘书正好不在，呈递诉状的士兵也不识字。宫殿里有一位侍从，他是国王最喜爱的男仆，于是国王传他过来。这位侍从是朝廷中一位贵族的儿子，但他的朗读能力非常差劲儿。

首先，他发音不清，当他朗读的时候，总喜欢把好几个词挤在一起，就好像它们是一个长单词的几个音节，必须尽快把它们读完了。他发音也不准确，而且他从来不变化声调，别人根本听不懂他朗读的东西是什么意思。他的声音低沉而单调，一点儿没有起伏变化。

“停下！”国王不耐烦地说道，“你在读拍卖物品清单吗？把你的同伴叫过来。”站在门旁边的另一位侍从走过来，国王把诉状交给他。这第二位侍从非常做作地嗽了嗽嗓子，这让国王开玩笑地问他，他昨晚是不是在公共花园里敞着门睡的觉。

但是，这位侍从非常自负，没有理睬国王的嘲笑，他决心不犯他的同伴所犯的错误。于是他开始慢慢地、故弄玄虚地朗读诉状，拖着长音，着重强调每个词。他这样子太令人生厌了，国王嚷道："停下！你在读幼儿识字课本吗？滚出去！不，等等，留下来！把坐在喷泉旁边的那个小女孩叫到我这儿来。"

国王指的这个小女孩是皇家花园园丁雇佣的一位工人的女儿，她是来帮助父亲播撒花种的。就像普鲁士的很多穷人一样，她受过良好的教育。她被带到国王面前，显得有些惊慌。国王告诉她，他的眼睛不好，希望她能帮他朗读诉状，小女孩这才开始平静下来。

欧内斯婷（小女孩的名字）喜欢大声朗读，很多邻居经常围在她父亲的房子周围，听她朗读。那些自己无法阅读的人，在收到远方亲戚或孩子的来信时，也经常来找她帮忙，所以她逐渐形成了很好的习惯，能熟练而清楚地朗读各种笔迹的内容。

国王将诉状递给她，她先快速浏览了一下开头，了解一下诉状的大概内容。她看着看着，眼睛开始闪闪发亮，胸脯上下起伏。"怎么了？"国王问道，"你到底知不知道怎样朗读？""哦，当然，陛下，"她回答道，还没忘了用人们习惯的头衔称呼他，"如果可以的话，我现在就读。"

两位侍从想离开房间。"留下！"国王命令道。小女孩开始朗读诉状。诉状是一位可怜的寡妇写的，她唯一的儿子应征入伍，但他的身体不好，难以适应军营生活。他的志向也不在于此。他的父亲在一场战役中牺牲了，儿子非常想做一位肖像画家。

这位寡妇以简单、朴素的语言讲述了她的故事，感人至深。欧内斯婷朗读的时候也倾注了很多感情，吐字不紧不慢，音调纯正清楚，等她读完的时候，国王眼里已满是泪水。他说："啊！现在我明白了，但是，如果我让那两位年轻的绅士给我读的话，我就永远不会明白这篇诉状的意思。现在，我将命令他们用一年时间去学习朗读，这段时间内他们不用来为我服务。”

“至于你，年轻的女士，”国王接着说，“我知道，对你来说最好的奖赏就是派你去向这位可怜的寡妇传达我的旨意，立即免除她儿子的兵役。让我看看，你的书写能力是不是与你的朗读能力一样优秀。给你这支笔，照我说的写。”然后他口授了一道命令，欧内斯婷写完，他签了字。然后他叫来一位士兵，命令士兵护送女孩完成命令。

欧内斯婷用自己的朗读能力帮助了别人，而且受到了国王的赏识，她多么高兴呀！首先，对于那些穷苦的邻居，她可以教给他们知识，或者让他们开心。而那个写诉状的可怜寡妇，现在不仅她的儿子回到了她身边，而且他还奉命为国王画像。这样，这个男孩很快就出名了，很多人请他为自己画像，他都快忙不过来了。他和他的母亲对小女孩的感激之情是无法用语言表达的。

欧内斯婷还帮助了她的父亲，他成了国王的首席园丁。国王当然也没有忘记她，他亲自支付她所有的学费，让她接受良好的教育。至于那两位侍从，她也间接帮助了他们。他们对自己差劲的朗读水平感到非常羞愧，因此开始如饥似渴地学习，最后终于克服了最初的缺点。后来，他们两个人一个成了一名律师，另一个成了一位政治家，两个人都很有名气，而他们的成就，主要归功于他们优秀的演说能力。

The Good Reader

It is told of Frederick the Great, King of Prussia, that, as he was seated one day in his private room, a written petition was brought to him with the request that it should be immediately read.

The King had just returned from hunting, and the glare of the sun, or some other cause, had so dazzled his eyes that he found it difficult to make out a single word of the writing.

His private secretary happened to be absent; and the soldier who brought the petition could not read. There was a page, or favorite boy servant, waiting in the hall, and upon him the King called. The page was a son of one of the noblemen of the court, but proved to be a very poor reader.

In the first place, he did not articulate distinctly. He huddled his words together in the utterance, as if they were syllables of one long word, which he must get through with as speedily as possible. His pronunciation was bad, and he did not modulate his voice so as to bring out the meaning of what he read. Every sentence was uttered with a dismal monotony of voice, as if it did not differ in any respect from that which preceded it.

"Stop!" said the King, impatiently. "Is it an auctioneer's list of goods to be sold that you are hurrying over? Send your companion to me." Another page who stood at the door now entered, and to him the King gave the petition. The second page began by hemming and clearing his throat in such an affected manner that the King jokingly asked him whether he had not slept in the public garden, with the gate open, the night before.

The second page had a good share of self-conceit, however, and so was not greatly confused by the King's jest. He determined that he would avoid the mistake which his comrade had made. So he commenced reading the petition slowly and with great formality, emphasizing every word, and prolonging the articulation of every syllable. But his manner was so tedious that the King cried out, "Stop! are you reciting a lesson in the elementary sounds? Out of the room! But no: stay! Send me that little girl who is sitting there by the fountain."

The girl thus pointed out by the King was a daughter of one of the laborers employed by the royal gardener; and she had come to help her father weed the flower beds. It chanced that, like many of the poor people in Prussia, she had received a good education. She was somewhat alarmed when she found herself in the King's presence, but took courage when the King told her that he only wanted her to read for him, as his eyes were weak.

Now, Ernestine (for this was the name of the little girl) was fond of reading aloud, and often many of the neighbors would assemble at her father's house to hear her; those who could not read themselves would come to her, also, with their letters from distant friends or children, and she thus formed the habit of reading various sorts of handwriting promptly and well.

The King gave her the petition, and she rapidly glanced through the opening lines to get some idea of what it was about. As she read, her eyes began to glisten, and her breast to heave. "What is the matter?" asked the King; "don't you know how to read?" "Oh, yes! sire," she replied, addressing him with the title usually applied to him: "I will now read it, if you please."

The two pages wore about to leave the room. "Remain," said the King. The little girl began to read the petition. It was from a poor widow, whose only son had been drafted to serve in the army, although his health was delicate and his pursuits had been such as to unfit him for military life. His father had been killed in battle, and the son had a strong desire to become a portrait painter.

The writer told her story in a simple, concise manner, that carried to the heart a belief of its truth; and Ernestine read it with so much feeling, and with an articulation so just, in tones so pure and distinct, that when she had finished, the King, into whose eyes the tears had started, exclaimed, "Oh! now I understand what it is all about; but I might never have known, certainly I never should have felt, its meaning had I trusted to these young gentlemen, whom I now dismiss from my service for one year, advising them to occupy their time in learning to read."

"As for you, my young lady," continued the King, "I know you will ask no better reward for your trouble than the pleasure of carrying to this poor widow my order for her son's immediate discharge. Let me see whether you can write as well as you can read. Take this pen, and write as I dictate." He then dictated an order, which Ernestine wrote, and he

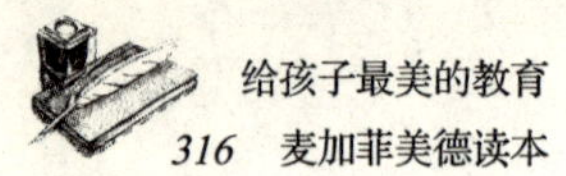

signed. Calling one of his guards, he bade him go with the girl and see that the order was obeyed.

How much happiness was Ernestine the means of bestowing through her good elocution, united to the happy circumstance that brought it to the knowledge of the King! First, there were her poor neighbors, to whom she could give instruction and entertainment. Then, there was the poor widow who sent the petition, and who not only regained her son, but received through Ernestine an order for him to paint the King's likeness; so that the poor boy soon rose to great distinction, and had more orders than he could attend to. Words could not express his gratitude, and that of his mother, to the little girl.

And Ernestine had, moreover, the satisfaction of aiding her father to rise in the world, so that he became the King's chief gardener. The King did not forget her, but had her well educated at his own expense. As for the two pages, she was indirectly the means of doing them good, also; for, ashamed of their bad reading, they commenced studying in earnest, till they overcame the faults that had offended the King. Both finally rose to distinction, one as a lawyer, and the other as a statesman; and they owed their advancement in life chiefly to their good elocution.

如何去阅读

诺亚·波特（1811～1892），出生于康涅狄格州法明顿。波特于1831年毕业于耶鲁大学，毕业后留在纽黑文，一边在耶鲁大学担任指导老师，一边在神学院读书，一直到1836年他担任牧师为止。1846年，波特被耶鲁大学召回，并担任伦理学和纯粹哲学教授。他于1858年又担任神学系教授，长达七年之久。1871年，耶鲁大学校长伍尔西退休，波特当选为耶鲁大学第十一任校长，直到1886年。

《人类的智慧：关于哲学和人类的灵魂》是波特校长最优秀的著作。这本书不但展现出清晰的思考和明智的判断，还有作者宽广的学识。因此被认为是“用人类语言所能表述的关于人类灵魂认知能力的最完全与详尽的展示”。他的其他重要著作有：《自然科学和人文科学》，这是对赫伯特·斯宾塞的经济学说的重新探讨；《美国大学和美国政府》；《书籍和阅读》，本文就是从此书中节选出来的。除了这些，波特还在期刊上发表了数量众多的论文等。在他的教授生涯，他最重要的工作就是作为《韦伯斯特辞典》的首席编辑对辞典进行修订。1864年，在波特认真的主持之下，编辑工作完成。《韦伯斯特辞典》之后的版本修订工作也在其主持下进行。

在读书的时候，向我们自己提出一个确定的目标和意图是非常好的一种做法。在读书时，我们越是明白我们自己想要知道的和期望知道的，我们获得的知识就越持久和确定。所以说，在读书的时候，我们要形成一个良好的习惯，我们要不断地问自己："我为什么要读这本书、散文，或诗歌？或者我为什么要现在读这本书，而不是在其他任何时候？"也许我们能获得一个比较满意的回答，因为这时候读比较方便；这本书刚好在我们手边，或者读这本书仅仅是为了打发时间。这些理由通常来说都是没问题的，但这些理由不应该总是让我们感到满意。但就是这么一个提出这些问题的习惯——无论这些问题我们是否能够给出一个满意的回答，会让我们说出我们读书的原因，从而使我们更有责任感，使我们变得更加有才智。

我们的这种某种目标或目的的清楚意识能够激起对任何书本内容的极大兴趣。这种意识赋予读者一定的力量、一种吸引力，就是由于这吸引力的存在，才使得读者专心致志、一心一意地读书，使读者不知不觉地朝着他所预定的目标努力。任何一个人，只要他读一个故事的目的是向另外一个朋友讲述，或者读一篇论文或者报告的目的是为了在辩论中能够引经据典，或者读一首诗的目的是为了获得一种意境，吟诵它最好的诗句，这样的人都能够意识到这一点。事实上，一般来说，只有带有一定目的，即便有时并不是为了直接的应用的读书方式才是最有效的。

历史上每一个自学成功的人，从富兰克林到以前的人，证实他们不仅仅学习认真刻苦，而且还对他们的读物有一定的"选择"，他们选择那些能够用得上的书，他们每个人在选择书本的时候都有一个明确的目的。事实上，大多数自学成功的人之所以在读书方面能够比接受他人训练的人更加有效或者更成功，就是因为他们知道自己读书和学习的目的，有确定的目标。那些随便什么、不管三七二十一，什么都拿来读的读者，同时又是一个毫无目的、被动的读者，主要是为他的好奇心所驱使，因此他永远也不会成为一个卓有成效的读者。

另外一个良好的习惯就是坚持不懈地读下去。身边总是放着一本厚厚的书，一天天或一小时一小时地持续读下去，直到读完为止。尽管许多成功的读者并没有这样做，但这也是一个非常有效的读书方法。

一天大清早，本人曾经去拜访一个兴趣广泛、不屈不挠的现代旅行家，同他一起步行到一个遥远的村子里去。吃过了早饭之后，尽管这个旅行家仅仅有几分钟可以利用的时间，他还是坐下来读着一本书——一本非常厚的历史书，这本书他几乎每天都要读。他说，“在我多年的旅途当中，我一直这样读书，这已经成了我的读书习惯。这种习惯使我的知识更加丰富，并使我的生活更加丰富多彩。只有通过这种方法，在每日变换的人和风景之前，我才能克服挥霍时光、注意力不集中的倾向。

我们已经明确了一点——读书需要有明确的目标。我们还可以加上一条——让你的手中随时牢牢地握着一本书，除非为了休息而停止工作，或者为了享受生活而去放松、娱乐的时候。有句话说的好，始终将一块铁放在炉火中，每天至少一次去照看下炉子。

前边还提及读者在读书的时候一定要有一个明确的主题，用一定的方法或比例来选择图书。如果目前我们只有一个目标，那这个目标就有必要指定我们选择什么样的书本来读，并根据这一核心来安排我们的读书计划。

对我们来说，如果有多个主题看起来都很重要，也都能引起我们的兴趣的话，那么我们就应当一个接一个地去完成。这种道理是不言而喻的。“一次做一件事情”，对所有的活动都是一种最为有效的方法，无论是对于做事，还是思考问题，还是读书。如果五个或者十个分散的主题吸引了我们同等的兴趣，如果我们要将每一个都当做一个

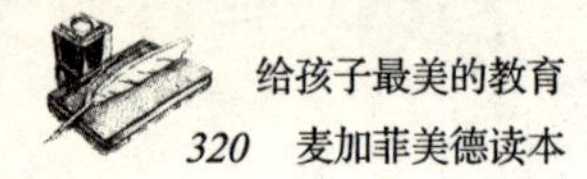

阅读的中心主题，那每一个主题都应该有足够的理由。否则很容易产生厌倦的危险。

大多数单一的主题要求阅读相当数量的书本，每一本书都与其他书本不同，每一本书又都是其他书本的补充。在这种情况下，阅读每一个能够帮助我们理解这个主题的作者的作品将是最好的方法之一。比如说，如果我们现在正在阅读《英国叛乱史》，如果可能的话，我们就不应当只读一个作者的作品，如克拉伦登的作品，我们还应当阅读另外六七个或者十多个作者的作品，他们当中的每一个都会站在自己的角度去写这些历史，他们当中的一个会补充另一个作者省略掉的，或者其中的一个纠正另外一个作者的说法。

当然，除了比较正式的历史著作外，还有各种小说，即以那个时代的人物为背景的小说，如斯科特的《伍德斯托克》；还有日记，如那些由伊夫林、佩皮斯和伯顿写的日记；还有随笔集，如由哈钦森写的随笔；另外，还有诗歌，如安德鲁·迈威尔、弥尔顿和德莱顿写的诗；除了以上提到的外，还有多如牛毛的传单、小册子、招贴和讽刺漫画等。

我们提到这些各种不同的作品和各种类别的读物，不是因为所有这些对于那些远离公共图书馆的读者来说都是唾手可得的，或者因为我们建议那些可以借阅到这些书的读者都把这些书拿来读，而是因为我们要说明众多的读物与阅读材料是如何围绕一个主题、在一个时期去分类的。

每一个人必须判断他解决一个单一主题需要多长时间，或者关于这个主题的书有多少需要去读才是最明智的一种做法。但对于这一点，每个人都可以确保：越容易做越好，越合适越好，越节省时间与精力越好，只有这样，才能集中注意力在一定的时间内对某一主题进行研究。阅读一些与主题相关的、为数不多的书本要比阅读众多的、与主题不大相关的书本有趣、有效得多。

无需争论以上的那些习惯和方法是否只对学者或者拥有很多空余时间进行阅读的人才适合。那些阅读量或者阅读时间相当少的人，更应该注重自己阅读的目的和方法。将自己有限的时间和分散的精力集中到一个感兴趣的中心点上，只有这样，才能达到事半功倍的效果。

感恩节

感恩节（Thanksgiving Day），每年11月的第四个星期四是感恩节。感恩节是美国人民独创的一个古老节日，也是美国人合家欢聚的节日，因此美国人提起感恩节总是倍感亲切。感恩节是美国国定假日中最地道、最美国式的节日，它和早期美国历史密切相关。

1620年，著名的“五月花号”船满载不堪忍受英国国内宗教迫害的清教徒102人到达美洲。1620年和1621年之交的冬天，他们遇到了难以想像的困难，处在饥寒交迫之中，冬天过后，活下来的移民只剩五十来人。基于“来者是客”的信念与习俗，印第安人给这些移民送来了生活必需品，并且教导他们狩猎、捕鱼和种植玉米、南瓜等等生存方法。

在印第安人的帮助下，来自欧陆的新移民逐渐习惯了在当地的生存方式。在欢庆丰收的日子，欧陆新移民邀请印第安人一同感谢上天的赐予，举行了三天的狂欢活动。从此，这一习俗就延续下来，并逐渐风行各地。

烤火鸡和南瓜馅饼是感恩节大餐中必不可少的两道佳肴。

A Definite Aim in Reading

Noah Porter, 1811–1892, was born at Farmington, Conn., and graduated at Yale in 1831. He remained in New Haven as a school–teacher, a tutor in college, and a student in the theological department until 1836, when he entered the ministry. In 1846 he was recalled to the college as Clark Professor of Moral Philosophy and Metaphysics; and in 1858 he also assumed the duties of the professorship of Systematic Theology, for a period of seven years. Upon the retirement of President Woolsey in 1871, he was elected to fill the office, which he held until 1886, being the eleventh president of the college.

President Porter's greatest literary work is entitled, "The Human Intellect: With an Introduction upon Psychology and the Human Soul." It is remarkable for the clear thought and sound judgment it displays, as well as for its broad scholarship; and it has been pronounced "the most complete and exhaustive exhibition of the cognitive faculties of the human soul to be found in our language." His other important works are: "The Sciences of Nature versus the Science of Man," which is a review of the doctrines of Herbert Spencer; "American Colleges and the American Public;" and the book from which the following selection is taken, namely, "Books and Reading."

Besides these he wrote numerous essays, contributions to periodicals, etc. During his professorship he was called upon to act as chief editor in the important work of revising "Webster's Dictionary." The edition of 1864 was the result of his careful oversight, and the subsequent revisions were also under his superintendence.

In reading, we do well to propose to ourselves definite ends and purposes. The more distinctly we are aware of our own wants and desires in reading, the more definite and permanent will be our acquisitions. Hence it is a good rule to ask ourselves frequently, "Why am I reading this book, essay, or poem? or why am I reading it at the present time rather than any other?" It may often be a satisfying answer, that it is convenient; that the book happens to be at hand: or that we read to pass away the time. Such reasons are often very good, but they ought not always to satisfy us. Yet the very habit of proposing these questions, however they may be answered, will involve the calling of ourselves to account for our reading, and the consideration of it in the light of wisdom and duty.

The distinct consciousness of some object at present before us, imparts a manifoldly greater interest to the contents of any volume. It imparts to the reader an appropriate power, a force of affinity, by which he insensibly and unconsciously attracts to himself all that has a near or even a remote relation to the end for which he reads. Anyone is conscious of this who reads a story with the purpose of repeating it to an absent friend; or an essay or a report with the design of using its facts or arguments in a debate; or a poem with the design of reviving its imagery, and reciting its finest passages. Indeed, one never learns to read effectively until he learns to read in such a spirit—not always, indeed, for a definite end, yet always with a mind attent to appropriate and retain and turn to the uses of culture, if not to a more direct application.

The private history of every self-educated man, from Franklin onwards, attests that they all were uniformly not only earnest but select in their reading, and that they selected their books with distinct reference to the purposes for which they used them. Indeed, the reason why self-trained men so often surpass men who are trained by others in the effectiveness and success of their reading, is that they know for what they read and study, and have definite aims and wishes in all their dealings with books. The omnivorous and indiscriminate reader, who is at the same time a listless and passive reader, however ardent is his curiosity, can never be a reader of the most effective sort.

Another good rule is suggested by the foregoing. Always have some solid reading in hand; i. e., some work or author which we carry forward from one day to another, or one hour of leisure to the next, with persistence, till we have finished whatever we have undertaken. There are many great and successful readers who do not observe this rule, but it is a good rule notwithstanding.

The writer once called upon one of the most extensive and persevering of modern travelers, at an early hour of the day, to attend him upon a walk to a distant village. It was after breakfast, and though he had but few minutes at command, he was sitting with book in hand—a book of solid history he was perusing day after day. He remarked: "This has been my habit for years in all my wanderings. It is the one habit which gives solidity to my intellectual activities and imparts tone to my life. It is only in this way that I can overcome and counteract the tendency to the dissipation of my powers and the distraction of my attention, as strange persons and strange scenes present themselves from day to day."

To the rule already given—read with a definite aim—we could add the rule—make your aims to be definite by continuously holding them rigidly to a single book at all times, except when relaxation requires you to cease to work, and to live for amusement and play. Always have at least one iron in the fire, and kindle the fire at least once every day.

It is implied in the preceding that we should read upon definite subjects, and with a certain method and proportion in the choice of our books. If we have a single object to accomplish in our reading for the present, that object will of necessity direct the choice of what we read, and we shall arrange our reading with reference to this single end. This will be a nucleus around which our reading will for the moment naturally gather and arrange itself.

If several subjects seem to us equally important and interesting, we should dispose of them in order, and give to each for the time our chief and perhaps our exclusive attention. That this is wise is so obvious as not to require illustration. "One thing at a time," is an accepted condition for all efficient activity, whether it is employed upon things or thoughts, upon men or books. If five or ten separate topics have equal claim upon our interest and attention, we shall do to each the amplest justice, if we make each in its turn the central subject of our reading. There is little danger of weariness or monotony from the workings of such a rule.

Most single topics admit or require a considerable variety of books, each different from the other, and each supplementing the other. Hence

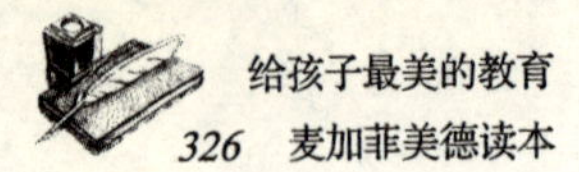

it is one of the best of practices in prosecuting a course of reading, to read every author who can cast any light upon the subject which we have in hand. For example, if we are reading the history of the Great Rebellion in England, we should read, if we can, not a single author only, as Clarendon, but a half dozen or a half score, each of whom writes from his own point of view, supplies what another omits, or corrects what he under– or overstates.

But, besides the formal histories of the period, there are the various novels, the scenes and characters of which are placed in those times, such as Scott's Woodstock; there are also diaries, such as those by Evelyn, Pepys, and Burton; and there are memoirs, such as those of Col. Hutchinson; while the last two have been imitated in scores of fictions. There are poems, such as those of Andrew Marvell, Milton, and Dryden. There are also shoals of political tracts and pamphlets, of handbills and caricatures.

We name these various descriptions of works and classes of reading, not because we suppose all of them are accessible to those readers who live at a distance from large public libraries, or because we would advise everyone who may have access to such libraries, to read all these books and classes of books as a matter of course, but because we would illustrate how great is the variety of books and reading matter that are grouped around a single topic, and are embraced within a single period.

Every person must judge for himself how long a time he can bestow upon any single subject, or how many and various are the books in respect to it which it is wise to read; but of this everyone may be assured, that it is far easier, far more agreeable, and far more economical of time and energy, to concentrate the attention upon a single subject at a time than to extend it to half a score, and that six books read in succession or together upon a single topic, are far more interesting and profitable than twice as many which treat of topics remotely related.

Nor should it be argued that such rules as these, or the habits which they enjoin, are suitable for scholars only, or for people who have much leisure for reading. It should rather be urged that those who can read the fewest books and who have at command the scantiest time, should aim to read with the greatest concentration and method; should occupy all of their divided energy with single centers of interest, and husband the few hours which they can command, in reading whatever converges to a definite, because to a single, impression.

图书在版编目（CIP）数据

给孩子最美的教育：麦加菲美德读本 /（美）麦加菲 编著；依妮，苍松 译. --北京：新世界出版社，2011.12
ISBN 978-7-5104-2408-3

Ⅰ.①给… Ⅱ.①麦… ②依… ③苍… Ⅲ.①品德教育－小学－课外读物 Ⅳ.①G624.153

中国版本图书馆CIP数据核字（2011）第242050号

给孩子最美的教育：麦加菲美德读本

策　　划：青豆书坊
作　　者：［美］麦加菲 编著
译　　者：依 妮　苍 松
责任编辑：余守斌　熊文霞
特约编辑：苍 松
责任印制：李一鸣　黄厚清
出版发行：新世界出版社
社　　址：北京市西城区百万庄大街24号（100037）
发 行 部：（010）6899 5968　（010）6899 8733（传真）
总 编 室：（010）6899 5424　（010）6832 6679（传真）
http://www.nwp.cn
http://www.newworld-press.com
版权部电话：+8610 6899 6306
版权部电子信箱：frank@nwp.com.cn
印　　刷：北京金瀑印刷有限责任公司
经　　销：新华书店
开　　本：660mm×940mm　1/16
字　　数：250千字　　印 张：21.5
版　　次：2012年1月第1版　2012年1月第1次印刷
书　　号：ISBN 978-7-5104-2408-3
定　　价：39.90 元